MATTER AND SPIRIT

Their Convergence in Eastern Religions,

Marx, and Teilhard de Chardin

RELIGIOUS PERSPECTIVES

Planned and Edited by

RUTH NANDA ANSHEN

BOARD OF EDITORS

RELIGIOUS PERSPECTIVES · VOLUME EIGHT

MATTER AND SPIRIT

Their Convergence in Eastern Religions,

Marx, and Teilhard de Chardin

by

R. C. Zaehner

HARPER & ROW, PUBLISHERS

NEW YORK AND EVANSTON

To

ELIZABETH JENNINGS

CONTENTS

Religious Perspectives
Its Meaning and Purpose   *page* 11

Introduction   15

1. Solitary or Solidary?   21

2. The Shattering of the Image   44

3. Refashioning the Image   68

4. Encounter   98

5. Solidarity in God   130

6. Solidarity in Matter   157

7. The Convergent Spirit   183

RELIGIOUS PERSPECTIVES

VOLUMES ALREADY PUBLISHED

I. *The Historic Reality of Christian Culture*
by Christopher Dawson

II. *International Conflict in the Twentieth Century*
by Herbert Butterfield

III. *The Limits of Reason*
by George Boas

IV. *Nihilism*
by Helmut Thielicke

V. *The Way of Israel*
by James Muilenburg

VI. *No Absent God*
by Martin C. D'Arcy, S.J.

VII. *Islam: Its Meaning for Modern Man*
by Muhammad Zafrulla Khan

VIII. *Matter and Spirit*
by R. C. Zaehner

RELIGIOUS PERSPECTIVES

Its Meaning and Purpose

RELIGIOUS PERSPECTIVES represents a quest for the rediscovery of man. It constitutes an effort to define man's search for the essence of being in order that he may have a knowledge of goals. It is an endeavor to show that there is no possibility of achieving an understanding of man's total nature on the basis of phenomena known by the analytical method alone. It hopes to point to the false antinomy between revelation and reason, faith and knowledge, grace and nature, courage and anxiety. Mathematics, physics, philosophy, biology and religion, in spite of their almost complete independence, have begun to sense their inter-relatedness and to become aware of that mode of cognition which teaches that "the light is not without but within me, and I myself am the light."

Modern man is threatened by a world created by himself. He is faced with the conversion of mind to naturalism, a dogmatic secularism, and an opposition to a belief in the transcendent. He begins to see, however, that the universe is given not as one existing and one perceived but as the unity of subject and object; that the barrier between them cannot be said to have been dissolved as the result of recent experience in the physical sciences, since this barrier has never existed. Confronted with the question of meaning, he is summoned to rediscover and scrutinize the immutable and the permanent which constitute the dynamic, unifying aspect of life as well as the principle of differentiation; to reconcile identity and diversity, immutability and unrest. He begins to recognize that just as every person descends by his particular path, so he is able to ascend, and this ascent aims at a return to the source of creation, an inward home from which he has become estranged.

It is the hope of RELIGIOUS PERSPECTIVES that the rediscovery of man will point the way to the rediscovery of God. To this end a rediscovery of first principles should constitute part of the quest.

These principles, not to be superseded by new discoveries, are not those of historical worlds that come to be and perish. They are to be sought in the heart and spirit of man, and no interpretation of a merely historical or scientific universe can guide the search. RELIGIOUS PERSPECTIVES attempts not only to ask dispassionately what the nature of God is, but also to restore to human life at least the hypothesis of God and the symbols that relate to him. It endeavors to show that man is faced with the metaphysical question of the truth of religion while he encounters the empirical question of its effects on the life of humanity and its meaning for society. Religion is here distinguished from theology and its doctrinal forms and is intended to denote the feelings, aspirations, and acts of men, as they relate to total reality.

RELIGIOUS PERSPECTIVES is nourished by the spiritual and intellectual energy of world thought, by those religious and ethical leaders who are not merely spectators but scholars deeply involved in the critical problems common to all religions. These thinkers recognize that human morality and human ideals thrive only when set in a context of a transcendent attitude toward religion and that by pointing to the ground of identity and the common nature of being in the religious experience of man, the essential nature of religion may be defined. Thus, they are committed to re-evaluate the meaning of everlastingness, an experience which has been lost and which is the content of that *visio Dei* constituting the structure of all religions. It is the many absorbed everlastingly into the ultimate unity, a unity subsuming what Whitehead calls the fluency of God and the everlastingness of passing experience.

These volumes seek to show that the unity of which we speak consists in a certitude emanating from the nature of man who seeks God and the nature of God who seeks man. Such certitude bathes in an intuitive act of cognition, participating in the divine essence and is related to the natural spirituality of intelligence. This is not by any means to say that there is an equivalence of all faiths in the traditional religions of human history. It is, however, to emphasize the distinction between the spiritual and the temporal which all religions acknowledge. For duration of thought is composed of instants superior to time, and is an intuition of the permanence of existence and its metahistorical reality. In fact, the symbol[1] itself found on cover and jacket of each

[1] From the original design by Leo Katz.

volume of RELIGIOUS PERSPECTIVES is the visible sign or representation of the essence, immediacy, and timelessness of religious experience; the one immutable center, which may be analogically related to Being in pure act, moving with centrifugal and ecumenical necessity outward into the manifold modes, yet simultaneously, with dynamic centripetal power and with full intentional energy, returning to the source. Through the very diversity of its authors, the Series shows that the basic and poignant concern of every faith is to point to, and overcome, the crisis in our apocalyptic epoch—the crisis of man's separation from man and of man's separation from God—the failure of love. The authors endeavor, moreover, to illustrate the truth that the human heart is able, and even yearns, to go to the very lengths of God; that the darkness and cold, the frozen spiritual misery of recent time, are breaking, cracking, and beginning to move, yielding to efforts to overcome spiritual muteness and moral paralysis. In this way, it is hoped, the immediacy of pain and sorrow, the primacy of tragedy and suffering in human life, may be transmuted into a spiritual and moral triumph.

RELIGIOUS PERSPECTIVES is therefore an effort to explore the *meaning* of God, an exploration which constitutes an aspect of man's intrinsic nature, part of his ontological substance. The Series grows out of an abiding concern that in spite of the release of man's creative energy which science has in part accomplished, this very science has overturned man's conception of the essential order of nature. Shrewd as man's calculations have become concerning his means, his choice of ends, which was formerly correlated with belief in God, with absolute criteria of conduct, has become witless. God is not to be treated as an exception to metaphysical principles, invoked to prevent their collapse. He is rather their chief exemplification, the source of all potentiality. The personal reality of freedom and providence, of will and conscience, may demonstrate that "he who knows" commands a depth of consciousness inaccessible to the profane man, and is capable of that transfiguration which prevents the twisting of all good to ignominy. This religious content of experience is not within the province of science to bestow; it corrects the error of treating the scientific account as if it were itself metaphysical or religious; it challenges the tendency to make a religion of science —or a science of religion—a dogmatic act which destroys the moral dynamic of man. Indeed, many men of science are confronted with unexpected implications of their own thought and are beginning to accept, for instance, the trans-spatial and trans-temporal nature of events and of matter itself.

RELIGIOUS PERSPECTIVES attempts to show the fallacy of the apparent irrelevance of God in history. The Series submits that no convincing image of man can arise, in spite of the many ways in which human thought has tried to reach it, without a philosophy of human nature and human freedom which does not exclude God. This image of *Homo cum Deo* implies the highest conceivable freedom, the freedom to step into the very fabric of the universe, a new formula for man's collaboration with the creative process and the only one which is able to protect man from the terror of existence. This image implies further that the mind and conscience are capable of making genuine discriminations and thereby may reconcile the serious tensions between the secular and religious, the profane and sacred. The idea of the sacred lies in what it *is*, timeless existence. By emphasizing time-less existence against reason as a reality, we are liberated, in our communion with the eternal, from the otherwise unbreakable rule of "before and after." Then we are able to admit that all forms, all symbols in religions, by their negation of error and their affirmation of the actuality of truth, make it possible to experience that *knowing* which is above knowledge, and that dynamic passage of the universe to unending unity.

The volumes in this Series seek to challenge the crisis which separates, the crisis born out of a rationalism that has left no spiritual heirs, to make reasonable a religion that binds and to present the numinous reality within the experience of man. Inso-far as the Series succeeds in this quest, it will direct mankind toward a reality that is eternal and away from a preoccupation with that which is illusory and ephemeral.

For man is now confronted with his burden and his greatness : "He calleth to me, Watchman, what of the night? Watchman, what of the night?"[1] Perhaps the anguish in the human soul may be assuaged by the answer, by the *assimilation* of the person in God : "The morning cometh, and also the night : if ye will inquire, inquire ye : return, come."[2]

RUTH NANDA ANSHEN

[1] Isaiah 21:11.
[2] Isaiah 21:12.

Introduction

THE APPEARANCE IN 1955 OF PIERRE TEILHARD DE
Chardin's *Le phénomène humain* and its English translation in
1959 as *The Phenomenon of Man* amounted almost to a revolution in Christian religious thought. For perhaps the first time in
this century a fundamentally religious and Christian book made
a profound impression on a predominantly non-Christian public.
For what Teilhard de Chardin had done was to situate the
Christian religion within its evolutionary context : religion was
to be no longer the enemy of science but its very culmination;
and science itself became "tinged with mysticism and charged
with faith." This was new and exciting.

Exciting too was Teilhard's interpretation of Christianity in
evolutionary terms and the irrepressible optimism with which,
both as a scientist and as a Christian, he viewed the future. In
the heyday of the cold war, with Stalin still alive, such buoyant
optimism and such a glowing faith in the triumphant destiny of
mankind can have seemed little short of quixotic : yet his book
had an immediate success, for it supplied the perfect antidote to
the modern existentialist disease, bidding man look out upon the
world of which he was part rather than contemplate the nasty
mystery of his own individual being, and urging Christians too to
think a little less about their individual salvations and to concentrate ever more on the building up of the mystical body of
Christ here on earth : he was asking professing Christians if not
to be, at least to appear to be, a little less selfish.

Teilhard de Chardin was a paleontologist and a Jesuit priest,
and his books can perhaps be fully understood only in both a
Catholic and an evolutionary context; yet some of the severest
criticism that has been leveled at him has come from the Catholic
side, for the Roman Catholic Church is ever wary of what seems
to be wholly new. He is, however, despite all this, a profoundly
Catholic writer, and succeeds in giving a new and compelling

meaning to the ancient doctrine of the mystical body of Christ, seeing in it the culminating point of the evolutionary process itself. This is an emphasis that has not been wholly lacking in modern Catholic thinking, but it needed the genius of a Teilhard de Chardin to make this most "collective" of all Christian doctrines comprehensible to the collective age that is now being born. He met a religious need that reaches out beyond personal salvation to the vision of a coherent and integrated whole; he brought the sacrificial Christ of the altar down into the laboratory, the workshop, and the factory; he brought the promise of sanctification to a material world re-created by man. He not only brought out what had been for too long latent in the Church herself but also filled up what is totally lacking in the only creed that seriously rivals Christianity, Marxian materialism : he made us aware of the Spirit of cohesion and reconciliation that he saw working everywhere throughout the whole unmeasured sphere of matter.

Teilhard de Chardin was a mystic as well as a scientist, and his mysticism is essentially Christian : it is a mysticism of affirmation, not of negation, of solidarity, not of isolation—a mysticism of action which, in the last analysis, is compatible only with a theology that sees in God not only Being but Act. His mysticism is no longer concerned simply with the transports of individual souls; it is the mysticism of the integration of souls not only with their ground which is God but also with each other and with all things through God : he looks forward with a rational confidence to what the Church has always called the Communion of Saints of which the Church herself is the too often unconscious vehicle.

Again, from the purely cultural point of view, Teilhard opens up a totally new perspective. A scientist himself, he concerns himself little with the arts, and, in the secular world, sees only science, in its disinterested pursuit of truth and in its ever clearer perception of the rational structure of matter, as being the only real ally of religion, however unwilling, in religion's own struggle to bring together all that seems broken into one intelligible whole. This concern with what is verifiable and real in the material world as it is being discovered by science, gave him no time to study or to interest himself deeply in what nowadays passes for culture. He had literally no time to try to make sense of the fragmentation of the arts and of philosophy itself which has been characteristic of the first half of the twentieth century : he had time neither to spare nor to waste. He stands on a watershed between a dying civilization based on an individualism, once arrogant, now abject, that has shown itself bankrupt and stands self-condemned, and a collective civilization yet to be born in which the "free development of each [will be] the condition for the free development of all."[1] He marks the passage from an epoch of individual despairs to one of shared hope in an ever richer material and spiritual life.

Yet he was not without precursors : and it will be the purpose of this book to show how, from the beginning, there have been, within religions, two tendencies in dialectical tension with each other—the one drawing the individual ever deeper into himself, down into the "kingdom of God" that "is within you," and the other integrating him ever more closely with the religious community. In Christian terminology this means the tension between preoccupation with the salvation of the individual soul on the one hand and the building up of the body of Christ in the Church on the other. The first was the almost exclusive preoccupation of the Indian religions as we hope to show, while in ancient times the second became the vision of the Zoroastrian state-church in Iran shortly before its collapse, and in modern times it has re-emerged in the Marxian hope of an infinitely perfectible world which is to come into being once the last of the social contradictions has been surmounted and man is no longer exploited by man. From a purely evolutionary point of view Teilhard de Chardin claimed that he could show that all creation converged upon itself in man and the whole human phylum was, in its turn, destined to converge ever more intensely upon itself within what he calls the "Christian phenomenon." In this book we will try to show that the same process is discernible only in what we can call religious evolution, and that this crisis of convergence is perhaps very near at hand. Now for the first time the religions of the world confront each other directly, and it is to be assumed that just as, on the purely secular plane, world unification cannot be long delayed, so, on the religious plane, the present melting pot of religions must, in the long run, simmer down into a coherent whole; and just as we cannot see how the antagonisms of personal, national, and ideological wills can be vanquished by any purely human agency, so we cannot see how first a divided

[1] K. Marx and F. Engels, *The Communist Manifesto*, ed. H. J. Laski (London 1948), p. 146.

Christianity can be united, nor how, beyond Christendom, the non-Christian religions can either absorb or be absorbed into Christianity. This, however, is to reckon without a power that is greater than man, greater than nations, and greater than individual religions—the power Teilhard attributed to evolution and which he believed operates among us conscious beings as much as it does in unconscious matter, the power that Marx identified with matter itself and which the present author would identify with the "Spirit of God" that "moved upon the face of the waters" before ever time began, the "convergent Spirit" that is ever busy kneading mankind into a coherent mass however much individual men may kick against the pricks.

This unity toward which mankind is converging the Catholic sees already there in embryo in the material and sacramental structure of the Catholic Church. How all mankind will ultimately be fitted into this structure he would not presume to say, but he would scarcely be a Catholic at all if he doubted that this was so. Else he would be false to Him who prayed "that they all may be one, as thou, Father, in me, and I in thee; that they also may be one in us." For the Catholic this unity has never ceased to exist—visibly and palpably—ever since the Catholic Church first came to be, and that it will continue to exist and grow until it embraces within itself all mankind, he cannot but believe and hope. If he did otherwise he would be less than "Catholic." That others not in communion with the See of Rome interpret the whole concept of the Church very differently is a matter for regret; but whatever our interpretations of the Church may be, it would be folly to expect the full unity of the Church to be manifest to all so long as the body of the Church itself is not wholly cleansed from the cancer of sin which ever works to destroy it from within; and that will not be till the end of time.

The great service of Pierre Teilhard de Chardin to Christianity lies in this, that he has put the concept of the growing into fullness of the mystical body of Christ in his Church into the forefront of his whole conception of Christianity, thereby diverting the individual's gaze from a too self-regarding preoccupation with his own soul and directing it ever more intently to the communal role he is called upon to play in a world in which each depends on all and all on each. His was an integral and therefore "Catholic" vision of reality which, as the enthusiastic reception of *The Phenomenon of Man* in the non-Catholic world showed, corresponded to a real need that conventional religion had hitherto failed to supply. The present work can claim no originality, for it is little more than an attempt to see the religious situation as it has existed and exists today through Teilhard de Chardin's eyes; and this can only mean to see it as the slow convergence of all man's religious thinking into the Catholic Church which is now in the process of being built up and which, under the "convergent Spirit" that informs it, must ultimately reach its full expansion in that it will come to include all men and "God will be all in all." Teilhard de Chardin has been criticized from the Catholic side for paying little or no attention to sin and evil : in the present book we have attempted to remedy this defect in that we have tried to look at sin too from an evolutionary point of view. The book itself, of course, does not attempt to be an objective study on comparative religion, rather it is a subjective interpretation of the religious history of man seen from an individual angle within the overall structure of the Catholic Church.

I

Solitary or Solidary?

IT IS AS DIFFICULT TO PINPOINT THE EXACT DATE at which a new era is born as it is to define at what precise point a small child becomes a fully self-conscious and rational being. That we are in fact witnessing the birth of a new era, different not only in degree but also in kind from all that has gone before in the long history of mankind, most of us obscurely feel. Something is changing—and changing very fast. Something is dying and something else is being born; and birth means pain, and through pain, hope and joy. With St. Paul we obscurely sense "that the whole creation groaneth and travaileth in pain together until now. And not only they, but ourselves also, which have the first-fruits of the Spirit, even we ourselves groan within ourselves, waiting for the adoption, to wit, the redemption of our body."[1] Perhaps that is what is happening now and the kingdom of heaven is at hand. Or perhaps we are only lapsing into deeper contradictions and more preposterous absurdities, the most absurd of which would be the destruction of man by man himself.

What makes our world different in kind from all the "worlds" that have preceded it is that, thanks to the enormous technological achievements of the last hundred years, it has become literally *one* world—actually one in space through the abolition of distance by the fantastic speed of modern communications, potentially one in social organization in that, despite the acute birth pangs of a new age, mankind is visibly moving toward an ever-closer union.

It can of course be argued that the emergence of the new nationalisms in Africa and Asia gives the lie to any such facile optimism; but this is to see only the surface, for these individual nationalisms are expressions of a single trend and a single will—the will to modernize and industrialize and by these means to achieve a real, and not merely asserted, equality with those

[1] Rom. 8: 22–23.

materially advanced societies which had formerly ruled, and maybe exploited, the former colonial nations. In Europe, still the
advance guard of world civilization, despite the pessimism of the
Spenglers and Toynbees who would disown her, the trend toward unification is already an established fact. The old nationalisms are fast subsiding into innocuous and purely parochial
patriotisms within a more complex union which is more and more
seen as a common fatherland. The trend is there, and in recent
times it has been analyzed as an inevitable trend dictated by the
evolutionary process itself by that most astonishing of Jesuits,
Pierre Teilhard de Chardin. In the remote past his vision had
been foreshadowed by the Zoroastrian "Church"; in more recent
times by Karl Marx and Friedrich Engels, the founders of international Communism, allegedly the mortal foes of all religions
against whose ideas, therefore, all religions are urged to unite.

Man, however, left to himself, is not very good at uniting and
will only do so willingly when he feels himself threatened not
only in his values but in his very existence. Hitler united Europe
by force and administered her by tyranny. His defeat, however,
did not lead to a resurgence of the old parochial nationalisms,
but to an ever-closer integration of Western European society into
what is on the way to becoming a unity in multiplicity in which
the individual nations, putting aside their particularistic attitudes
in a common oblivion of a nightmare past, look forward to living
and prospering together in a shared well-being and a common
harmony. As was only natural, this has been the achievement of
a resurgent and once again self-confident Christianity, and its
architects have been, in the vast majority of cases, sons of the
Catholic Church, for the Catholic Church is the mother of that
very Western Europe which, ever since Luther nailed his theses
on to the church door at Wittenberg, has so often denied and
decried her.

The essence of Catholicism is unity : the Church sees herself
as a living organism, visible, tangible, and alive, and like any
other living organism she has but one brain—one authoritative
center which controls the rest of the body, and which the other
members of the body, if the body itself is healthy, must obey.
But just as no purely human organism will ever be free from
disease, so must the Church be vitiated in her members by the
sickness of sin until her mission is completed and God becomes
"all in all."

In the Middle Ages the Catholic Church preserved the unity of Western Europe—religious, cultural, and, in so far as Latin remained the language of learning, linguistic. It was, then, inevitable that the successful revolt against the Church in the sixteenth century, supported as it was by the secular arm for reasons of purely local sovereignty, should give rise to the local nationalisms, once so highly esteemed, but now seen in their true perspective as first the scourge and secondly the ruin of Europe. It took the savagery of the Nazis under the leadership of a gang of Catholic apostates, which all but destroyed everything that Western Europe had so long stood for, to bring Europe back to a sense of her Catholic heritage and spurred her on to rebuild, as best she could, her shattered unity.

With the Reformation Europe lost her sense of being a single and indivisible civilization because great parts of her had been estranged from the visible symbol of her unity—the Church that had her center in Rome. The era of religious, dynastic, and then of national wars had set in : and with the wars came the industrial revolution which caught both the Catholic Church and the Protestant bodies off their guard. The Reformation had led ultimately to the division of Europe into self-conscious, self-righteous nation states : the industrial revolution introduced a deeper cleavage—the cleavage between the man who had nothing to sell except the work of his hands and the man fortunate enough to be able to buy his labor cheap. The rift between the social classes, never for long below the surface, became patent for all to see. The birth pangs of the modern world had begun.

Man, as Aristotle had long ago remarked, is a social animal, and the more he organizes himself and the greater his mastery over Nature, the greater and the more urgent does his instinctive craving for unity become. With the fragmentation of Christianity in the sixteenth century the reality of Christian unity had disappeared, and Protestant theology had perforce to resort to the unreal idea of one undivided but invisible Church to which all Christians of good faith invisibly belonged. The Catholic Church of the Counter-Reformation had no longer any right to describe herself as Catholic : at best she might be referred to condescendingly as the "Roman" Catholic Church, less politely and more oddly she had become the Popish apostasy. Quite apart from Protestant indelicacies, however, the Catholic Church had indeed become more evidently and more specifically the "Roman"

Church than she had ever been in the course of her long history. She was no longer the center of European unity, though through the tireless and inconspicuous efforts of her missionaries overseas she was installing herself, very slowly and not always surely, in every corner of the globe.

The industrial revolution, when it broke over Europe and America, as we have seen, caught both the Catholic Church and the Protestant churches off their guard. Neither the one nor the other was equipped to deal with the problems of the new urban working class. They did little—very little—to alleviate the sufferings of the newly created urban proletariat—they did less to adapt the Christian message to the totally new needs of a class whose roots in the soil and in nature had been suddenly and violently ripped up. Religion came to lose all relevance for the uprooted workingman. In England the flood of irreligion had for a time been stemmed by the evangelical zeal of the non-conformist sects, but once these sects lost their enthusiasm and in their turn became conformist and institutionalized, they too failed to inspire later generations. The cause of Christianity was going by default.

The year 1848 was a landmark in European history, for it was not only a year of revolution, it was also the year in which Marx and Engels published for the first time their *Communist Manifesto*. Their message passed far beyond a mere call to proletarian revolution; it presented the working class not only with the hope that the future was in its hands if only it learned how to use them, but it conjured up the vision of an earthly paradise in which the exploitation of man by man would forever be done away with and "all tears would be wiped away." And not only this: the millennium would come to pass with the inexorable certainty of an iron necessity, for the establishment of this classless society would not in the last analysis depend on the will or the power of proletarian man but on forces inherent in the very structure of the material world which had been working from the beginning of time for this apocalyptic denouement. The workingman, then, in his masses, is the weapon chosen not only by history but by nature herself for the destruction of the old order of iniquity and for the establishment, not at the end of time nor in another order of existence, but here and now on this earth, not indeed of the kingdom of God but of the commonwealth of man.

We shall be returning to the religious message of Marxism at the end of this book, but there are things that here, at our beginning, must be said. Marxism is not simply an economic system that substitutes state capitalism for private monopoly capitalism, any more than the Communist Party is just one among several political parties : Marxism is an apocalyptic that not only brings the kingdom of heaven down to earth, but also looks to the fulfillment of the promise not in the remote future but in the lifetimes of many of us; it is a religion (or ideology if the word is preferred) that sees individual salvation only in collective salvation—the part cannot be saved except in the context of the whole. Collective salvation, that is, the healing of the wounds of a society at war with itself, is not only here upon us, it is the fine flower of the whole process of cosmic evolution, the culmination of the whole evolutionary drive that has been moving inexorably forward for billions and billions of years. It is nothing less than "The whole creation groaning and travailing together until now waiting for the adoption, to wit, the redemption of our body," and not of *our* body only but of the "collective body" of all mankind. This is a faith—and a hope; and it is very far from contemptible. Had there been charity too, it might have been most admirable.

What is more, it is in tune with what seems to be an irreversible trend of our times—the trend, through technological achievement, toward the unification of the planet in which we live. Therein lies its strength. But Marxism in practice has not worked out along the lines foreshadowed by its founders. From the moment it ceased to be a revolutionary party and found itself in full control of the apparatus of state of potentially the most powerful country in the world, it was false to the deeply humanistic insights of its founders, false to their empiricism, above all false to their vision of the Communist society in which "we shall have an association in which the free development of each is the condition for the free development of all." Stalinism was a radical distortion of Marxism in that it set up as its idol a monolithic state—the direct antithesis of a society composed of free individuals co-operating toward a common goal—and put a tyrant in the place of God. While Stalin lived there could be no possible rapprochement between the Communist and non-Communist worlds.

But Stalin is dead : and Dulles is dead. The spirit of intransigence and willed misunderstanding, though very far from dead, is nonetheless sickening. The mass of mankind is patient, but the will to survive of the totality of men is as strong as the will to survive of the individual; and the angry reaction of the ordinary man (if such exists) on either side of the iron curtain at the foolhardy U-2 flight over Russia, at the clumsy handling of the affair, at Nikita Khrushchev's vulgar histrionics at the stillborn summit meeting, showed that even the Soviet leaders will henceforth have to take into account more and more the opinions and above all the will to survive of both ordinary and not so ordinary men. Co-existence is not the ideal nor even the natural state of affairs in a technologically united world. The ideal state is rather "an association in which the free development of each is the condition for the free development of all." To quarrel with this definition of the ideal society which is no less Christian than it is Communist simply because it was penned by Marx amounts to a willful refusal of all points of contact with a significant and frequently sincere portion of our fellow men : it is mortal sin.

The faults of the Communists both in Russia and in China have been so frequently and so zestfully pointed out to all good democrats that it would be useless to repeat them here. This does not, of course, mean that in our effort to understand the inner dynamism of Communism, we should blind ourselves to the anti-human atrocities committed by both Stalin and Mao Tse Tung. The trials of the 1930s, the executions, the mass deportations of the war years, not to mention the fearful suffering imposed on the peasantry during collectivization, are crimes as gigantic as any committed by Hitler—crimes the less pardonable in that they were committed in the name of a theoretically humanist ideology, which, rather than destroy the dignity of man, should have sought to restore it by rescuing it from what it conceived to be the tyranny of things.

The Russian ruling class has always been acutely suspicious of the outside world; and this evil Tsarist heritage has been enthusiastically taken up by the Communists. As hate breeds hate, so does suspicion breed suspicion : and both breed fear. The Western world is fond of boasting of its Christian civilization, but Christ never bade us meet hate with hate or suspicion with suspicion. "Love your enemies" was his message as much as it was the Buddha's; but since the day he died upon the Cross for the redemption of the world, no Christian, except the highest athletes in Christian virtue, has dared to take him at his word.

On what is meant by love we shall have much to say in the

sequel, but to "love your enemies" can scarcely mean less than to wish them well, and this in turn implies an effort to understand why they are as they are and why they behave as they do. It would be foolish to give up the effort to try to understand what makes Communism work simply because the Communists have been guilty of atrocities as vile as Hitler's. The Communist Party has been in power for only four decades in the Soviet Union, but its list of atrocities is already impressive. It is, however, not for Christians of any of the major denominations to be self-righteous about the antihuman conduct of the modern totalitarianisms : their past is far too murky for that. Few Catholics are now proud of the Sack of Constantinople, the Albigensian Crusade, the Inquisition, or the Wars of Religion, nor, for that matter, of the Crusades themselves. It has taken us a long time to realize that we cannot save a soul by destroying the body, or remove the mote from our brother's eye without first getting rid of the beam in our own.

The so-called "free" world likes to speak of Christian values, and Americans will still speak of their civilization as a Christian civilization, though in Great Britain it is more generally spoken of as post-Christian. And how do these values and this Christian civilization appear to the non-Christian world? The churches, it is said, have never been so full, yet in his literature, his films, his comic strips, and in the reputation of his soldiery abroad, the American advertises himself as a brainless thug devoted to sexuality and violence. American religion and American morality seem strangely out of step; for morality, though part of religion, is not all of it. Each, rather, is dependent on the other, and the quality of each is bound to affect the quality of the other. Protestantism, in its Puritan manifestation, distorted Christian ethics, not so much because it so often adopted a ruthlessly uncharitable view of sexual weaknesses in direct violation of Our Lord's precept and practice as because it mistook self-righteousness for righteousness : it exalted pride, the deadliest of the seven deadly sins, on to a pinnacle of virtue. For this censorious attitude toward sexuality we are paying now, since with the usual swing of the pendulum, Puritanism has turned into its opposite, license. It would, of course, be grossly unfair to judge American civilization by the less admirable productions of Hollywood, but it is precisely American films and American comic strips by which the uncommitted world judges American civilization. If the

American way of life is so inextricably bound up with sex and
violence, what, the Asian may well ask himself, is there of value
in it? And America is a Christian nation; and if this is the way
Christians behave, is not Communism, with its decent prudery,
far better? "Woe unto you, scribes and Pharisees, hypocrites!"

As we shall see in the sequel, man is a strange being, composed
of soul and body; and unless he has succeeded in integrating and
harmonizing his total personality, his soul and his body do not
march in step. Only the born ascetic can browbeat the body into
submission : in the long run it is beyond the power of the average
man (I leave out of consideration for the moment the operation
of divine grace), and it is no accident that Hinduism, the religion
which, more than all others, reverences ascetic practices *per se,*
should also find room for such productions as the *Kāma-sūtras,*
probably the lewdest book ever written. Similarly in its attempt
to suppress all bodily pleasure, Puritanism paves the way for the
opposite and no less pernicious vice—sexual license. And just as
Puritanism has its roots in pride, so does sexual license have its
roots in blasphemy. The natural result of the sexual act is the
creation of new life and by that act man becomes co-creator with
God—with the Holy Spirit who is the "Lord and giver of life."
By indulging in the act simply for his own pleasure and without
any intention of creating new life, he blasphemes against life
and thereby against the giver of life. He desecrates a holy thing
and blasphemes against the Holy Ghost. Sooner or later, and
without recourse to religion, he will realize this instinctively, and
this is what the Communists have done in the Soviet Union.
There, at least, sex is seen in its due perspective, as one of the
many things that are important in a man's life, not as an all-
consuming and often self-destructive obsession; nor is it ruthlessly exploited at its most brutish and forced down the throats
of a bemused public for commercial ends as it too often is in our
"Christian" West. Soviet decency in sexual matters is, indeed,
more in conformity with traditional Christian values and the
deepest instincts of man than is the frank exploitation of sex so
characteristic of a civilization that still claims to be Christian.

Again, how far can a civilization that attaches so much importance to the accumulation of money rightly be considered a
Christian civilization? "Ye cannot serve God and Mammon." Or
what is one to make of the thirst for status so widespread among
the Anglo-Saxons? Is it not just this that Christ condemned in

the Pharisees of his time—the man who "loved the uppermost rooms at feasts, and the chief seats in the synagogues, and greetings in the markets"[2]? For this rather pathetic hankering for status he had nothing but scorn : "whosoever shall exalt himself shall be abased; and he that shall humble himself shall be exalted."[3] Any civilization that makes the possession of money or social status a criterion of value is not a Christian civilization : it stands condemned by Christ himself.

We in the West must learn to see ourselves as others see us; and the resultant picture is not beautiful. In our relations with the non-Christian world we should never have presumed to describe ourselves as a Christian civilization : such a thing has never existed and probably never will exist till the end of time. Everywhere Christianity has been seen not so much as a religion the merits of which are to be weighed against those of any other religion, but as the religion of the European conqueror whose sole motive seemed to be the exploitation of subject peoples and whose personal conduct seemed so often to be singularly at variance with the precepts propagated by the missionaries. Christianity's association with the great surge of European expansion and the disrupting of traditional values in ancient lands that that expansion entailed, did it nothing but harm. And it was a tragedy too that Christian expansion outside Europe should have taken place at a time when the unity of Christendom had been shattered in Europe herself; and so not only was this deep cleavage between Catholic and Protestant exported from Europe overseas, but the increasing proliferation of the sects within Protestantism itself followed it wherever it went. What sort of image of Christ's Church was presented to Asia and Africa that could be recognized as the Church of Him who prayed "that they all may be one; as thou, Father, art in me, and I in thee, that they also may be one in us; that the world may believe that thou hast sent me."[4]

In contrast to Christian sectarianism Islam, despite the survival of the Shī'a and other sects, presented a more or less united front; and, again unlike Christianity, it brought with it an uncomplicated creed, demanding only absolute subservience to God and the recognition of Muhammed as his Prophet, and promising to all who submitted to God by accepting Islam, an eternity of bliss. More impressive still was the impact of Com-

[2] Matt. 23 : 6-7.   [3] *Ibid.*, 23 : 12.   [4] John 17 : 21.

munism, truly international in a sense that neither Christianity nor Islam were, owing, like the Catholics, allegiance to a central and near-infallible authority, and bringing with it a message of hope to all who were exploited and who had nothing to lose but their chains. Communism spoke of concrete realities, it offered immediate relief to appalling want : it spoke of this world and its regeneration here and now, not of the next. This, rather than the language of sin and redemption, the oppressed and exploited could readily understand.

The strength of Communism has hitherto lain in its unity. The price paid for this unity in terms of the suppression of independent thought cannot detain us now : the unity is there. Over against this unity the West has nothing to offer. We are very fond of extolling the virtues of "democracy" and "freedom," but rarely bother to define these terms. Moreover, a "democratic" form of government is no longer required for membership of the "free" world, and everywhere the newly emancipated and under-developed countries are turning to a dictatorial form of government as being the most efficient way of modernizing their economies, so inept and corrupt have their experiments with parliamentary government proved to be. As to freedom : there is freedom "to," and freedom "from." There is a whole array of freedoms, from the freedom to do exactly what you please whatever the cost to others may be and the fatuous *acte gratuit* of Gide, Sartre *et hoc genus omne,* to the more humble freedom from want the desirability of which all would concede. Thus when all is said and done, the "free" world has nothing constructive to offer, neither Christianity, nor freedom, nor democracy. It has nothing to offer except anti-Communism—which is neither more nor less sensible than the anti-Fascism of the Communists themselves.

In the Western world there is only one organization that is in any way a match for international Communism—not in material strength indeed (for it has none) but in closeness of organization, internal cohesion, and ideological power. This is the Catholic Church. And they have much in common. Whether it was Marx's intention or not (and in fact it certainly was not), in its forty-two years of political power Communism has developed into an authoritarian regime; so too has the Catholic Church. Both the Communists and Catholics are intensely interested in the "correct" education of their children in accordance with the tenets of their respective creeds : in other words, neither shrinks from indoctrination. Both Communists and Catholics, whether or not they admit it in public, regard heresy as an evil, and both have persecuted it when they have had the power, the Communists understandably, for they operate in time only and believe themselves alone capable and enlightened enough by their grasp of Marxian principles to bring about the final abolition of the exploitation of man by man with which all creation has been travailing since Cain slew Abel and man enslaved his fellow man; the Catholics understandably perhaps, but not excusably, for the Catholic Church makes the enormous claim that she alone is the repository of the Christian faith in its fullness and that she alone holds the key that infallibly unlocks the doors of salvation, she alone is the Church founded on the rock of Peter against which the gates of hell shall not prevail. Guided, as she claims to be, by the Holy Spirit, she is false to her mission and shows little faith in that same Spirit when she stoops to persecute those who, through no fault of their own, cannot see the justice of her outrageous claims : for does she not claim that she has the guarantee of God himself that the truth of which she believes herself to be the enshrinement must in the end prevail?

The mutual menace of the nuclear deterrent has made it virtually impossible that war can ever again become an instrument of policy unless, of course, power in either the United States or the Soviet Union should fall into the hands of a criminal maniac. At the moment this does not seem likely, and the mere fact that each side knows that the destruction of the one means the destruction of all should give mankind some confidence that in the end the will to survive of all must win the day. Even more important than the abolition of war must be the cessation of persecution. Marxism is not old enough yet to realize that it has no essential quarrel with religion, for, as we shall see, it is too akin to some of the Oriental religions at least to need to fear any danger from that quarter. Nor is Christianity necessarily opposed to Marxism as an economic system : on the contrary, it has every reason to welcome it as an ordered alternative to unbridled capitalism. When, however, Marxism not only proclaims itself atheist but persecutes religion itself in defiance of its founders' prediction that religion would automatically disappear once the social order on which it was allegedly founded was made away with, then Christians can and must react in self-defense and in defense of what they hold to be true. Less negatively, however, it is open to them to show that, by admitting the existence of eternal Law beneath the world of perpetual change, the Marxists are themselves drawing nearer than is perhaps comfortable for them not only to the immanent God of Oriental religion but also to the Holy Spirit, immanent in the world, who is the third Person of the Christian Trinity.

Marxism, as developed by Engels after Marx's death in accordance with what he conceived to be Marx's own thought, is itself a powerful religious force for reasons we have briefly outlined above and which we shall survey in greater detail below. Christianity, on the other side, and particularly the Catholic Church which still constitutes the "Great Church" and, as such, the central axis of Christendom around which the immobilism of the Eastern Orthodox and the individualism of the Protestant bodies uneasily revolve, shows more vitality now than would have seemed credible a hundred years ago. Marx and Engels were wrong in thinking that Christianity or, for that matter, any of the higher religions could be laughed out of court once they had been deprived of their revenues. This has not happened in Russia itself, much less in Poland. And since it has not happened and the prophecy has proved false, the Marxists, foolishly, prefer to ignore Engels' warning that "persecution is the best means of promoting undesirable convictions" : they have forgotten that "the only service that can be rendered to God today is to declare atheism a compulsory article of faith and to outdo Bismarck's *Kirchen-kulturkampf* laws by prohibiting religion generally."[5] It is true that they have not quite gone to this extreme, but by forbidding religious propaganda and putting every obstacle in the way of religious education they tacitly admit the power of religion and have only themselves to blame if they have been unable to destroy what they had so confidently proclaimed to be an illusion.

Communism set out to destroy the bourgeoisie as the last remaining exploiting class—and with the bourgeoisie was to go the whole superstructure of bourgeois civilization which the economic realities of the capitalist system supported. In actual fact, of all the so-called "bourgeois" values so savagely and, considering the time of writing, so rightly arraigned by Marx and Engels in the *Communist Manifesto,* it is only religion that Communism has tried to eradicate. The fiery prophetic genius of Karl Marx and

[5] Marx and Engels, *On Religion* (Moscow, 1957), p. 142.

the deep insights of Friedrich Engels into the secrets of matter, which they saw to be not only a moving but a living thing, were never allowed by their epigoni to develop into an immanentist religion that might have done something to replace what of Orthodox Christianity and Islam they had succeeded in destroying. Instead they contented themselves with persecution, but still the old order dragged on diminished but alive. In the sphere of morals the proletarian dictatorship reverted to a modified Puritanism which is much to its credit, while in the sphere of the arts, so far from creating anything new, they tended to cling to outmoded bourgeois forms so suspicious were they of everything new that emanated from the still unliquidated bourgeois West.

Marx and Engels were not only materialists, they were also Romantics, Marx the Prophet and Engels the Seer. They were humanists who believed in the dignity of man both as an individual and as one element among many working harmoniously with, and for the good of, his class first, and then, with the abolition of class, the whole human race. They were neo-Zoroastrians.[6] For them "the criticism of religion ends with the teaching that man is the highest essence for man, hence with the categoric imperative to overthrow all relations in which man is a debased, enslaved, abandoned, despicable essence."[7] For them the great scandal of bourgeois society was the enslavement of man by man. The answer was to humanize industrial society, for "if man is shaped by his surroundings, his surroundings must be made human. If man is social by nature, he will develop his true nature only in society, and the power of his nature must be measured not by the power of separate individuals but by the power of society."[8] The vision of Marx and Engels foreshadowed, among other things, the vision of Teilhard de Chardin who saw what he considered to be the inevitable socialization of society as the convergence of the whole human phylum upon itself in accordance with the evolutionary drive in living things toward ever more "improbable" constructions. For Teilhard the convergence of humanity upon itself is the final phase in the development of organic life to which all creation has been striving; and in his stupendous vision which we shall have to consider in more detail later, he follows unwittingly in the path that Marx and Engels had trod before him : he is the first Marxist Christian.

[6] Below p. 181.   [7] Marx and Engels, *On Religion*, p. 50.
[8] *Id.*, *The Holy Family* (Moscow, 1956), p. 176.

Marxism meanwhile has become ossified into an ideology, and the works of Marx and Engels are granted an authority usually bestowed only on a sacred book—a thought that would have horrified them both. Marxism as a living faith was destroyed by the dead hand of Stalinism, and it is all the more to the credit of Nikita Khrushchev that he has publicly declared that what Lenin (himself a sacred figure) said about world revolution being possible only through war no longer applied to present-day conditions. This is a revolution in post-Stalinist thought and, it must be hoped, a first sign that Marxism will once again step out of its fossilized shell and regain the intellectual dynamism it has long since lost. It is true that Stalin betrayed Marx, and that under him Communism became a ruthless form of state capitalism conducted as a tyranny. Russia, however, is in the throes of change; and though the change may seem slow and erratic to our eyes, the fact remains that the colossus moves. Marxism, like Christianity, paid the usual penalty when it achieved political power : it betrayed the spirit of its founders; but enough of the old idealism remains for it to cause Western statesmen endless unease. If, then, the Communist sector of the world is beginning to shake off the Stalinist nightmare and to take its first faltering steps toward the creation of a world community for which co-existence can be only the first stage, how do matters stand with the "free" world?

Here again we are confronted with a totally new phenomenon. With the gradual opening up of the East to Western commerce and, above all, with the establishment of British rule in India, a whole new religious world opened up to the Western mind. Many formerly religious people, impressed by the Darwinian interpretation of the evolution of man from lower animal forms of life and distressed by the total inability of a predominantly fundamentalist theology to meet this new challenge, drifted away from Christianity into a complete religious agnosticism. On minds such as these both the Hindu scriptures and the Buddhist texts, as they gradually became available, made a tremendous impact; for in neither of them were embarrassing doctrines to be found such as the creation of the world *ex nihilo,* let alone the physical resurrection and ascension of a God-Man—doctrines that seemed to fly in the face of what the self-confident science of the day regarded as scientific fact. Western man for the first time became interested in the religions of the East.

Having lost faith in his own God, he was amazed to find that here were religions, some of them of immeasurable antiquity, which had succeeded in getting on very nicely with no clearly formulated idea of a personal God at all, and for which, in the last analysis, "man was the highest essence for man." Here were religions that knew nothing of the humiliating doctrine of Original Sin, religions which, while granting that man in his strictly human condition was enslaved to powers that not only did not belong to his true essence but were also actually hostile to it, taught that he had immortal life within his own grasp if only he knew the secret of how to lay hold of it. Man, so far from being totally corrupt and incapable of producing good of any kind from himself, so far from being entirely dependent on the grace arbitrarily mediated through the blood of Jesus Christ or equally arbitrarily withheld, was himself an immortal soul, eternal in essence, beyond all the vicissitudes of this world, beyond space and time, and therefore beyond birth and death.

And how could this be so?

It is, I think, fair to make the following very broad generalization: according to both the Upanishads which constitute the kernel of Hindu scripture and what are generally considered to be the most ancient Buddhist texts, man is regarded as being a composite creature: he is composed of a material part which includes not only the body but also the senses, emotions, and mind, all of which can operate only through bodily, that is, material organs. All of these must disintegrate at death. Connected with this material apparatus is the "soul" which, in essence, is totally distinct from it. Of the soul nothing positive can be stated except that it is eternal, and, being eternal, it can neither be born nor die: it cannot act nor can it be acted upon. Its connection with the body is only apparently real; absolutely, there is no connection, for the soul is, of its very nature, free, autarchic, and eternal. The object of religion is, then, not reconciliation with God (since either he does not exist or at best is no more than a well-meaning ally of the soul in its quest for its eternal ground), but the realization of the eternal essence of the soul itself as distinct from all that binds it to matter, and this can be achieved only by the complete withdrawal of the soul from all that binds it to matter and the universal flux which is the permanent yet unstable condition that makes matter what it is.

This is a broad generalization that will have to be qualified in the sequel; but it is typical of the mainstream of both Hinduism and Buddhism. In practice it means that neither religion, in its classical formulation, pays the slightest attention to what goes on in this world. Whatever theories may be put forward about the nature and origin of this world, all sects are agreed that attachment to the world is the greatest obstacle to the soul's realization of its own eternal essence. Indian religion, in its classical formulation at least, is altogether other-worldly.

It was largely the sympathetic interest of European scholars, as well as the extravagances of the Theosophical Society, that rekindled among the Indians themselves an enthusiasm for, and a pride in, their ancient religion. First the Ārya Samāj, which made the extravagant claim that the Indian Vedas were the source of all religion, and then the Rāmakrishna Mission put Hinduism on the map as one of the "highest" of the world religions, if not the highest of all. For the first time in history Hinduism took the offensive and missions were sent to Europe and the United States. The Buddhists were even more successful : Buddhist societies sprang up in the West, and a general interest in Buddhism and the Buddhist way of life grew up among agnostics who had rejected Christianity as being irrational and who were therefore ready to welcome in Buddhism a religion that dispensed with God, that was devoid of rigid dogmas, and that placed man's own salvation and the realization of his own immortality in bliss squarely in his own hands. Such a religion, they felt, did not run counter to the scientific spirit of the age. The whole Hindu and Buddhist cosmology, for instance, which had never been geocentric or even heliocentric, but which conceived the universe as being limitless in space and infinite in time and had never found any difficulty in peopling both with uncounted "worlds," seemed to prefigure the immensities of space and the countless galaxies that roam throughout it which science was at that time discovering. Buddhism made its impact on the West as being a religion that did without both God and dogma, and it continues to do so as the never-ending spate of popular works on Buddhism conclusively shows.

Even more spectacular was the impact of Zen Buddhism, a type of Buddhism developed first in China and then more concentratedly in Japan. The propagation of Zen Buddhism in recent years was due very largely to the tireless efforts and enormous literary output of Professor Suzuki, and the appeal his writings made was to the pronounced nihilistic tendency that swept, is sweeping, and, one may justifiably hope, will very shortly cease sweeping the literary bourgeoisie. It has been seized upon to justify almost any idiocy and excess : it is deeply anti-intellectual and antidogmatic and would have us believe that the release of the eternal soul from the bonds of materiality can be achieved only by "passing beyond" the discursive intellect into a world where nonsense, we are told, makes sense.

The climate of opinion of the modern "intellectual" bourgeoisie was ripe for such an invasion. In contrast to the Soviet Union where cultural life has hitherto been driven to conform to the standards of nineteenth-century bourgeois philistinism, the bourgeois "intellectuals" of the West developed an acute form of schizophrenia. For the description of this, as is usual in cases where the nature of the complaint is ill-defined, they resorted to the German language and found the word *Angst* (the concept having been invented by a Dane a century ago); and *Angst*, unlike *Weltschmerz*, a more noble condition because concerned, however indirectly, with the world and not merely with self, is the deep anxiety and unhappiness the modern intellectual feels because he neither knows how to connect with the people and things that go to make up his environment and the greater world beyond his environment, nor is he in a position to sort out the conflicting instincts, drives, and inhibitions that war with one another in his own deeply divided personality. His symbol, characteristically, is one single capital letter,—K—the hero of Kafka's two great novels, *The Trial* and *The Castle,* the real horror comics, in the most literal sense of those words, of the modern age.

Soviet man is more than encouraged—he is driven to see himself as part of a collective whole, but until now the function of the collectivity has been regarded so exclusively as being to build up a purely material civilization which should first equal and then surpass that of the United States that all the arts have suffered thereby; or is it simply that the coercive regime of terror of Stalin's time so stifled even orthodox enthusiasms that they not only dared not but were unable to express themselves in the way most natural to them? Even the fiery spirit of Marx could scarcely have expressed itself in the atmosphere of "terror that walks by night" that for so long held Russia captive. Now things are changing in Russia, but they are changing very slowly, and no immediate flowering of the Russian genius is perhaps yet to be expected; but when it comes, we can be fairly sure that it will be something quite other than the ingrowing pessimism that has for so long characterized the literatures of the West.

The whole existentialist literary movement in France and elsewhere today takes it for granted that the world is meaningless or "absurd" as they prefer to call it, and that each individual man must come to grips with it as best he can, thereby trying to impose a partial meaning on to it for himself. Perhaps I am being unjust, but the whole movement seems to be obsessed by an egoism so extreme that it regards everything outside the individual's ego not as something existing and having value in its own right but as a means toward solving one's own personal predicament. This explains both the alternate acceptance and rejection of Communism by a series of French intellectuals and the wholesome contempt of the Communist Party for intellectuals as such and for the left-wing variety in particular. And it is not without significance that the best, because the most humble, of the French left-wing intellectuals, Albert Camus, should lump Christians and Communists together as sharing a common long-range optimism concerning the destiny of man and a common pessimism about individual men.[9] This is typical of the whole movement, and it is precisely because the modern intellectual cannot see any meaning in a world that has been the scene of so much senseless violence and cannot accept the existence of a God who connives at evil that he so often turns to Buddhism which is unencumbered with a God and sickened by a world in pain; for not only does Buddhism admit the existentialist premise of the absurdity of the world, it also points the way that leads to release from the world into a timeless Nirvāna where all suffering is snuffed out. It provides for individual salvation and, except in its more unfashionable Mahāyāna form, does not concern itself greatly with the collective redemption of mankind : it has nothing to correspond to the "communion of saints." "Work out your salvation with diligence" are the last words attributed to the Buddha; and this is precisely what the existentialist tries to do.

He usually fails : and his last state is more often than not worse than his first; for Camus alone, it would seem, among the French existentialists had his intimations of immortality, and in this he came nearer to the Buddhists than most; for to taste of immort-

[9] *Actuelles* (Paris, 1950), p. 216.

ality and to shake off the trammels of space and time is the Buddhist's certain hope. To the best of my knowledge Camus had no direct or even indirect acquaintance with Buddhism, but no one who is not a "natural" Buddhist could have written these words :

"In every man there is a deep instinct which is neither the instinct to destroy nor the instinct to create. It is simply a question of being like nothing else."[10]

". . . Being like nothing else" : this is perhaps what the Buddhists mean by Nirvāna—something that no words can adequately describe, but the attainment of which brings certain immortality, and with that certainty release from anguish and quiet joy.

The impact of Indian religion on the West in recent times has, however, been greatly exaggerated. It has been popularized by the so-called "beats" and adopted in its Zen form (based on the smaller of the two Zen sects in Japan) because the more traditional forms of Buddhism demand an intensive moral and mental training—a "vigilance" that is too much like hard work for the nihilists of today.

It is true that the non-Communist East is going through some kind of religious revival. During the last hundred years Hinduism has succeeded in almost completely transforming itself, and, mainly through Gandhi, himself largely responsible for the change, it has developed a sense of social responsibility it totally lacked before. Buddhism too has witnessed a marked revival in Burma and Ceylon, and also in Japan; but it should not be forgotten that both the revival of Hinduism and the revival of Buddhism are as much manifestations of nationalism as they are of religion. As such they are suspicious of Christianity not only as a rival creed but also as being the religion of the former colonial power. Any question of a "higher synthesis" being created out of the "higher insights" of the "higher religions" as Professor Toynbee thinks might come to pass is ruled out by the brute facts. There is at present no sign of the great religions of the world drawing together with a view to sharing their spiritual resources. For a religion, in so far as it is a religion and not simply a matter of personal faith, is almost invariably associated with a social organization, so that it is not meaningless to speak of a Catholic, Muslim, Hindu, or Buddhist "world"; and such "worlds," as social organizations, cannot combine without

[10] *L'Été* (Paris, 1954), p. 61.

destroying themselves as separate entities. It is true, however, that "salvation" is for some religions very much more an individual affair than it is for others—much more so, for instance, for the Buddhist than it is for the Jew; and it is true too that on the individual level one religion can borrow much from another. But it is also true that no religion can survive and grow except as a community, and it is the harmony or tension that exists between the purely individual approach to the divine and the communal organization in which the individual must operate that gives each religion its distinctive flavor.

In one of his short stories Camus describes how a painter who had not much faith in his own talents anyhow, is suddenly besieged by friends and "fans" who successfully prevent him from doing any worthwhile painting at all. In despair he finally retires to an attic where he works at what is to be his masterpiece in complete solitude. Finally he collapses, and the masterpiece is found to be a perfect and absolute blank, except that in the center of it one word is written in a microscopic hand; and this one word was clearly enough written except for one letter. Had he written *solitaire* or *solidaire*?

This is true of religion too. Does it concern itself primarily with individual salvation (however this word is understood) or with that of the "nation," the "Church," and beyond that of the whole human race? Of the Western religions Judaism, in its Old Testament phase, conceived of salvation as being that of the Jewish people—the salvation of an historical community which, under God's rule and despite countless backslidings on the part of the chosen community, worked itself out here on this earth in time. Primitive Zoroastrianism, however, which made close contact with the Jews during and after the Babylonian captivity, saw salvation primarily as the continued existence of the individual soul after death, and that existence was conditioned by the quality of a man's life on earth, "an evil lot for evil [done] and a good one for a good [deed]." Later, however, perhaps influenced in its turn by Judaism, it developed a grand doctrine of collective salvation which, despite the unremitting attacks of the powers of evil, worked itself out through the ages until all was made new in the last days.

In Christianity both ideas were present from the beginning, the salvation (or damnation) of the individual soul and collective salvation through the Church which is the sum total of all

Christians and the mystical body of Christ of which each Christian forms an organic member inseparable from the whole. In Islam, too, both aspects are present, and the sense of belonging to a community distinct from, and superior to, the rest of mankind is probably stronger in Islam than in any other religion.

Hinduism is held together by the caste system and by the fact that certain essential rites (birth, coming of age, marriage, death, etc.) must be performed by a Brahman. With the disintegration of the caste system which may take a long time yet but which will become inevitable once India is fully industrialized, Hinduism will be driven back onto what is most essential to it and most characteristic of it—the Yogic techniques (which it has inherited from an immemorial past) of enabling the individual soul to realize its own eternity. Buddhism, on its side, has, far more than Hinduism, concentrated on the individual aspect of salvation (which it understands in much the same way as Hinduism). It has never succeeded in developing as a homogeneous community held together by a uniform system of rites or a coherent system of beliefs. More elusive than any other religion and capable of adapting itself to almost any situation without losing its essential nature, it has hitherto been, from an organizational point of view, too closely identified with its own tightly-knit monastic communities for it to survive once a really ruthless enemy has set about destroying the monasteries themselves and slaughtering and scattering their inmates. This the Muslims achieved with complete success in India and parts of Central Asia, and the Communists, one must assume, are pursuing the same end with equal success in China.

Thus, while Neo-Hinduism and Neo-Buddhism may seem attractive ways of escape from an increasingly intolerable world to an intelligentsia already conditioned by existentialist attitudes, the native religions on their native soil are doing probably no more than hold their own. The Westernized intelligentsia of the Asian countries has turned its back on them, and they are unlikely to play any significant part in an age in which solidarity is likely to loom far larger than solitude.

Christianity was able to adapt itself slowly and painfully to the first onslaughts of the scientific and technological age and has emerged from it, weakened in numbers certainly, but greatly strengthened in spirit. The other religions have had too little time, and Islam, the only one among them that is solidary in outlook rather than solitary, has shown itself wholly incapable of adapting itself to the new secular and scientific civilization which it can neither assimilate nor stave off.

It is sad but it is nonetheless true that Asia is at present far more interested in bringing herself up to date technologically, that is to say, she has far more interest in achieving material parity with the West than she has in preserving a religious heritage which many of her more "advanced" sons already regard as being obsolescent. In the second half of the twentieth century, then, we are likely to see not only the total industrialization of Asia and, indeed, the rest of the world, but also a total reappraisal of religious values. Private religion and private meditation will, of course, continue to exist, for whatever the fate of the totality of mankind, the salvation of individual souls must always remain one of the chief preoccupations of religion. Only those religions, however, which already have a deeply ingrained tradition of communal solidarity as well as an intense care for the dignity of the individual person, can hope to retain their vigor in a world that is fast and visibly becoming one. Leaving aside Islam which can hope to make further progress only in what of Africa is still primitive, there would seem to be only two world-wide organizations that fulfill the bill—the Catholic Church with her two-thousand year tradition of unity behind her, and the Communist International, the new religion of collective man, which, like the Catholic Church, is represented in nearly every country of the world. At present it looks as if neither side will or can compromise. But this is to reckon without a power that is greater than they— a power which the Church has known from her foundation and still knows as the Holy Spirit and which Marx and Engels, though they did not recognize it for what it was, discovered working silently within matter itself.

In a former book[11] I tried to show how the great religions of India and Iran prepared the way, confusedly sometimes, sometimes more surely, for the coming of Christ. In this book the task is very different, more bold perhaps and certainly more difficult. Leaning heavily on the work of Pierre Teilhard de Chardin, I would show that Marxism itself, as understood by its two founders, has within it elements of natural religion which, given some relaxation of the present rigid attitudes, could be slowly absorbed and transformed in the body of the Church. Stranger

[11] *At Sundry Times*, London, 1958

things than this have happened before, for "the Spirit bloweth where it listeth," and man is astonishingly obtuse in foreseeing where it will blow next. And this is how it should be, for the Spirit, good commander as he is, loves the element of surprise.

2

The Shattering of the Image

IN THE BEGINNING GOD CREATED THE HEAVEN AND
the earth. And the earth was without form, and void; and darkness was upon the face of the deep. And the Spirit of God moved
upon the face of the waters.[1]

From the very beginning when matter was as yet no thing, the
Spirit of God brooded over it. Matter, so vague and elusive a
thing that Greek philosophy could not be sure whether it truly
existed or not, became energy, because moved by the Spirit of
God. "The Spirit of God moved upon the face of the waters,"
and the waters stirred into life. From the beginning of time Spirit
was wedded to matter, and matter to Spirit. What was dead became alive, and finally, when consciousness was born, matter
"smiled at man with poetical sensuous brightness."[2] Matter
from the beginning received the impress of the Holy Spirit and
was sanctified. Matter, because the Spirit of God moves upon its
face, was thereby rendered holy.

Very slowly, in the course of billions of years and in units of
space that are literally inconceivable to the human mind, the
dust of the universe, breathed upon by the Holy Spirit, formed
itself into galaxies separated from each other perhaps by hundreds
of thousands of light years. Further billions of years were required
for a tiny grain of dust to be flung off from our own sun to form
this earth on which we live and die, millions more for the
appearance of life from a "dead" but intensely active matter,
and millions more again before living matter became conscious
of itself as man.

Until the eighteenth century Western man, unlike his brothers
in India who from the beginning conceived of the universe as
being indefinitely extended and peopled with a myriad worlds,

[1] Gen. 1.1.
[2] Marx and Engels, *The Holy Family*, p. 172.

lived in the cosy atmosphere of a geocentric world : the earth was the center of a spatially finite universe, and man was the earth's crowning glory. Though the literal interpretation of the first chapters of Genesis was impugned long before science proved it to be manifestly absurd, the scale of values which those chapters take for granted, was not seriously disputed. Man was thought to be the highest achievement of all nature and as such he was the lord of the universe.

So God created man in his own image, in the image of God created he him; male and female created he them. And God blessed them, and God said unto them, Be fruitful, and multiply, and replenish the earth, and subdue it: and have dominion over the fish of the sea, and over the fowl of the air, and over every living thing that moveth upon the earth.

And God said, Behold, I have given you every herb bearing seed, which is upon the face of all the earth, and every tree, in the which is the fruit of a tree yielding seed; to you it shall be for meat. And to every beast of the earth, and to every fowl of the air, and to every thing that creepeth upon the earth, wherein there is life, I have given every green herb for meat: and it was so.

And God saw every thing that he had made, and, behold, it was very good.

The only difference between the concept of man in the first chapter of Genesis and the eighteenth-century Enlightenment was that the latter dispensed with God : he was no longer relevant. Man thereby became the central phenomenon of the universe and, by the mere fact that he alone was a rational animal, the lord of the universe because he alone could bend his environment to his will.

The revolutionary discoveries of astronomy changed all that : for not only did the old theory of the primacy of man as the crown of creation now seem absurd, but the immensities of time and space that the new astronomy revealed reduced his significance to that of a worm.

I am a worm, and no man; a reproach of men and despised of the people. All that see me laugh me to scorn.[3]

These words of the Psalmist took on a new and terrible meaning; for it was seen that they could be applied not only to the Biblical figure of the Suffering Servant, but also, and with a

[3] Ps. 22 : 6-7.

more frightening relevance, to man himself. Man, so proud and
so sure of his mastery over all creation, had himself become the
target of the inhuman and antihuman mockery of an indifferent
universe, blindly pursuing its senseless course and gloating, without heart or brain, over the absurdity of the human predicament
and inevitable disappearance of an accident of evolution that
had given birth to the phenomenon of life and thought on a tiny
speck of cosmic dust called earth. Man, who had sought to seat
himself upon the throne of a dying God, now saw himself, against
an infinitely extended and lifeless cosmos, as an insignificant
epiphenomenon, a silly little freak, which chance had thrown up
from the evolutionary stream—a dirty little bubble that could
have no destiny at all but to burst and be forgotten. *L'immensité
de ces espaces infinies m'effraie*—"The immensity of these infinite
spaces frightens me," Pascal had said; and we have been
frightened ever since. The universe is no longer our home, but a
terrifying, mechanical immensity in which thought, which distinguishes us from all other living things, and life itself, are just
an unhappy mistake.

No less disconcerting is the consideration of the infinitely small.
Here everything is not only in flux—as Heraclitus long ago
intuitively sensed—but moving at incredible speeds, so fast indeed that each atom cannot be assigned a durable individuality.
"Indeed our sensory experience," that is, the specifically human
experience of matter through the five senses, "turns out to be a
floating condensation on a swarm of the undefinable. Bewildering
in its multiplicity and its minuteness, the substratum of the
tangible universe is in an unending state of disintegration as it
goes downward."[4]

Man, then, finds himself suspended in an abyss between the
infinitely great and the infinitely small, in a kind of no man's
land between the spacial immensities revealed by astronomy and
the incomprehensible tumult of the infinitely small with which
modern physics is making us familiar and to which the normal
categories of time and space seem to have no relevance. Worse
still, those scientists who resolutely refuse to see in consciousness
more than an epiphenomenon in the general trend of the universe, assure us that "in every physico-chemical change, ... a
fraction of the available energy is irrecoverably 'entropized,' lost,

[4] Pierre Teilhard de Chardin, *The Phenomenon of Man* (London and New
York, 1959), p. 41.

that is to say, in the form of heat."[5] It is true that living organisms build themselves up into ever more complex forms, and the higher the degree of consciousness the greater the complexity of the matter through which it operates. But, according to orthodox science, "the same wearing away that is gradually consuming the cosmos in its totality is at work within the terms of the synthesis, and the higher the terms the quicker this action takes place. Little by little the *improbable* combinations [that is, those least expected by the scientists themselves] that they represent become broken down again into more simple components, which fall back and are disaggregated in the shapelessness of *probable* distributions."[6] Consciousness, that is, the emergence of the Spirit within matter itself, is then doomed to a final relapse into an inert chaos, and the Spirit of God will have moved upon the face of the waters in vain.

But is this the whole story? Teilhard de Chardin, and an increasing number of scientists whose agnosticism has not blinded them to other and more exciting possibilities, see that the second law of thermodynamics (the law of increasing entropy) is counterbalanced by another law—the law of ever-increasing complexity typical first of life and then of consciousness. Of all the complex constructions into which matter has evolved the human brain is by far the most complex as well as the most concentrated upon itself. The greater the complexity, the greater the degree of consciousness—and with consciousness comes the power to think, the sense of responsibility, the power to choose, and conscience itself, each stage representing a "qualitative leap" which natural science of itself cannot explain. In man matter becomes conscious of itself through the Spirit that from the beginning indwelt it. Thus man, though poised between the infinitely great and the infinitely small, has an infinite dimension of his own—an infinity of biological complexity, increasingly concentrated upon itself and increasingly aware of itself : poised midway between the great and the small he has the potentiality of comprehending both, and in this he remains the measure of all things.

And the Lord God formed man of the dust of the ground, and breathed into his nostrils the breath of life; and man became a living soul.

[5] *Ibid.*, p. 51.   [6] *Ibid.*, p. 52.

How are we to explain this second infusion of the Spirit in evolutionary terms?

Matter from the beginning was and is inseparable from motion. Aristotle would have declared that matter could not be said to exist until it had received "form"; and for him there could be no science of matter as such since it cannot be grasped apart from the "forms" that are impressed on it. Marx, more scientifically, saw that matter and motion or change are inseparable. "The first and most important of the inherent qualities of matter is motion, not only mechanical and mathematical movement, but still more impulse, vital life-spirit, tension, or, to use Jakob Boehme's expression, the throes (*Qual*) of matter. The primary forms of matter are the living, individualizing forces of being inherent in it and producing the distinctions between the species."[7] Thus not only is matter not inert, it cannot, by definition, be inert. It is a living thing, and when not actually imbued with physical life as we understand it, then pregnant with life. Once the ideally favorable conditions arise, then matter, hitherto characterized by only mechanistic and mathematical movement, bursts into life, proliferates, and fills the world with living things. How this qualitative leap (to use the Marxian phrase) can come about, and come about only once, science has so far been unable to explain; for, the further it advances, the less clear does the dividing line between the highest form of inorganic matter and the lowest form of organic matter appear, yet that a qualitative distinction between the two exists can scarcely be denied. Science, indeed, by the mere fact that it moves forward with so breath-taking a velocity, must become increasingly specialized and departmentalized, and no scientist can have a firm grasp of the whole field of the individual sciences; no scientist, *qua* scientist, is in a position to see the wood for the trees. It needed the almost prophetic vision of a Teilhard de Chardin to draw our attention not only to the "without" of things—mechanistic and mathematical movement—but also to the "within"—the evolution of life and consciousness from the potential to the actual within the ever-increasing complexity of matter itself and of its subsequent involution upon itself. Although both he and Marx—for different reasons—avoid the term "spirit," they both speak of matter as of something in which life and consciousness *and purpose* inhere.

Marx and Engels, *The Holy Family*, p. 172.

Matter "gropes,"[8] nature "thinks up" processes[9]; and by groping Teilhard understands "directed chance."[10] These circumlocu-
tions are no doubt employed to throw dust in the eyes of those
"materialist" scientists whose philosophical materialism has not
advanced beyond the French Encyclopaedists of the eighteenth
century. If "chance" is "directed," then it must be directed not
only by something but by some*one* who has the will and the power
to direct, and this the Bible calls the "Spirit of God"—the Spirit
that is immanent in the evolutionary process itself, which is able
to guide it, by a *natural* process of trial and error, to ever more
"improbable" combinations and so to make the qualitative leap
from organized nonliving molecules to the living cell and, millions
of years later, to make the no less astonishing leap from the
unconscious to consciousness.

And man became a living soul.

About man's appearance in the world science can again tell
us nothing that we can represent to ourselves in a concrete way.
It is difficult enough to say at what stage a child becomes first
a conscious, and then a thinking, rational being. The development is so gradual that the exact point eludes us. How much
more true, then, must this be of the origins of man when all we
have to guide us are fossils and the first crude tools used by the
earliest men. Anatomy can tell us very little, for the human brain,
though more developed, certainly, than that of the other primates,
is not different in kind from them; but the difference of the
capabilities of the two is totally incommensurate with the in-
considerable difference in structure and size. Once again we have
a qualitative leap in the "within" of matter which science cannot
as yet explain.

That the human race or *Homo sapiens* derives from a single
couple as represented in the Book of Genesis no scientist today
believes : and there seems no reason why a Christian should believe
it either. St. Thomas himself admitted that scripture was first
written for untutored minds and that the Biblical myths had to
be modified in accordance with the views of contemporary
science. So too with the myth of Adam, "in the eyes of science,
which at long range can only see things in bulk, the 'first man' is,

[8] Teilhard de Chardin, *op. cit.*, p. 110.   [9] *Ibid.*, p. 104.
[10] *Ibid.*, p. 110.

and can only be, a crowd, and his infancy is made up of thousands
and thousands of years."[11]

We cannot, then, even imagine how consciousness first emerged
in man or how consciousness transformed itself into thought, nor
can we imagine why or how man, from the very earliest times,
came to believe in a world beyond the world he experienced with
his senses, how, that is to say, religion itself arose. The myth in
the second chapter of Genesis, however, is instructive, for it deals
expressly with the emergence of man from a childlike state of
innocence into full self-consciousness, the "knowledge of good and
evil." Let us consider the myth itself and its interpretation by
orthodox theology. For what the myth tells us is very strange
indeed; for man, who achieved consciousness through the
operation of the Spirit of God, was forbidden by God himself to
taste of the fruits that consciousness was bound to bring him.

It is not surprising that the Gnostics made the Lord God the
villain of the piece and regarded the serpent as being a saviour
who sought to release mankind from the yoke of an unjust God,
for it was he who caused them to make the qualitative leap into
full consciousness by persuading them to eat of the Tree of the
Knowledge of good and evil, the result of which would be that
they would become "as gods." Had the story no sequel God would
show up in a very bad light indeed.

What religious views the first men had we shall never know—
whether they believed in one God, or many, or none, or merely
sensed the "sacred" in what they could not explain. The Book of
Genesis, however, like all the rest of the Hebrew Bible, assumes
that God had dealings with man from the very beginning. Man,
on his side, had the innocence of a child—and of the animals : he
knew neither good nor evil. Not having reached self-consciousness,
he could have no sense of right and wrong : he was innocent and
therefore unashamed. God, according to the legend, invited man
to stay a child and not to make the final breakthrough into the
consciousness of good and evil and the moral responsibility that
that would entail.

But the Spirit of God was already working within him, preparing him for the moment when he would be a "living soul"—
an individual human being. We can have no conception of what
human beings were like before the breakthrough into consciousness became a fact, and man could stand alone outside the group

[11] *Ibid.*, p. 186.

and say "I am." It is generally agreed among scientists that the coming to consciousness of the human species was a process lasting perhaps thousands of years. To speak, then, of a first man does not really make sense. Whatever we say about this twilight period is bound to be a myth, and the myth of Genesis, taken as an allegory which yet figures forth a profound truth, thereby loses none of its value.

Let us assume, then, in accordance with what the paleontologists tell us, that *Homo sapiens* was everywhere springing up over the whole face of the earth and that everywhere he was quivering on the brink of consciousness. We must assume that the Spirit was everywhere working within him, preparing him not only for the freeing of his hands to serve as tools to fetch and carry and hold and for the further expansion of the brain that this freeing would indirectly make possible, but also for a transformation of his whole being by a qualitative leap he could not possibly understand in advance. Perhaps we can best compare the state of man at the dawn of consciousness to the state of the human adolescent just before puberty. Something in his body is changing; new, hitherto unfelt and unheard of forces are striving within him; they trouble him, he is filled with anxiety, and is a little afraid. The facts are usually explained to him beforehand, but, however well and sympathetically explained, they can have no meaning for him until he has actually made the leap from boyhood into manhood and lived through the violent change. Something similar must have been experienced by the first men as they became aware of themselves as individuals. Let us see how paleontology analyzes the birth of consciousness in *Homo sapiens*. Teilhard de Chardin writes,

It is true that in the end, from the organic point of view, the whole metamorphosis leading to man depends on the question of a better brain. But how was this cerebral perfecting carried out—how could it have worked—if there had not been a whole series of other conditions brought together at just the same time? If the creature from which man issued had not been a biped, his hands would not have been free in time to release the jaws from their prehensile function, and the thick band of maxillary muscles which had imprisoned the cranium could not have been relaxed. It is thanks to two-footedness freeing the hands that the brain was able to grow; and thanks to this, too, that the eyes, brought closer together on the diminished face, were able to converge and fix on what the hands held and brought before them—the very gesture which formed the external counterpart of reflection. In itself this marvellous conjunction should not surprise us. Surely the smallest thing formed in the world is always the result of the most formidable coincidence—a knot whose strands have been for all time converging from the four corners of space. Life does not work by following a single thread, nor yet by fits and starts. It pushes forward its whole network at one and the same time. So is the embryo fashioned in the womb that bears it. This we have reason to know, but it is satisfying to us precisely to recognize that man was born under the same law of maternity. And we are happy to admit that the birth of intelligence corresponds to a turning in upon itself, not only of the nervous system, but of the whole being. What at first sight disconcerts us, on the other hand, is the need to accept that this step could only be achieved *at one single stroke*.[12]

The birth of consciousness is thus a true birth prepared by the Spirit in the womb of space-time for billions of years; and like all births it is a time of shattering distress. Before the advent of self-consciousness the life of man must have been a life of what is now called the "unconscious"; and, if we are to believe Jung, it must have been a life controlled by what he calls the "collective unconscious," the shared experience and shared memory of the whole prehuman race that was trembling on the brink of consciousness. With no reasoning ego as yet developed, the whole race can be imagined as being in a state of what Lévy-Bruehl called *participation mystique* in all that lives. As yet there were no men to speak of themselves as "I," there was only consciousness of a common animating principle, the Spirit of Life that cannot die. Man was not yet *a* living soul, but living Soul or Spirit by participation. And then his blissful sense of participation seems to jerk out of place and become unhinged. Something terrifying and unimaginable is in preparation, and man could not know what : he is about to become an individual person with the freedom to make choices. This is the terrible moment described in the *Brhadāraṇyaka* Upanishad, where we read : "Looking round he saw nothing else but himself. He first said 'I am.' . . . He was afraid. . . . Verily he had no delight : and henceforth the man who is alone has no delight. He desired a second. In size he was as large as a man and a woman in close embrace. He split himself in two; and from thence man and wife came to be. Hence a human being is like a half-fragment."[13]

[12] *Ibid.*, pp. 170-71.
[13] *Bṛhadāraṇyaka* Unpanishad, 1.4.1-3.

This is the Hindu account of man's entry into self-consciousness—the birth of reflection. Individual man turns in upon himself and, for the first time detaching himself from the spirit of life in which he is bathed, sees that he is in his own right a "living soul." He says "I am" : and this means not only "I exist as an individual person," but also "I am alone, standing on my own feet, responsible, and unaided." This is terrifying.

Man is now conscious and, because conscious, isolated. Consciousness brings loneliness, and loneliness the sense of being cut off from one's environment—the malaise of existentialist man no less than of Adam when consciousness was first born. This, for a being whose preconscious experience had been all of participation in the unity of life, is unbearable. So conscious man reflects again and turns both instinctively (for he inherits it from the animals) and rationally to the one physical act which blurs the distinction between two living and thinking beings—the act of sexual union : "he cohabited with her, and from thence was mankind born."

The Book of Genesis puts it differently, for there man is not entirely alone but created and protected by God. The difference between Creator and creature, however, is too great to be borne, and so it is God himself who seeks to ease man's aching loneliness by giving him a wife :

And the Lord God said, It is not good that the man should be alone; I will make him an help meet for him. . . . And the Lord God caused a deep sleep to fall upon Adam, and he slept: and he took one of his ribs, and closed up the flesh instead thereof; and the rib which the Lord God had taken from man, made he a woman, and brought her unto the man. And Adam said, This is now bone of my bones, and flesh of my flesh: she shall be called Woman, because she was taken out of Man.

It is curious that in India, Iran, and Israel we should find that the first man is represented as being one creature in which both sexes are present : he is androgynous. In Genesis we read, "God created man in his own image, in the image of God created he him; male and female created he them." This is the usual translation, but it has been suggested that originally Adam was androgynous (as he is in the second chapter of Genesis where Eve is formed out of his rib), and this would conform to the normal type of myth concerning the nature of man. In the Upanishad again the primal man is originally undifferentiated

sexually, and then splits himself in two : "hence a human being
is like a half-fragment." In the Iranian myth too the first human
couple grow out of the earth, "and they were joined the one to
the other, joined in limb and form. . . . So closely were they linked
together that it was not clear which was the male and which the
female. . . . Then the two of them developed from plant form
into human form."[14]

These myths can be interpreted psychologically or in an evolutionary sense. According to Jung (and this part of his teaching
at least seems to be generally accepted) the human psyche is
essentially androgynous, the psyche of the male being balanced
by an *anima* or female psychic element and the psyche of the
female being balanced by an *animus* or male psychic element.
The close union of the two will mean psychic integration; their
division, which usually means the suppression of the *anima* in
male persons and the suppression of the *animus* in female, leads
to neurosis. The ideal psychological balance is, then, represented
in mythology by the union of the two sexes in the single person
of the first human being.

From the point of view of evolution the myth may be interpreted in this way. For thousands and thousands of years Adam,
that is, the Hominidae, proliferated across the surface of the
globe held together by *participation mystique* in an unconscious
harmony. Like animals they were not conscious of themselves as
individuals, and, again like animals, the death of an individual
among them could mean nothing to them. Lives were lost, but
life went on. The falling of the odd leaf from the tree of life was
a matter of no consequence since life renewed itself eternally;
each was part of all and, because each was a living creature, each
was life itself. But when the awful moment of awakening into
self-consciousness came and individual men realized they stood
alone, man instinctively turned to woman who, through sexual
union, could restore to him that sense of *participation mystique*
he had so largely lost. Through woman and through the rearing
of children man, become self-conscious, could participate again,
though on a more limited because a less indefinite scale, in the
unity of life. True, for the first time he would have to face up to
the reality of his own individual death, but the fact that his life
continued in his children, made the acceptance of death bearable.
Immortality was no longer the felt participation in all living

[14] R. C. Zaehner, *The Teachings of the Magi* (London, 1956), pp. 75-76.

things but the perpetuation of the newly-won "selfhood" of the individual person in his progeny. The immortality of the mass in space gave way to the immortality of the person prolonging himself in his offspring in time. In this way perhaps did man become a "living soul."

God created man in his own image, in the image of God created he him; male and female created he them.

How is this passage to be understood? and how can man be said to be "in the image of God"? The stock answers we already know, and perhaps find them none too satisfactory. Man is said to resemble God in his soul rather than in his body; but since God is defined by Christians as a "pure spirit," this is little more than a tautology. He is said to resemble God in his higher faculties—his reason and his will. More basically still, as the Indians tell us (and we shall have to discuss this later) he resembles him in his essence, which is eternal Being. Conscious man, according to the Indian way of thinking, is, like the Christian God, a triune being : he is Being, thought or reason, and will transmuted into love and perfect happiness. So much for the individual.

Evolution, however, teaches us that the emergence of consciousness in man must have been a slow process, spanning many thousands of years, and we are no longer permitted to accept monogenism, that is, the emergence of one single fully self-conscious couple from among the prehuman Hominidae. The myth of Adam and Eve, then, must be drastically reinterpreted in accordance with evolutionary theory. Sensible Christians have long ago accepted the fact that man's origins can and must be traced back not only through the Hominidae to the common ancestors of men and apes, but also right back beyond these to the metazoa, the protozoa, and then back again beyond the living cell, to organic and then inorganic molecules, and finally to the atom itself.

"God formed man of the dust of the ground." So says Genesis, and Genesis, like science, is right. The scale of time is different : that is all—and yet not so different, for Christians should not have forgotten that "one day is with the Lord as a thousand years, and a thousand years as one day."[15] The Hindus, on their side, have always thought astronomically in terms of space and time

[15] II Pet. 3 : 8.

and account one "day of Brahman" to be a thousand ages of the gods, one "day of the gods" being twelve thousand human years. Add to this one "night of Brahman" of the same length.[16] and we have one day and night of Brahman equal to twenty-four million years. This is indeed more in the perspective of modern evolutionary theory.

What, however, is the second chapter of Genesis trying to tell us in the myth of the Tree of the Knowledge of good and evil? We have seen that it was evolution itself which brought man right up from the "dust of the ground"—inorganic matter—through the simplest living cell to the most complex and highly organized animal organism the world had ever seen and so to the brink of consciousness—and beyond. Man became a rational animal, an individual freed from the mass, capable of thought—but an animal still : and a thinking animal is a dangerous thing. To cure his loneliness and, one cannot help thinking, to distract him from too intense a preoccupation with his new-found powers, God gave man woman, and through woman, children. A wholly self-conscious human race had come to be. All this was brought about by the "Spirit of God," the directive power of evolution which transforms the "dust of the earth" into a "living soul." This Spirit the Church calls the "Lord, the Giver of Life."

The motives ascribed by the author of the Book of Genesis to the Lord God seem to be far from creditable. Mankind is in the process of crossing the threshold of consciousness; and this has happened to him through the operation of the Spirit in living matter. Self-consciousness brings with it the apprehension of the divine—for *homo sapiens* was also *homo religiosus* at least from paleolithic times as the evidence of the caves at Lascaux and elsewhere conclusively shows. But this time the apprehension of the divine is not the apprehension of the spirit of life working within man himself and within all living things and linking them together in a felt unity, it is an apprehension of the divine as something other than himself to which obedience is due.

And the Lord God planted a garden eastward in Eden; and there he put the man whom he had formed.... And the Lord God commanded the man, saying, Of every tree of the garden thou mayest freely eat : but of the tree of the knowledge of good and evil, thou shalt not eat of it : for in the day that thou eatest thereof thou shalt surely die.

[16] *Laws of Manu*, I.69-72.

One of the commonest themes in all mythology is that man came into the world not only innocent but immortal. And this is, perhaps, natural; for in these twilight years in which man was still groping toward consciousness—since he had no thought of himself as an individual—he could not be disturbed by the deaths of others or the fear of his own death : he was assured of eternal life in the universal life that everywhere pulsated around him. Passing across the threshold of consciousness, but still having the mind of a child, he must have been as certain of his own immortality as he previously had been of that of the group. And even today it seems to be a fact that children, often up to puberty and sometimes long after, cannot grasp the fact of death even when it strikes within their own family, nor can they at all conceive that they themselves will ever die. So must it have been with those first fully conscious human beings whom Genesis calls Adam and Eve; it seemed to them incredible that they should ever die, and God's threat must therefore have seemed idle.

In the Garden they were still innocent; they were like children as yet uninstructed in what is right and wrong; and, being children, they could not sin, for sin implies responsibility. And this myth too, though valueless as an account of the origins of man, nevertheless reflects a deep nostalgia within the human mind. For man has never ceased to be haunted by the vision of an innocence that he himself and, with him, the whole human race has irremediably lost : he hankers after the lost childhood of the world. He longs to say with Rimbaud, *Apprécions sans vertige l'étendue de mon innocence*—"Let us scan, without giddiness, the full extent of my innocence." For man knows that despite the load of guilt that weighs upon him and his whole race, this innocence still persists somewhere deep down within his psyche. Somehow or other "original innocence" must co-exist with Original Sin.

This vision of innocence which Jung symbolizes as the archetype of the *puer aeternus,* has a quite extraordinary hold on men's minds. In mythology it will turn up in myths concerning the golden age at the beginning of time, in which there was neither disease nor sin, old age nor death, while in poetry and fiction the type will turn up over and over again—in the Prince Myshkins of this world whose simplicity nothing seems able to corrupt. "Is there such a thing," Bernanos asks, "as carnal innocence—an innocence that is capable of standing up to every kind of experience, an innocence which vice itself cannot blight?"[17] That such an innocence does exist most of us know by experience, for all of us must have known people who carry with them an atmosphere of innocence and purity that seems to transcend not only their environment but also their own sometimes considerable imperfections. The type of all such is, of course, St. Francis of Assisi who, in his purity and gaiety and love of simple things, puts us in mind of the dawn of human life, the "age of innocence" before consciousness of self and the experience of good and evil that only individual selves can know, came to be. This age of innocence, the myth of Genesis has it, was the original state of man, and it was this state that Adam's disobedience, his insatiable and quite natural curiosity to *know,* forever shattered.

Before the Fall man was conscious as a child is conscious : he had not yet grown to full moral stature. Knowing neither good nor evil he could not be held responsible for his acts. His Eden was a child's Eden but without the miseries that usually attend childhood, for these seem to stem in large measure from the intervention of grownups : and in Eden there were no grownups— except only the Lord God.

The Lord God was, of course, omniscient and therefore familiar with the ways of children. He must, then, have been perfectly aware that if he told them not to do something, they would almost certainly do it; or, to put it more philosophically, the Fall must have been present before him in his eternal consciousness (for in God there can be neither past nor future but only an eternal now), and before him too were the dire consequences that the Fall was bound to bring about : yet all this seemed to him "very good."

Now the serpent was more subtil than any beast of the field which the Lord God had made. And he said unto the woman, Yea, hath God said, Ye shall not eat of every tree of the garden? And the woman said unto the serpent, We may eat of the fruit of the trees of the garden: but of the fruit of the Tree which is in the midst of the garden, God hath said, Ye shall not eat of it, neither shall ye touch it, lest ye die. And the serpent said unto the woman, Ye shall not surely die: for God doth know that in the day ye eat thereof, then your eyes shall be opened, and ye shall be as gods, knowing good and evil. And when the woman saw that the tree was good for food, and that it was pleasant to the eyes, and a tree to be desired to make one wise, she took of the

[17] Georges Bernanos, *Un mauvais rêve* (Paris, 1951), p. 43.

fruit thereof, and did eat, and gave also unto her husband with her; and he did eat. And the eyes of them both were opened, and they knew that they were naked; and they sewed fig leaves together, and made themselves aprons. And they heard the voice of the Lord God walking in the garden in the cool of the day: and Adam and his wife hid themselves from the presence of the Lord God amongst the trees of the garden. And the Lord God called unto Adam, and said unto him, Where art thou? And he said, I heard thy voice in the garden, and I was afraid, because I was naked; and I hid myself.

In this simple story we have the sole Scriptural authority for the Christian doctrine of the Fall and Original Sin; and by the standards of the world Adam's sin was no sin at all, for all he wanted was to increase his intellectual grasp of reality, to know and understand more, even if that meant disobeying what seemed to be a totally unreasonable command. Adam was the first free-thinker, and for freethinkers it is not Adam but God who stands in need of justification. It is true that God had warned Adam that to eat of the tree of knowledge meant death. Man must choose between achieving intellectual maturity with death at the end of it and an indefinite prolongation of the age of innocence which would spare him forever the pain inseparable from the process of growing into manhood. God had, however, not warned him of the miseries and the dislocations that intellectual maturity would bring with it; he had not warned him of the violent and often intolerable stresses he would be subjected to once his "eyes were opened" when he would not only "know good and evil" but be in the terrible position to know the good and choose the evil. Nor did he warn him of the nature of evil itself which is at once a boomerang and a snowball; for it both recoils upon the evildoer and starts a chain reaction of further evil the end of which cannot be foreseen. This is something self-conscious man would have to find out for himself. It is the price that all have to pay for intellectual quest pursued in isolation from God.

The serpent in the parable is the intellect, newly born and thirsting to test its young muscles in a totally virgin field— intellect proud and supremely self-confident, seeing in God no longer a father but rather a jealous tyrant determined to keep his unwilling subjects in a beatific coma of invincible ignorance. The serpent is the fruit of that same Spirit which from the beginning "moved upon the face of the waters"—the Spirit which transformed matter into energy, energy into life, and life into thought, the Spirit that directs and guides evolution itself toward self-consciousness and against which God himself seems to be powerless. The serpent, then, *is* in a sense the Holy Spirit as the Gnostics were not slow to point out. Orthodox Christianity, however, has preferred to see in the serpent not the Holy Spirit, but Satan, man's eternal enemy; and the myth of Genesis must then mean not that God intended to keep man forever from investigating the mysteries of nature, to keep him from making the qualitative leap to which the Spirit was itself leading him, but that he wished to spare him the inevitable bewilderment and disorientation the leap was bound to bring if it was made not in co-operation with God but against his express command. The human race does not of itself "choose" to eat of the fruit of the tree of knowledge, it is beguiled thereto by the serpent, forced, as it were, by the very nature of things to make the qualitative leap from ignorance which is innocence to full self-consciousness which is knowledge, responsibility, and intellectual progress. Who could resist this "tree to be desired to make one wise"? What possible harm could there be in eating its fruit? And then, as the serpent pointed out to Eve, what were God's motives in seeking to hold man back from the leap into consciousness for which the whole universe had been working since time began? Surely, nothing but jealousy, "for God doth know that in the day ye eat thereof, then your eyes shall be opened, and ye shall be *as gods, knowing good and evil.*" With the attainment of knowledge man would be able to shake off the tutelage of God and set up house on his own, "going it alone in defiance of the grace of God." These consequences the infant human race had not realized : they ate of the sweet fruit of the tree of knowledge and were astonished that at once it turned bitter in their mouths.

And what were the results of the eating of the fruit? First man became conscious of his nakedness—he had lost his innocence and felt disarmed in the face of both God and the world outside him. Gone was the feeling of *participation mystique* which had given him the sense of immortality through his solidarity with all living things. Gone was his sense of fellowship with a transcendent God with whom he had walked in the Garden; gone the sense of unity he had felt with his own kind; gone the bond that once had bound man and woman into "one flesh."

Worse still, he now knew that he must die, and he saw that life itself, now no more than a prelude to death, was no longer the pleasure garden he had known as a child, but a hard road that leads only to bodily extinction and from which there is no return. Lastly, and we shall be returning to this later, the unity of man's own being was shattered. The "breath of life" that God had breathed into him when he "formed him from the dust of the ground" no longer directed and lived in harmony with the psychosomatic frame he had inherited from the animals. The brain, the locus of his newborn consciousness, thought, and will, was no longer subject to his immortal soul.

All this is represented in the Biblical story as happening in a moment. Science teaches us that the emergence of man into full consciousness was a process that lasted thousands of years; but the larger perspective does nothing to diminish the gravity, or impair the truth, of the doctrine of the Fall. Science, however, could never regard man's crossing of the threshold of consciousness as being a "fall" at all, and from the point of view of science, of course, it is not : for science is the fruit of the Fall and the serpent its guiding genius. But science is not everything; and in terms of human happiness it cannot be denied that a state of innocence in which the individual is barely conscious of his own separate existence and conscious of his built-in solidarity with the living mass is a happier state than individual consciousness in which all is striving and frustration. In the parable of the "Grand Inquisitor" in the *Brothers Karamazov* Dostoevski arraigns the Catholic Church for its alleged preoccupation with human happiness at the expense of human endeavor and the deepening of the human spirit. This may or may not be a fair description of the teaching of the Catholic Church; it is certainly a fair description of the Lord God's attitude to Adam : it is better to be an ignorant child than to pursue knowledge without reference to God.

In the Easter rite of the Catholic Church the Fall is spoken of as a *felix culpa*, a "happy fault"; and that is just as it should be seen. And perhaps it could not have been otherwise for the history of the human race, at least as interpreted by many modern physicists, seems to be strangely reflected in the life of the human individual; and just as a child, if he is a true child, must long to stay a child forever—no child wishes to put away childish things —so must the human race have been reluctant to pass from the age of innocence to the age of experience and responsibility. Yet, on reaching the age of reason, the child has perforce to accept his new condition, and, if he is sensible, he will make the most of the responsibilities he cannot evade. In nine cases out of ten the adolescent will rebel against his father, and that is precisely what the infant human race, symbolized by Adam, the "All-Man" as Julian of Norwich calls him, is represented as doing. He could scarcely have done otherwise, for the transition from life to consciousness, even though it may have occupied a period of thousands upon thousands of years, cannot but have been a violent affair, nor can it have produced anything but bewilderment and turmoil, and therefore resentment at whatever divine authority was felt to exist. "Adam's" reaction is precisely that of an intelligent adolescent, and the results were the same.

Cursed is the ground for thy sake; in sorrow shalt thou eat of it all the days of thy life; thorns also and thistles shall it bring forth to thee; and thou shalt eat the herb of the field; in the sweat of thy face shalt thou eat bread, till thou return unto the ground; for out of it wast thou taken: for dust thou art, and unto dust shalt thou return.

This is a terrible judgment which many may think unjust. And so it would be had Adam and Eve really been a single pair of human beings who one day decided to disobey an arbitrary command and ate of the fruit of a tree that was to make them wiser and, if wiser, then surely better people. But the story has a deeper meaning than that. Nowadays, we are practically forced by the paleontologists to accept the fact that although in geophysical time the passage from life to consciousness must have been a sudden and violent affair—a qualitative leap that happened once and for all—it nevertheless must have taken place throughout most of the globe, and it must have happened to a great many Adams and Eves spread out not only in space but also in what is by our standards a very long time. It is not too farfetched to assume that this gradual passage from subconsciousness through group consciousness to self-consciousness—from the sense of belonging to the All and through the All to its source which is God to total self-consciousness and self-confidence—resulted not only in the isolation of man from his fellow men but also from any sense of intimate communion with his environment. The human race was split up into fragments: in Biblical terms the "image of God" was shattered. Man, henceforward, being but a shattered fragment of the "All-Man," cut off from all intimate relationship with the whole, cut off too from any sure knowledge of God as the author of his being, had no alternative but to go it alone. At the same time, it may be assumed, he had memories of a life in which he was not conscious of his own individuality and in which his solidarity with the whole had guaranteed his own immortality in the context of the whole. His religious quest would therefore now be divided : first he would try to restore his lost sense of solidarity through social means, since he no longer *felt* the oneness of all things, and secondly he would delve deep down within himself in an effort to discover immortality within his own being. Intermittently too a deep nostalgia for a vanished age of innocence would make itself felt and men would, on rare occasions, catch a fleeting glimpse of a vanished golden age.

To sum up, then, we may take the doctrine of the Fall as related in the Book of Genesis to mean the full emergence of the human race into consciousness. Since so far we have taken Genesis as our text, we must be excused, even in allegorizing it, for taking the reality of the central figure of the drama—the Lord God—as given. The Biblical picture of man as the image of God we accept on other grounds that will become apparent in the sequel. Here it will suffice to say that if we take the minimal definition of God as being the eternal and changeless substrate of all that is subject to change, then the "image of God" in man must mean, among other things, that in him which is changeless and eternal. The shattering of the image will mean the fragmentation of human "soul-stuff" into an infinity of self-enclosed eternities, turned in upon themselves and unable, therefore, to participate in the eternity of each other or of God.

Let us pursue the simile further. Let the Sun symbolize God, and an absolutely pure and translucent mirror the soul of man-kind as it was before the Fall. The whole mirror will perfectly reflect the Sun : this is the age of innocence before man stumbled into self-consciousness and fell. When he falls, the mirror falls with him : it is smashed into millions of tiny bits, some remaining relatively clean and unsmirched. Others, however, falling into the mire, are immediately covered completely over with mud, and the crystal beneath is completely hidden from sight. Others are

only slightly soiled, while yet others are cracked and reflect only
a distorted image of the Sun. Our fragments are, of course, conscious entities; and except for those which have sunk deep into
the mire, they will try to reassemble themselves into the perfect
whole they once were, or, if they have been too badly damaged,
they will try to polish themselves clean so that they will be able
to reflect the Sun in their own individual way. In other words
they will try to unite socially, or they will try to rediscover their
own eternity alone. These two trends, in fact, form the dominant
streams of the so-called higher religions in historical times. They
are never entirely separate, but, broadly speaking, it can be said
that the Indian religions concern themselves mainly with the
polishing of the mirror, the Semitic religions mainly with the reintegration of the mirror into a perfect whole that will once again
enshrine a perfect image of the Sun.

This dual quest which will be the subject of our next chapters,
however, was to take place only in the remote future. The shattering of the mirror had meant that each individual now stood
alone, suspicious of his neighbor, resentful against God, full of
guilt and *Angst*, but knowing only dimly in what his guilt
consisted.

And "unto Adam and his wife did the Lord God make coats
of skins, and clothed them"—clothed them to hide their guilt and
shame, clothed with a new set of rules, taboos, and beliefs to distract them from knowing their own nakedness and lift from
them for a little while the intolerable burden of being alone and
of contemplating the defiant loneliness of one another.

And the Lord God said, Behold, the man is become as one of us, to
know good and evil: and now, lest he put forth his hand, and take
also of the tree of life, and eat, and live for ever: therefore the Lord
God sent him forth from the garden of Eden, to till the ground from
whence he was taken. So he drove out the man; and he placed at the
east of the garden of Eden Cherubims, and a flaming sword which
turned every way, to keep the way of the tree of life.

Gone was the garden of innocence forever, gone the very state
of innocence, gone the sense of being part of a greater whole,
of being "one in Adam" as St. Paul puts it, when the death of the

one was felt to be no diminution of the whole not even by the
one who died, gone the day when it was still true to say,

> If the slayer think to slay,
> If the slain think himself slain,
> Both these understand not:
> This one slays not, nor is slain.[18]

Those were the days when the individual was still merged in
the mass and could therefore have no consciousness of a duty to
his neighbor. On emerging into consciousness, however, his terror
of his neighbor was such that he must strike him down; for only
by actually committing murder could the murderer feel a
murderer's guilt.

And Cain talked with Abel his brother: and it came to pass, when
they were in the field, that Cain rose up against Abel his brother,
and slew him. And the Lord said unto Cain, Where is Abel thy brother?
And he said, I know not: Am I my brother's keeper? And he said, What
hast thou done? The voice of thy brother's blood crieth unto me from
the ground. And now art thou cursed from the earth, which hath
opened her mouth to receive thy brother's blood from thy hand. . . .
And Cain said unto the Lord, My punishment is greater than I can
bear. Behold, thou hast driven me out this day from the face of the
earth; and from thy face shall I be hid; and I shall be a fugitive and a
vagabond in the earth; and it shall come to pass, that every one that
findeth me shall slay me.

Such are the unpromising beginnings of the story of the
brotherhood of man. Self-conscious man comes face to face with
his brother as a separate individual. He sees him, fears him, and,
fearing him, lays him low. Things have not changed much since,
except that in our more collective civilization it is not only individual men who hate each other, but nations, classes, and
ideologies. Adam, by his disobedience to the Father, became the
symbol of disunity. Christ, the second Adam and Son of God,
by his perfect sacrifice of self, became the symbol of unity
renewed; and once-Christian nations, by turning their backs on
the second Adam and the unity of his Church, repeat the Fall
on a far grander scale. Having dissolved the bond of unity that
held them together, Christian nations have been forced, as Adam
was forced, to accept a minimum moral code lest they should
utterly destroy each other. Slower to learn than Cain, even this

[18] *Kaṭha* Upanishad, 2.19.

may prove too much for them. Again it is Camus who best depicts the aftermath of this second Fall :

There can be no love without a little innocence. And where was innocence? Empires collapsed, nations and men were at each other's throats. Our very mouths were defiled. First we were innocent and knew it not : now we were guilty and wanted no part in it. The mystery only increased with the increase of our knowledge. So, fools that we were, we busied ourselves with morality. Being weak, I dreamt of virtue. In the age of innocence I did not know there was such a thing as morality. I knew it now, and I could not live up to it.[19]

Things have not changed : the lament of Camus is the lament of Cain. For as in Adam all sinned by pushing individuality to a point where it severed the bond that had linked us together, so do we in our turn look back with longing to the age of innocence when conscience had not convicted us of sin. And that is what the "Lord God" stands for in those first chapters of Genesis : he is the conscience of individual man before which, deep down and no matter what his beliefs, he stands naked and ashamed.

Two aspects of deity—the Father and the Holy Spirit, the moral imperative and the "Giver of Life" : and the miracle is that, using matter as its raw material, the Spirit forces us, however slowly and gently, toward an ultimate encounter with the Father. It starts with motion, and motion burgeons into life, and life into consciousness. By sin consciousness stumbles on conscience, and by conscience we acknowledge the justice that is of God. In the end, as we shall later see, the Spirit urges matter on yet further, and, through the Incarnation of the Son of God, redeems and sanctifies the whole material universe. According to the second law of thermodynamics the universe is running down, but over against this downward drag, science is beginning to tell us, there is the dialectically contrary law of the progress of life toward ever greater complexity and ever greater consciousness, the end of which we cannot yet foresee : and this is surely the operation of the Holy Spirit in the order of nature. But over against this "Spirit of God" that "moved upon the face of the waters" and the "breath of life" which God breathed into man stands that God himself who is man's Lord and Father—and his conscience : and it is this God who not only convicted but convinced man of the awful reality of sin; and without this

[19] L'Été, pp. 148-49.

conviction and the knowledge that it is sin that separates him from God and therefore from happiness, man cannot even hope for salvation which means the reassembling and perfect cleansing of God's shattered image into the unity to which the Spirit drives us on.

3

Refashioning the Image

"SIN," IN GERMAN, IS *SÜNDE*; AND THE WORD *SÜNDE* is etymologically connected with *sondern*, "to sever or separate," and *Sonderung* "separation." Sin, then, is not only "error" (for that is the meaning of the Greek *hamartia*), it is also separation. In Christian theology Original Sin, which we allegorized in our last chapter, results in bodily death, the separation, that is, of the "living soul" which is of the breath or Spirit of God and the psychophysical organism which constitutes the body. It results, then, in the dichotomy of man's own nature. A word, however, must now be said about the nature of the soul as it is understood first in the West and secondly in India.

The Hebraic view of the soul right up to the time of the exile and the first contacts between Jew and Zoroastrian was that it formed an indissoluble whole with the body. When the body died, the soul to all intents and purposes died with it : it went to Sheol, the "pit" of the grave, where it led an existence so shadowy as to be almost unreal, cut off from the "living" God and the whole world of the living. This gloomy view of the state of the dead the Hebrews shared with the Babylonians (from whom they may have derived it) and with the Homeric Greeks. For them the soul was the breath of life through which the body lived, and this was its sole function. Soul and body fused together constituted man, and once the two were separated no man remained : the soul in Sheol was a shadow or a memory of a man, it was not a man, for it had no contact with living things, and life, except in God, is possible only when a material substrate is animated by spirit. Neither matter nor spirit alone can properly be considered to be alive. Body and mind too were as indissolubly linked as body and soul, and with the disintegration of the body the mind disintegrated with it. Death, that is, the disintegration of the human person, was the result of the Fall, and this primitive Judaism accepted without demur; for had not the Lord God himself said, "Of the tree of the knowledge of good and evil, thou shalt not eat of it: for in the day that thou eatest thereof thou shalt surely die"? And death meant the breaking up of man into his component parts.

Starting with so stark an acceptance of the finality of death, Israel might well have lapsed into as dismal a pessimism as prevailed in neighboring Babylon where man was seen simply as the infinitely expendable slave of the gods. In Israel, however, things worked out differently; for though man had been driven out of the Garden of Eden, God did not then leave him to his own devices. Very much the reverse: he was ever present with his people, but the relationship between the two was changed—and changed very much for the worse. Man no longer walked with God as Adam had once done, but waited upon the word of God. God was no longer man's father and companion but his Lord and Master to whom absolute obedience was due and against whom there could be no appeal. To the early Israelites the supreme sin was disobedience, and disobedience meant, as it had meant in the case of Adam, to engage in any enterprise however attractive and however seemingly worthwhile without reference to God. The Fall had brought man not only death but disunion, and the re-creation of the shattered unity must then have been one of man's principal preoccupations. The symbol of this is the Tower of Babel, the representation in myth of man's supreme attempt to recover the lost unity of the age of innocence by social organization.

And they said one to another, ... Go to, let us build us a city and a tower, whose top may reach unto heaven; and let us make us a name, lest we be scattered abroad upon the face of the whole earth. And the Lord came down to see the city and the tower, which the children of men builded. And the Lord said, Behold, the people is one, and they have all one language; and this they begin to do: and now nothing will be restrained from them, which they have imagined to do. Go to, let us go down, and there confound their language, that they may not understand one another's speech. So the Lord scattered them abroad from thence upon the face of all the earth: and they left off to build the city.

In the Koran we read, "And they were crafty: and God was crafty—and God is the best of the crafty ones."[1] And the idea

[1] Koran, 3.47.

of the "craftiness" or "guile" of God shocks us. The idea, however, is as characteristic of the Old Testament as it is of Islam : no human endeavor can hope to succeed, however good the intention, if it is pursued in defiance of the will of God. Both in the story of Adam and in the story of the Tower of Babel man's aspirations are not only laudable but inspired by the Spirit that directs his evolutionary development, tirelessly urging him on toward a greater unity. But each evolutionary advance is compensated by a loss. Individual self-consciousness is paid for by the loss of all sense of participation in the whole; and similarly any artificial attempt to imitate the age of innocence when mankind formed one single organic whole must fail until such time as humanity has overcome its individualistic phase and has reached a stage where, transcending self, it can combine to form a single living organism in which there will be no clash between the individual and the whole, and each will work for all, and all for each. An organism is not just an efficient organization, for it is "totalitarian" in the sense that if one part is diseased, the whole will suffer : the individual members cannot opt out. In an organization, however, the parts work independently and never constitute an organically united whole. It was not the concept of the Tower of Babel that was wrong, for it was noble, but the timing, for it was vastly premature.

On the superficial level God's action in driving Adam out of Paradise and in destroying the Tower of Babel is both petty and spiteful : he fears the latent power of man and is not ashamed to say so. In the first case he justifies himself in these words :

Behold, the man is become as one of us, to know good and evil: and now, lest he put forth his hand, and take also of the tree of life, and eat, and live for ever.

He is afraid that man may outstrip him in knowledge and deprive him of his throne. In the second case he fears that "now nothing will be restrained from them, which they have imagined to do." Here again he shows that man, by the unrestricted use of reason and through an efficient social organization, may so order his own affairs that the Lord God himself will become redundant. So ungodly did the God of the Old Testament seem to be that the third century heretic, Marcion, while admitting divine inspiration for the Old Testament, came to the not wholly surprising conclusion that the two Testaments were inspired by different gods : the first was the work of the "God of the Law" who, though not downright evil, was nonetheless a petty tyrant and, though not himself the Supreme Being, was foolish enough to believe himself to be so. In reality the Supreme Being was the God of Love and Gnosis, the Father of Jesus Christ and he it was who inspired the New Testament, or rather those parts of it that Marcion found to his liking. Marcion was condemned as a heretic, but his is a heresy that many find not unreasonable; for the Old Testament, if allowed to speak for itself without any authoritative interpretation, shows us a God at times so arbitrary, so "jealous," and so petty as scarcely to be reconcilable with the God of Love revealed in and by Jesus Christ. To put such a book into the hands of an uninstructed laity is surely to court disaster.

On a deeper level, however, God's action can be seen not so much as the action of a power both stupid and jealous as the inevitable result of man's own original sin—"disobedience" in the language of the Bible, *hybris* in the terminology of the Greeks. In the case of the Tree of Knowledge it is man's own arrogant conceit that he is sufficient in himself to control and direct his new-found consciousness, that precipitates his Fall and throws him into internal disarray. In the case of the Tower of Babel it is the same self-conceit that leads him to believe that, relying on his own resources alone, he can create a perfect state. In the first case he is wrecked by intellectual pride in that he thinks that he knows better than God, in the second by an ineradicable selfishness which makes it impossible for him, unless aided by God, to work in harmony with his fellows.

The story of the Tower of Babel is typical of the Hebrew way of thinking. For us it is a story with a moral : for the Hebrews it was history—an episode in the slowly unfolding story of God's dealings with man and more particularly with his chosen people. In the Old Testament the individual plays no significant part at all : the story is all of God's dealings with the Jewish people which he has chosen out of all the peoples of the world as his vessel of election. The Jewish religion is thus "solidary" and collective, the unity that was lost through the sin of the "All-Man," Adam, being partially reconstituted in the communal obedience owed by the chosen people to God. So too God's covenant is with Israel as a whole, not with the individuals who compose it. The individual Jew was, of himself, of no consequence; his privilege and his responsibility were collective, he had importance only as being part of the people privileged to be the elect of God. Of personal immortality he knew nothing, and it was only by his membership of the race and by the race's confrontation with the living God that he could conceive of himself as participating in the Eternal. This participation was, however, in no sense a mystical communion; rather it was the experience of transcendence, the awed awareness of the presence of One, who, in his unutterable holiness, is totally other than man.

This sense of religion as being a collective activity is fundamental to all the religions of Semitic origin. It is as true of Catholic Christianity and Islam as it is of Israel. Except in so far as Hinduism is also a social system, it is totally foreign to the religions of India.

So long as Israel maintained this collective view of religion, she did not worry herself over the fate of the individual soul at death : it did not seem particularly relevant. During the Babylonian captivity, however, and after the overthrow of Babylon by Persia, she made contact with another monotheistic faith not dissimilar to her own—Zoroastrianism. So close did the Jews feel the religion of the Persian kings to be to their own that the second Isaiah saw nothing incongruous in hailing Cyrus as the "Lord's anointed." Zoroastrianism at this stage, however, was not a collective religion in the sense that Israel was. On the contrary, the Prophet Zoroaster had, more than any of the Hebrew prophets, insisted on the personal responsibility of each individual to choose between the forces of "Truth" and the forces of the "Lie." If there is one thing that marks out Zoroaster's message and distinguishes it not only from the neighboring religions to East and West but also from "Zoroastrianism" as it was later to develop, it is his rigorous insistence on the freedom of the individual will to choose between good and evil and his confident affirmation that good will be rewarded and evil punished in postmortem states he calls the Best Existence and Evil Existence respectively, that is to say, heaven and hell. What Judaism had hitherto lacked was any picture of individual afterlife that was consonant with either the divine justice or the divine mercy. This lacuna Zoroastrianism could fill in, for, unlike the peoples with whom the Jews had been in close contact in the past, the Zoroastrians were not idolaters but monotheists, and so extraordinary must this have appeared to the Jews that they may have conceded that they too had received a revelation of some sort from the one true God to whom they themselves owed allegiance. Were this not so, it is difficult to see how they could have called Cyrus the Lord's anointed. Hence it would not be unnatural for them to assimilate from the Zoroastrians doctrines which were lacking in their own religion but which nonetheless corresponded to a deeply-felt human need. So, from this period on we find what we so often think of as being typically Christian doctrines appearing for the first time in Judaism—the rewarding and punishment of the souls of the dead in accordance with the good and evil deeds they had performed on earth, the resurrection of the body, and the final renewal of existence in the last days.

Moreover, the Zoroastrians' ideas concerning the nature of man were very similar to those of the Jews. Unlike the Indians they did not conceive of the soul as an entity that has its being outside space and time and is therefore eternal and immortal; they conceived of it as something that even after death has some material substrate, for the wicked are described as being condemned to a "long age of darkness, foul food, and cries of woe." Whatever the nature of the material substrate, however, the mind was certainly held to survive, for heaven is also described as the "House of the Good Mind" and hell as the "House of the Worst Mind." For Zoroaster was in no doubt at all that individuality continues after death, and this is just what you would expect in a religion which lays so overwhelming an emphasis on the individual's moral responsibility on earth.

For later Judaism and later Zoroastrianism, then, there was both an individual salvation and the salvation of the community. There was both a judgment of the soul at death and a final resurrection of all men in the last days when body and soul would once again be joined together. In the final analysis the destiny of the individual dovetailed into the universal destiny at the end of time. There is no fusion of the individual personality in the mass, but a harmonious interaction of persons turned toward the central point of a universe renewed by the saving power of the living God. Nowhere do we see this more clearly than in the later Zoroastrian texts; and since the Zoroastrian vision has so much in common with the contemporary vision of Teilhard de

Chardin and in a sense prefigures it, we shall be dwelling on it in some detail in a later chapter.

The principal criticism leveled against Teilhard de Chardin is that in his evolutionary assessment of the upsurge of humanity to ever greater peaks of consciousness he takes little or no account of sin or evil. This criticism seems perfectly fair, and *The Phenomenon of Man* reads far more like a more strictly scientific development of Engels' thought in *Anti-Dühring* and the *Dialectics of Nature* than it does of anything we find in orthodox Christianity. Neither Marxism nor Teilhard takes into account the evil that is within man; and this makes it impossible for them to explain why their reading of the laws of nature or, as Teilhard puts it, of the "irreversible trend of evolution," proves to be so tragically and repeatedly wrong. They have no alternative but to fall back on the concept of geophysical time, and to say that if the mere passage of man from life to consciousness took thousands upon thousands of years, then is it not probable that the passage from consciousness to hyperconsciousness, as Teilhard calls it, or the passage from capitalism to full Communism in the case of the Marxists, may not take an equivalent time? Against this must be set the incredible advances made by science in the last hundred years, which would seem to indicate that the evolutionary process within what Teilhard calls the "noosphere," that is, the collective scientific mind, is accelerating in almost geometrical progression, and time itself has acquired a new momentum. It is not that the qualitative leap that he foresees seems particularly improbable : what is in doubt is rather whether the human race is in any way prepared for it. And it is because the Zoroastrians had so clear a conception of the blighting action of evil even in the last days when it would finally be laid low, that we will have to consider their vision of the future before we pass on to the modern apocalypses of Engels and Teilhard de Chardin.

The Jewish and the Zoroastrian views of the origin of evil differ. In the Jewish account the origin of evil is man's disobedience to God—he tries to arrange his own affairs without reference to God. In the Zoroastrian account evil is either a separate principle, or a perverse but originated spirit (closely akin to the Lucifer of later Christian theology), or again it is a hidden canker in the heart of God himself. For both religions, however, evil is a factor that must always be taken into account in any interpretation of the story of mankind. For the Jew evil manifests itself primarily in the unaccountable stubbornness against God displayed by the Jewish people themselves; for the Zoroastrian it is rather an objective reality which man is free to choose at his peril. Both religions, moreover, are essentially this-worldly, because they regard body and soul, matter and spirit, as being an inner and an outer aspect of the same reality. Just as matter itself has a "without" and a "within," what Teilhard de Chardin confusingly calls a "tangential" and a "radial" aspect, that is, in more conventional terminology a "material" (observable) and a "spiritual" (not directly observable) aspect, so has individual man a "without" and a "within"—a body and a soul.

The reaction of Judaic man to the Fall, then, was to seek to restore a lost solidarity in a collective obedience to God, while that of Zoroastrian man was to prolong human life beyond the grave in a form of existence in which the soul, though deprived of its earthly body temporarily, would partake of the joys of heaven or suffer the pains of hell in accordance with deeds done on earth—and this in anticipation of the renewal of all existence in which evil would exist no more and the body would once again arise from the dead. In both religions salvation, if it is to be salvation at all, must be total—salvation of the body as well as of the soul, of matter as well as of spirit. In addition it must be collective as well as individual.

In India and China too we find the equivalent of both individual and collective salvation, but the two ideas develop *pari passu* like parallel lines : they never meet to form a single coherent world view. Thus in China we find two indigenous religions—Confucianism and Taoism. The first is almost exclusively a system of social ethics, possible only within one particular social structure, the Chinese Empire, while the second, in the classic formulations of Lao-Tzŭ and Chuang-Tzŭ, is essentially an esoteric doctrine applicable to the individual only. The two complement each other, for both of them, in the last analysis, would claim to be different facets of the one "Tao," which, though indefinable, is both the unchanging source of all that moves and lives, and the preordained "norm" of all human conduct. This norm the Neo-Confucianists claimed to reproduce in their elaboration of the code of ethics, etiquette, and ritual which for so many centuries dominated Chinese life. The Taoists, on the other hand, claimed esoteric knowledge of the "within" of the

Tao and saw individual salvation as simply letting oneself go and allowing one's personality to dissolve in the ebb and flow of the cosmos.

Yet, though the two religions may be the "without" and the "within" of the same indecipherable Tao, historically the "without" seemed so different from the "within" as to be antagonistic to it. Of all the great religions Confucianism is the most "this-worldly," so much so that the very title of religion has often been denied it. Its concept of deity is wholly nebulous; it is quite un-concerned with any personal survival after death—a matter, they held, it was futile to discuss since we know nothing about it; and in any case, "until you understand life, how can you understand death?"[2] All their emphasis was on the orderly regulation of life on this earth in accordance with gentlemanly standards, which, the Confucians considered (and who shall deny them?), reflected the Way (Tao) of heaven.

Taoism represents a much more generalized trend in the religious experience of the world. Basically it is indistinguishable from what is usually called nature mysticism; and this represents not an advance in any sense (indeed it does not claim to do so and would dismiss any such claim as being singularly wide of the mark), but a slipping back into the comforting embrace of that *participation mystique* which we have seen to be characteristic of the age of innocence before individual consciousness was born. It crops up not only in Taoism but in the Upanishads in India, in the Sūfī poets of Islam, in Western authors like Richard Jef-feries, Rimbaud, Proust, Hölderlin, and a host of others. It is some-times called nature mysticism, sometimes pantheism, and frequ-ently among its principal characteristics is a lofty contempt for conventional morality; for this experience of being one with all things annihilates time and destroys the validity of the distinc-tion between good and evil, for these concern the individual only; and what significance can they have for one who has not yet achieved individual consciousness or, having achieved it, lets it fall like an overripe apple to the ground, secure as he believes himself to be in nature's own deathlessness? Chuang-Tzŭ's instinct, then, serves him well when he situates the golden age of man's nonresistance to the "Way of Heaven" in the immemorial past, for before the rise of consciousness neither life nor death can have any particular meaning; both were equally good and

[2] *Analects,* xi.11.

accepted with a child's acceptance because there was nothing else to do.

The true men of old knew nothing of the love of life or the hatred of death. Entrance into life occasioned them no joy; the exit from it awakened no resistance. Composedly they went and came. They did not forget what their beginning had been, and they did not enquire into what their end would be. They accepted [their life] and rejoiced in it; they forgot [all fear of death] and returned [to their state before life]. Thus there was in them what is called the want of any mind to resist the Tao and of all attempts by means of the human, [that is, the self-conscious individual] to assist the heavenly. Such were they who were called the true men.[3]

This kind of mystical experience in which the individual seems to dissolve in the All brings wonderful peace and joy, but whether it comes unheralded (as is usual) or as a result of Yogic or similar techniques, it represents a retrograde step into the evolutionary past, not, as so many would-be mystics would have us believe, a "leap" into what they are pleased to call "super-consciousness." This, to their credit, the Taoists realized more clearly than anyone. Consciousness produces thought—individual thought, that is, which does not flow with the Tao of the unconscious—and thought produces the self-conscious and self-satisfied morality of the Confucians—and that too is not in accordance with the Tao. When the Tao was still able to operate without obstruction, that is to say, before the birth of intemperate individual thought,

On the hills there were no footpaths, nor excavated passages; on the lakes there were no boats nor dams; *all creatures lived in companies;* and all the places of their settlement were made close to one another. Birds and beasts multiplied to flocks and herds; the grass and trees grew luxuriant and long. . . . Yes, in the age of perfect virtue, men lived in common with birds and beasts, and were on terms of equality with all creatures, *as forming one family;*—how could they know among themselves the distinctions of superior men and small men? *Equally without knowledge,* they did not leave [the path of] their natural virtue; *equally free from desires,* they were in a state of pure simplicity. In that state of pure simplicity the nature of the people was what it ought to be.

But when the clever men appeared, limping and wheeling about in [the exercise of] benevolence, pressing along and standing on tip-toe

[3] Chuang-Tzŭ, vi.2.

in the doing of their duty, then men universally began to be perplexed. [The clever men too] went to excess in their performances of music, and in their gesticulations in the practice of ceremonies, *and then men began to be separated from one another.* If the raw materials had not been cut and hacked, who could have made a sacrificial vase from them? If the natural jade had not been broken and injured, who could have made the handles for the libation-cups from it? If the attributes of the Tao had not been disallowed, how should they have preferred benevolence and duty? *If the instincts of nature had not been departed from, how should ceremonies and music have come into use?* ... The cutting and hacking of the raw materials to form vessels was the crime of the skilful workman; the injury done to the character- istics of the Tao in order to practise benevolence and "do one's duty" was the error of the clever men.[4]

In this lovely, nostalgic passage is expressed as perhaps no- where else man's longing for a vanished age of innocence when all men were "equally without knowledge" and "equally free from desires." It was only with the rise of consciousness that men began to be separated from each other and a moral code became necessary to protect the individual from his more predatory fellow. To fall back into the stream of the eternal Tao means to merge consciousness once again into the collective unconscious, and this is what the nature mystics of all times and places have done and do; and in this loss of personality in what they conceive to be a more primeval and a more perfect state they experience a wonderful release from the responsibility that personality brings with it, a blissful letting-go in which individuality melts imper- ceptibly away and is once again swallowed up in the undifferentiated stream of life in which, if consciousness there is at all, it is a suffused consciousness of all that lives and, deeper down still, of all that moves. Without in any way wishing to belittle the experience (for in its way it is most precious), we can compare it to our wartime experiences in the armed forces. What- ever hardships we may have had to undergo and however great our initial resentment and rebellion may have been, most of us must have felt an unspeakable relief that the burden of respon- sibility, of independent thought, and of purposeful moral action had been lifted off our shoulders. Yet it was just this abdication of individual responsibility that made it possible for the Nazis

[4] *Ibid.*, ix.2.

to carry the German people with them into the vortex of their own unspeakable Tao.

> If the slayer think he slay,
> If the slain think himself slain,
> Both these understand not:
> This one slays not, nor is slain.

This saying from the *Katha* Upanishad was no doubt true of the age of innocence, and it is true too if, as Indian religion has always declared, the soul not only has its being outside space and time but also has only an accidental connection with the body. Given that the soul is thus secure and inviolable, it must follow that life as lived on earth has no ultimate significance, and it can matter little of what quality our actions be—whether they be good, bad, or indifferent—for life is a dream, a mirage, or an illusion, or, if it is none of these, then it is a hell from which we must at all costs escape. Whatever salvation may be, and in whatever terms we formulate the blessed release, one thing is agreed, and that is that intellect and sense must be transcended or suppressed. This is as true of "classical" Hinduism and Buddhism as it is of Taoism : but only Taoism has the courage and the honesty to castigate "benevolence" and "duty" as being the errors of clever men.

In no other country was the dichotomy between "this-worldli-ness" and "other-worldliness" more sharply etched than in the old China. Thus, in a Taoist text, Confucius is represented as accusing the Taoists of being enemies of life itself, though the Taoist would no doubt have replied that it was not so much life itself that wearied him as life as individually lived with all its suffering and anxiety, its impermanence and pain—a life which, even if passed in happiness had no other issue than death; and in the Tao there is neither life nor death. To the Confucians, ever preoccupied with morality and statecraft, their eyes firmly fixed on the doings of living men in this world, the Taoists appeared both irresponsible and frivolous. Confucius is represented as saying,

Those men occupy and enjoy themselves in what is outside the [common] ways [of the world], while I occupy and enjoy myself in what lies within those ways. *There is no common ground for those of such different ways;* and when I sent you to condole with those men, I was acting stupidly. They, moreover, make man to be the fellow of the Creator, and seek their enjoyment in the formless condition of heaven and earth. *They consider life to be an appendage attached, an excrescence annexed to them, and death to be a separation of the appendage and a dispersion of the contents of the excrescence.* With these views how should they know wherein death and life are to be found, or what is first and what is last? ... They occupy themselves ignorantly and vaguely with what [they say] lies outside the dust and dirt [of the world], and seek their enjoyment in the business of doing nothing. How should they confusedly address themselves to the ceremonies practised by the common people, and exhibit themselves as doing so to the ears and eyes of the multitude.[5]

In China the cleavage between the Way (Tao) of Confucius and the Way of Lao-Tzŭ and Chuang-Tzŭ was almost complete, the one striving to create a perfect social ethic which would owe its perfection to its supposed conformity to the law or Tao of nature, the other opting altogether out of life as humanly lived and humanly organized in order the better to sink back into the common life of the "Great Mass" and therein to breathe with the universal Spirit which gives life to all the material world.

In India things were rather different, and the reactions of Indian man to the results of the Fall, that is, the problem of what to do with human consciousness and how to face the certainty of bodily death, was overwhelmingly in the direction of transcending both. There are close resemblances both between Taoism and Buddhism and between Taoism and "classical" Hinduism from which Buddhism sprang; and this is enough to account for the phenomenal success of the Buddhist missionaries in the Chinese Empire. Buddhism, however, though no less insistent than Taoism in its contention that salvation could come about only when this world of matter *and mind* had been transcended, nevertheless considered moral conduct in this world as being an essential *propaideutikon*[6] to final release from the world. The pursuit of "benevolence" could not just be dismissed as a Confucian error unless, of course, it was the self-conscious benevolence of the "do-gooder" and social busybody whose motives are manifestly the reverse of selfless; rather it had to be actively pursued, for attention to the needs of others conduces to forgetfulness of self, and, for the Buddhist, consciousness of self is the root of all evil. Benevolence, in the Buddhist sense, consists in

[5] Chuang Tzŭ, vi.11.   [6] propaideutic: to teach beforehand.

wishing all men well, whether they love or hate you, agree with you or disagree with you, interest you or bore you : it consists in developing an attitude of mind toward your fellow men which is not one of excessive partiality or aversion; you must simply take them as they come and wish them all that is best. Love without attachment is, perhaps, the best way of describing this Buddhist virtue. But, in the Buddhist scheme of things, it is detachment from one's fellow creatures, not love of them, that leads to final emancipation from the ties of this world. For, despite its wonderful moral code of total self-denial, Buddhism remains, at least in its earlier development, supremely and sublimely, an other-worldly religion. The Buddha, the "Wholly Awakened One," is time and again compared to the lotus bloom flowering exquisitely a few inches above the muddy pool, detached from it and quite unsoiled by it, but connected nevertheless with the life-giving mud by the stalk that links its loveliness with the grime beneath. This state the Buddhists call "Nirvāna with a residue," for something of earthly attachment still remains. The final stage of "Nirvāna without residue" can be reached only when the flower is plucked and finally detached from the muddy water of the world of matter —the world of coming-to-be and passing away. The renunciation of individual life is the same in Buddhism as it is in Taoism, but is the goal necessarily the same? Is the Buddhist too simply reverting into that state of innocence where consciousness was not yet born? This is a question to which we shall have to revert. The down-to-earth Confucian, however, could see no difference : both Taoists and Buddhists were shirkers and impossible dreamers. This is how the Neo-Confucian Hu Yin, saw it :

Man is a living thing: the Buddhists speak not of life but of death. Human affairs are all visible: the Buddhists speak not of the manifest but of the hidden. After a man dies he is called a ghost: the Buddhists speak not of men but of ghosts. What man cannot avoid is the conduct of ordinary life: the Buddhists speak not of the ordinary but of the marvellous. What determines how we should behave in ordinary life is moral principle: the Buddhists speak not of moral principle but of the illusoriness of sense-perception. It is to what follows birth and precedes death that we should devote our minds: the Buddhists speak not of this life but of past and future lives. Seeing and hearing, thought and discussion, are real evidence: the Buddhists do not treat them as real, but speak of what the ear and eye cannot attain, thought and discussion cannot reach.

All this is true up to a point, but there is a big difference between Taoism and the form of Hinduism from which Buddhism sprang on the one hand and Buddhism itself on the other; for, whereas Taoism is openly contemptuous of the Confucian code of moral and social behavior and the Upanishads scarcely concern themselves with the moral order at all, Buddhism holds, and apparently held from the beginning, that the world, and with it the body and the discursive intellect, cannot be transcended unless and until all sense of self has been destroyed. And here we must pause for a moment and consider the concept of "self" as it appears in India; for until we are reasonably clear about how this word is used in the orthodox Hindu tradition, we will not be able to understand the Buddhist doctrine of "not-self" which European scholars seem largely to have misunderstood. And this brings us up against what the Indian tradition understands by the "self" or soul.

Let us quote the *Katha* Upanishad again :

> If the slayer think he slay,
> If the slain think himself slain,
> Both these understand not;
> This one slays not, nor is slain.

As everyone knows, the mainstream of Indian religion distinguishes itself from all others by its firm belief in the transmigration of souls. The verse quoted above, then, can mean no more than that since all individual souls which have already been born and reborn from time without beginning, are sure to be reborn again, to speak of "killing" a "soul" is absurd. The body, of course, can be and is killed—it can be deprived of the breathing spirit that gives it life; but the soul cannot be killed, since the body is no more than its clothing, and if that is destroyed, well then, it simply provides itself with a new suit of clothes. This, however, is not the real purport of the text as we shall see.

The *Katha* Upanishad is one of a remarkable set of treatises collectively known as the "Upanishads," meaning literally "sessions at the foot of or around [a teacher]." These form the latest stratum of the canonical Hindu scriptures known as the *Veda*, a word which means simply "knowledge" or "wisdom." To the earlier strata of the Veda—the four *Vedas* proper and the ritualistic texts called the *Brāhmanas*—lip service is still paid, but in actual fact it is the Upanishads that are the living source from which all later Hinduism draws its nourishment and inspiration. In them will be found, *in parvo*, the whole confusing, kaleido-scopic panorama of later Hinduism which, on the whole, abhors precision and shrinks from the drawing of hard-and-fast distinc-tions. In them too will be found the germs of four at least of the philosophical schools which, unlike Hinduism as a whole, posi-tively rejoice in drawing distinctions particularly when they are concerned with the formulation of the shape of ultimate reality.

The Taoist classics—the *Tao Tê Ching* ("The Way and its Power") attributed to Lao-Tzǔ and the works of Chuang Tzǔ—are nostalgic and backward-looking; through and through they voice a revolt against the claims of individuality and a longing for a golden age long past when men *naturally* submitted to the rhythm of the Tao and had not yet had the faculty of thought thrust upon them. They are at times brutally anti-intellectual and childishly philistine in their hatred of any form of creative individuality in man. The Upanishads are much more varied; for whereas some passages might come straight from the *Tao Tê Ching* or from Chuang Tzǔ in that they hanker back to a time when the individual was merged in the All, there are others which accept individuality and the reality of the indivi-dual soul and seek to define its relationships with the universe as a whole, and, beyond the universe, with what they sensed to be the changeless ground from which the universe had sprung.

The Taoists had complained that the "clever" Confucians "went to excess in their performances of music, and in their gesticulations in the practice of ceremonies." They did not realize, or feigned not to realize, that the Confucians, in their elaborate ceremonies, were themselves ritually reconstructing the rhythm of the Tao, re-creating on a smaller and human scale the ebb and flow of nature herself. In India, during the period immediately preceding the composition of the Upanishads, sacrificial cere-monial had taken on an enormous importance. The gods, many of them easily identifiable with natural phenomena or with functions within the divine hierarchy, itself reflecting the society of the Aryan invaders of India, had by now been dethroned, and the sacrifices that were theoretically offered them became of more importance than the gods themselves : they had taken on magical significance. According to a myth found in the last and latest book of the *Rig-Veda* (the earliest portion of the whole *Veda*), in the beginning there existed only a Primal Male from whom evolved one Virāj who reproduced the Primal Male again together with the gods. Whereupon the gods sacrificed the reborn Male, and from his dismembered parts the universe emerged in all its manifold variety. Creation, then—the emergence of the many from the one—was in origin a human sacrifice performed by the gods as priests on Primal Man as victim.

Sacrifice, performed by human priests, is thus a magical representation of the act of creation, the ritual act that ensures that evolution shall continue on its appointed course. It is an attempt to ensure that men, though now separated from one another by individual consciousness, shall put a brake on that consciousness and harness it back to the main evolutionary stream, or, to use the Chinese term, the universal Tao. It is a magical device designed to concentrate the individual "egos" of the community around the "self" of the tribe, and through the communal "self" evoked by the communal sacrifice, around the "self" of the whole universe, that is to say, around the Primal Man, himself the eternal victim whose dismemberment made possible the evolution of the cosmos. Through the magic of the sacrifice the individual is brought into a mystical *rapport* with the dismembered victim, and through the particular victim with the universal victim which is Primal Man.

The sacrificial ceremony, then, so far from being despised as it was by the Taoists in China, was the starting point of Upanishadic speculation. Slowly the theory of the exact correspondence between the macrocosm (the universe) and the microcosm (man) took shape—as indeed it did in practically every religion of the world—and so, through this magical correspondence the individual felt himself mysteriously identified with the All. This too is part and parcel of nature mysticism, for by participation in the All one, in a sense, *is* the All, and all things are, in the last analysis, identical. This sense of identity with the all, a constant undercurrent in Taoism and perhaps the main theme of the Upanishads, is probably due to the very nature of the material structure of which we are made, and it is only consciousness—the individual ego, ever intent on restricting us to the arduous business of living out our individual lives—that inhibits this blissful melting into the unknown. For, as Teilhard de Chardin remarks (and the fact is not disputed by scientists), "thanks to the prodigious biological event represented by the discovery of electro-magnetic waves, each individual finds himself henceforth (actively and passively) simultaneously present, over land and sea, in every corner of the earth."[7] But surely it did not need the discovery of electro-magnetic waves to enable man to be so universally present. Universally present he has always been, and only after the Fall, after the coming-to-be of individual consciousness, did he feel himself to be otherwise. The discovery of electro-magnetic waves explains, maybe, how this can be so, but in so doing it only confirms what nature mystics have consistently affirmed from the days of Lao-Tzŭ to our own day.

This sense, sometimes of participation in, sometimes of actual identity with the All, is, however, only one type of mysticism; and it is the type most characteristic of the Upanishads. In our figure of the shattered mirror we might say that it is an anamnesis on the part of the single fragment of the once unbroken whole.

Man was made "in the image of God." How are we to understand these words? Does it mean that all mankind, collectively one in Adam, was made in the image of God, or that every individual soul that reached separate consciousness after the Fall, is also made in the divine image? And in what sense is man "in the image of God"? The solutions of this problem advanced by the Indians may help us to answer these questions more clearly.

Here, however, we immediately run into a difficulty; for the Upanishads start not so much from any idea of God as from the idea of human immortality.

> From the unreal lead me to the real.
> From darkness lead me to light.
> From death lead me to immortality.[8]

This is basic to the whole of the Upanishadic literature. The stanza is in the form of a prayer, and prayers are usually addressed to a personal God; but until the latest of all the classical Upanishads it is very difficult indeed to discern such a being, for the old gods had proved inadequate, and the vacuum they left had not been filled. The situation in India was very much the same as it was in Greece at approximately the same time. The

[7] *The Phenomenon of Man*, p. 240.
[8] *Brhadāraṇyaka* Upanishad, 1.3.28.

Olympians had failed and a rudimentary physics had replaced an obsolescent mythology. And so we find the early Milesian philosophers speculating on what the original stuff can be from which the universe proceeds. Similarly, in India we find that the earliest Upanishads concern themselves not so much with the identity of the unknown God as with the problem of what it is that gives the ever-changing universe cohesion, what is the changeless ground beneath all change. And because these early thinkers had grown used to the idea that man, the microcosm, was closely akin to, and in some "mystical" sense identical with, the sum total of existence, the macrocosm, he quite naturally not only turned his eyes outward toward the external world, but also turned them in upon himself in deepest introspection. His first attempts to find this "Absolute" are frankly materialistic. The technical term used to signify the mysterious power that pervades all things and remains unchanged through all individual change, is *Brahman*; and one of the ideas that keeps recurring in the earlier Upanishads, as if it exercised a peculiar fascination on their authors, is that Brahman is food. "Food," however, is not regarded as being something static and "dead"; it is a dynamic process that keeps all things in being, it is ultimately the source of life and, through life, of thought.

Matter and spirit are interdependent; and the degree in which they are interdependent has in recent times once again been thrown into high relief by Teilhard de Chardin. "First of all, the dependence," he writes. "This is depressingly and magnificently obvious. 'To think, we must eat.' That blunt statement expresses a whole economy, and reveals, according to the way we look at it, either the tyranny of matter or its spiritual power."[9] The Upanishads themselves, unlike their most illustrious commentator, Śankara, saw in matter no tyranny—rather, they saw it as something inextricably intertwined with spirit, each depending wholly on the other. Their favorite symbols for the Absolute, at this stage, were "food" and "breath," for they, like Teilhard de Chardin and the modern materialists, saw clearly that "to think, we must eat"; and it was only when they came to realize there was something that lay outside and beyond both physical life and mental thought that they arrived at the idea that Brahman was not just a process or rhythm within a space-time continuum (and the jargon of modern physics is wonderfully

[9] *The Phenomenon of Man*, p. 63.

applicable here) but the constant and eternal ground from which
every process and every rhythm must arise.

The *Taittirīya* Upanishad is almost entirely devoted to the ex-
altation of food as being the principle which sustains both
physical life and thought. "Food" is the word the Upanishads
use for what we should call "matter" in the Marxian sense of that
word; it is a *process,* the inherent quality of which is motion, and
by motion is understood "not only mechanical and mathematical
movement, but still more impulse, vital life-spirit, tension, or, to
use Jakob Boehme's expression, the throes of matter."[10] For the
Taittirīya Upanishad it is Alpha and Omega; it is the origin of
all things, by it they are maintained in existence, and in it they
pass away.

> From food indeed are creatures engendered,—
> Whatever [creatures] dwell on earth.
> Then again by food they live,
> And again pass into it at the end.
> But food is the chief of beings,
> Whence it is called the elixir of all things.
> Whoso reverences Brahman as food
> Gains all food.
> For food is the chief of beings,
> Whence it is called the elixir of all things.
> From food are [all] creatures engendered;
> When born, by food do they grow up.
> It is eaten and eats all creatures.
> Therefore is it called food.[11]

"Food" is the stuff of the universe and, for the author of the
Taittirīya Upanishad, it is the focal point at which spirit and
intellect on the one hand and "dead" matter on the other meet.
To use Teilhard de Chardin's terminology, it can be said that in
the human person the "without" of "food" is the physical body,
while its "within" is mind and spirit; for, as the Upanishad goes
on to say, "within" the self whose essence is food is another
"self" which consists of "mind" (*manas,* that is, the faculty which
co-ordinates sense impressions). This in turn is indwelt by intellect
(*vijñāna*), and deep down at the heart of them all is an abiding
joy (*ānanda*). Body and breath, then, are the "without" of
"food," mind, intellect, and joy its "within."

[10] Marx and Engels, *The Holy Family,* p. 172.
[11] *Taittirīya* Upanishad, 2.2.

In the verses we have just quoted the Upanishad speaks of food as a universal process which is the source of the life of the whole universe, which keeps it in being, and into which it finally dissolves : it is the universal rhythm which regulates all material change within the whole macrocosm. In man it is the source of life and thought. The macrocosm, however, is reflected in man, the microcosm; and man, whatever may be said about the universe as a whole, manifestly has a "within" as well as a "without." He is not only a living body, he is also a "living soul." He eats food not only that he may live, but that he may think— and this means not only the correlation of sense data but abstract thought too. At the heart of all, however, there is joy; and although the Upanishad does not here tell us in what this joy consists, we know from other passages and from the later tradition that the Sanskrit word we have translated as "joy" is the joy that pure Being has in itself. If, then, God is pure Being and rejoices in himself, what could be more natural than to find substantial joy enshrined in the heart of man, God's image?

By analogy with the human person the Upanishad implies that the macrocosm too has a "within" as well as a "without"; but the inner dimension proceeds in a manner dialectically contrary to the outer. Outwardly matter, never static but always in motion, pushes purposively forward from the state of food (physics) to the state of life (biology), thence to sense perception, the correlation of sense data, and abstract thought (philosophy), and thence to an abiding joy (religion) which is his final cause.

Inversely, the inner nature of the macrocosm starts as the joy that Being has in itself; then it "expands", so to speak, into abstract thought, thence into the correlation of sense data and sense perception itself, thence into life, and finally into extended matter, the *material* substrate of all things which the Upanishad calls "food." Matter, then, is eternally pregnant of spirit, and spirit eternally acts as a magnet to matter. In man the two meet in the closest possible synthesis, for man is both the "image of God" in that he can seize upon his own essential being as existing outside space and time—and this is probably what the Upanishad means by "joy"—and he is the "image of the world," for he actualizes all the potentialities of matter in its evolutionary drive, through the development of ever more complex structures culminating in the human brain, toward conscious and reflective existence. His privilege as man is that he is a thinking animal : and this he can owe only to spirit, for though it is true that he must eat to think, the fact remains that the quality of his thought is dependent in only a minute degree on the quality and quantity of his food; for were one to feed an atomic scientist, a creative artist, and a perfect moron on identical diets, it is pretty certain that the atomic scientist would remain as he is, qualitatively distinct both from the artist and the moron, just as these two would remain qualitatively distinct from him. And this is what distinguishes man from all other material things. Again, he is by nature the "image of the world" in that he can sink himself, if he is prepared to abandon his privileged position of being an individual person, into the general rhythm of the cosmos, he can readapt himself to the mainstream of the great Tao from which he has emerged. He can see himself no longer as an individual but as a *process* within the universal process of matter within the space-time continuum. In the Upanishadic phrase he can see himself as "food," and then, conscious that he participates in the existence of all things, he can cry out without absurdity :

> O rapture, O rapture, O rapture!
> I am food, I am food, I am food!
> I am an eater of food, I am an eater of food,
>   I am an eater of food!
> I am a maker of verses, I am a maker of verses,
>   I am a maker of verses!
> *I am the first-born of the universal order,*
> *Earlier than the gods, in the navel of immortality!*
> Whoso gives me away, he, verily, has succoured me.
> *I, who am food, eat the eater of food!*
> *I have overcome the whole world.*[12]

This is still *participation mystique*, the mysticism of matter (or nature, for the two words are interchangeable, as Engels saw); or rather it is the mysticism of matter becoming aware of a spiritual dimension inherent in itself and realizing this wonder in the human brain; it is the pure joy that the Spirit gives when it uses the human brain, the most complex and highly organized material instrument it has yet brought forth, to break down its own limitations in order that it may understand in a flash the

[12] *Ibid.*, 3.10.(6).

electric unity of all material things. It is the encounter of heaven
and earth in man.

Indian man, however, did not rest content with this. He was
still not satisfied with his definitions of Brahman as "food" or
"breath"—as purely material processes, however intimately these
might be indwelt by life, thought, and joy. He wished to find an
Absolute that was independent of both matter and space-time,
the very condition of material existence.

In the *Maitrī* Upanishad[13] the theory of food is further
developed, but a new element is introduced. On the one side
stands "food," here explicitly identified with matter (*pradhāna*)
or nature (*prakṛti*), on the other stands the "person" (*puruṣa*)
who is the "eater of food," that is to say, the subject of experience.
Matter itself engenders the senses, the mind, and the emotions,
whereas the "person" or soul is possessed only of consciousness
(*caitanya*). The soul's contact with matter is maintained by the
eating of food : by eating, the soul is made to share in physical
life; it thinks, hears, touches, speaks, tastes, smells, and sees. All
this it does through the senses and through the mind which depends on the senses. *But*—and here a new element creeps in—
once the "person" abandons food, losing thereby his ability to
use his senses and his mind, once he lets go his grip on life, he becomes what the Upanishad calls a *performer of the sacrifice of
the self* (*ātman*)—and the "self" in this context is explicitly stated
to be "food," that is, matter, which here as elsewhere is held to be
the necessary substrate of life, sensation, and mind. The implica-
tion is that to cut oneself off from matter and thereby from life,
sensation, and mind, all of which depend on space-time, is to
achieve a form of existence that transcends space-time. Here we
meet with that tendency which was so soon to become so
characteristic of Indian religion—the ascetic tendency, which by
detaching itself from mind as well as matter, sought to transcend
death itself by breaking through the time barrier into a timeless
immortality.

This craving to pass clean out of an existence conditioned by
space and time can be explained only by the Indian's unquestion-
ing acceptance of the doctrine of the transmigration of souls. The
idea of starting life over again from scratch for all eternity is
unbearable. In Western mythology the same idea is represented
by the myth of Sisyphus who pushes the same stone up the same

[13] 6.10-12.

mountain only to see it roll down to the bottom each time the task had seemed to be achieved. Such a theory makes nonsense of all human endeavor; hence the Indian's passionate longing to escape from what he sees only as a senseless repetition of more or less miserable lives into a state of being in which there is no more birth, no more life, no more death, and no more rebirth. And this he cannot do unless he transcend time itself. And so, in the *Maitrī* Upanishad, the soul leaves the world of matter and space, and a fresh start is made with the consideration of time : "food is the source of the whole universe, and time is the source of food."[14] Time, therefore, should be reverenced as Brahman, for "whoso reverences time as Brahman, from him does time withdraw afar, for thus has it been said :

> 'From time flow forth created things,
> From time too do they advance in growth;
> In time too do they return home.
> Time is form and the formless too.' "

Thus there are two types of time—time as commonly understood, what Aristotle analyzed as the measurement of movement, and "timeless" time which "existed before the sun," that is to say, which lies outside the time sequence altogether. This is identical with the "infinitely great" spoken of elsewhere in the Upanishads, whereas our universe is simply "embodied time, the ocean of created things."

Brahman, however, is not only infinite time, but infinite space as well, "unlimited, unborn, beyond discursive reason, unthinkable. He is the very self (or soul, *ātman*) of space. When all collapses in ruin, he alone remains awake. From space itself he brings the world to consciousness (*bodhayati*),—[this world] whose matter is thought (*cintāmātram*). By him is this [world] thought [into existence] and in him it finds its rest (lit. 'sets,' *pratyastaṁ yāti*)."[15]

The universe, then, is a space-time continuum composed of matter and shot through with thought. It is thought into existence by a being who is timeless, not delimited or in any way qualified by space, and within this being it finds its final rest. So Brahman is said to be the "infinitely great."

The infinitely great and the infinitely small—the infinite and

---

[14] *Maitrī* Upanishad 6.14.
[15] *Ibid.*, 6.17.

the infinitesimal : poised between these two, man seems to lose
his bearings. From being master of the universe, he finds himself
of less significance than a worm. This was the predicament of man
as we analyzed it in the beginning of this book. It was no less the
predicament of Indian man in, perhaps, the fifth century B.C. :
but Indian intuitive thought, so marvellously in tune with the
mysteries of modern physics, did not lose its balance, for by intuition and by controlled meditation on his own innermost being,
Indian man came to realize that the incommensurably great and
the incommensurably small were ultimately one; the heart of the
"within" was co-extensive with the unmeasured vastness of space
and time "without"; and "to the unity of [this] One goes he who
knows this."

He who consists of mind, whose body is breath, whose form is light,
whose conception is the real, whose self is space, through whom are
all works, all desires, all scents, all tastes, who encompasses this whole
[universe], who does not speak and has no care, he is my self within
the heart, smaller than a grain of rice or a barley-corn, or a mustard-
seed, or a grain of millet, or the kernel of a grain of millet; this is my
self within the heart,—greater than the earth, greater than the
atmosphere, greater than the sky, greater than these worlds. . . . This
my self within the heart is that Brahman. When I depart from hence,
I shall merge into it. He who believes this will never doubt.[16]

So, it would seem, it is within the heart of man that the infinite
and the infinitesimal meet, and there is a certain fitness in this
if, as J. B. S. Haldane has pointed out, man himself is exactly
intermediate in size between the electron and the spiral nebula,
the smallest and the largest existing things at present known to
science.[17] But Indian thought did not stop here. It was not
content merely to assert that the human soul has an infinite
dimension : it also developed a technique whereby, it was
claimed, that infinite dimension could actually be captured; and
this, to break through into the infinite, is the goal not only of
Hinduism but of Buddhism as well. The technique is called Yoga,
and it is practiced by Hindus and Buddhists alike.

In the *Maitrī* Upanishad the Yoga technique is dealt with at
considerable length, but the goal to which it leads is not always
consistently described. All that can be said without analyzing the
passage in detail (which would be out of place here) is that the

16 *Chāndogya* Upanishad, 3.14.
17 R. G. Collingwood, *The Idea of Nature* (Oxford, 1945), p. 24, n. 1.

supreme goal is regarded as being a condition beyond space and time—the condition of Brahman, that is; and this is described also as "isolation" (*kevalatvam*), "selflessness," an inner light, "tranquil, without sound, fear, or sorrow, joyous, content, steadfast, immovable, immortal, unshaken, enduring."[18] Thus, in the *Maitri* Upanishad, this timeless state that the released soul is said to enjoy can be interpreted either as a complete identity with Brahman as the changeless source and ground of the whole universe, or as a participation in Brahman, or else as the isolation of its own eternal essence not only from the world of matter which includes the world of thought, but also from all other spiritual essences that have their being in Brahman.

Whatever the interpretation of the experience, the experience itself would seem to be the same; but it has probably nothing at all to do with the *participation mystique* of the Taoists and the nature mystics which is felt to be an expansion of the personality; for the Yoga technique is one of intense introspection and interior asceticism. Ethically it demands a complete denial of self, and this means a complete abandonment of all egocentricity, lust, and hatred, abstention from violence, falsehood, and theft, as well as the cultivation of the virtues of poverty and chastity : these form the indispensable foundation upon which the whole edifice of meditation and introspection is built; and they are essential because only through them can detachment from all worldly things and from one's own thoughts of worldly things be obtained.

These techniques were employed by the Buddhists and Jains outside Hinduism and by both the followers of the Vedānta and the Sāṁkhya-Yoga within it. The nature of the techniques is, in our present context, irrelevant : what is relevant is the transformation of consciousness that these techniques are said to produce and the metaphysical interpretations of this changed consciousness offered by the different sects. These must now be briefly considered.

Let us start with the strictly nondualist Vedāntins who are probably still the most influential philosophical school within Hinduism. For them the achievement of "liberation," as this timeless condition is habitually called, means that the soul experiences itself as actually identical with Brahman, the One than whom no other *is*. It sees thereby that the whole cosmic process which is governed by a personal God is illusory, or, at least, like the

[18] *Maitri* Upanishad, 6.23.

matter of both Aristotle and modern physics, it is incapable of
exact definition (*anirvacanīya*). Hence it follows that God too,
from the point of view of the Absolute, which, on the level of pure
being, is identical with the liberated soul, is also illusory. On
the level of relative being, however, he governs the universe,
including human souls still deluded by an illusory matter; but, in
the last analysis, he is himself illusory, and the liberated soul
who now knows himself to *be* Brahman, the One without a second,
knows that he is. In Judeo-Christian terms this would mean that
man, so far from being made "in the image of God," is himself
God in his essence, though not in his attributes. The essence of
God is nothing more nor less than the existence of man.

Early Buddhism prefers to leave ontological speculation on one
side altogether. It is enough to know that the state of Nirvāṇa
(the Buddhist technical term for "liberation") is immortal, unborn, not become, uncompounded, and timeless. All talk of union
with Brahman or identity with him or it is, the Buddha maintains,
"foolish talk,"[19] for no one has ever seen him nor had experience
of him. To achieve the "immortal," that is, to pass beyond space
and time, is all we need to do : it is an experience we cannot
describe but only savor once we have known it.

The classical Yoga, or Sāṁkhya-Yoga as it is usually called,
however, has views as well-defined and dogmatic about the nature
of ultimate being as does the Vedānta, and they are very different.
Being is divided into two distinct and mutually exclusive categories. On the one hand we have an infinite plurality of souls
(called *puruṣas* or "persons") and on the other we have matter
(*pradhāna*) or Nature (*prakṛti*). The souls are eternal in that
they have their being outside space and time, and matter too is
eternal in the sense that it has no beginning and no end : in time
it is infinite duration, in space it is infinite extension. It is in a
permanent state of flux and is conditioned by a permanent in-
stability and never-ending change. These two types of eternity
are really mutually exclusive, and yet they become mixed up with
each other, though it is not at all clear how. The souls get caught
up in matter which includes not only the phenomenal world without but also all the internal characteristics of the individual
person, such as intellect, will, and the ego or sense of individuality,
these characteristics being present on a cosmic scale as well. They
are, as it were, imprisoned there, and their "salvation" consists

[19] *Tevijjā Sutta*, §14.

in liberation from matter. Unlike the Sāṁkhya proper, the Sāṁkhya-Yoga admits of the existence of a God who is called the "Lord." The nature of the Lord is succinctly described as being "a special type of soul which is untouched by care, works, the fruits of works, or desire. In him the seed of omniscience is perfect. He is the *guru* even of the ancients, since he is not limited by time."[20] He is the only soul that has never been involved in the process of transmigration : he dwells in permanent isolation, outside time, and his only activity is that of a *guru* or spiritual director of souls still in bondage to matter. He is omniscient, keeps the world of matter in being, and causes both the union of souls with matter and their liberation from it. Despite this limited involvement, however, he is totally impassive and utterly serene in his splendid isolation. The soul, on its side, sunk in matter as it is, can nonetheless escape from it. This it can do on its own by pursuing the prescribed course of ethical and ascetical practices. Or it can be helped thereto by a rapt contemplation of God in his perfect isolation. Thus by the contemplation of him, he can himself break through the bonds of matter into a form of existence in which he is *like* God in that he is perfectly isolated in *his own* eternal being without, for that reason, participating in the being of God or of any other soul whatever. This he achieves by the contemplation of God who, though he sustains the material world for inscrutable reasons of his own, is nevertheless unique in that he has never been involved in matter or indeed can be. The serpent in the Garden of Eden, it will be remembered, promised Eve that by eating of the fruit of the Tree of Knowledge man would be "as God," and Yoga experience seems to show that what the serpent promised came true.

In our interpretation of the Fall we suggested that the breakthrough into consciousness resulted in the fragmentation of the human race unto dissociate and unharmonious individual units. The mirror was shattered and the fragments scattered abroad. How, then, could the unity be restored? This could be done in three ways, it would appear. Either the severed fragments could seek reintegration in the stream of life, thereby renouncing individuality as being something against nature and therefore evil; and this is the way of Tao. Or they could seek to find a new organic harmony between their individual organisms as newly developed and augmented by consciousness and the vast organism

[20] *Yagasūtras*, 1.24-26.

of the totality of existence comprised within the space-time continuum, finding thereby an identity of substance between the
infinitesimal in their own hearts and the infinitely great which
pervades the whole cosmos; and this is the general tenor of the
Upanishads. Or again they could seek the "image of God" within
their own fragmentary selves, and, by contemplating God, they
could win through to this God-image. Thereby they would restore
the timeless image on their own individual scales. In so doing they
cut themselves off from the whole advancing tide of evolution,
transcend matter and thought and individuality itself, and through
very selflessness win through to a new, immortal, and indestructible "self" that is beyond experience, beyond space and time,
beyond life and death—absolute, autarchic, and free. They have
in very truth become a faithful "image of God." But this they can
do only by casting off all the vices inseparable from egoism; for
if the fragment of the mirror is to become like God, it must be
purged of all dross and dirt, else the image it shows will be a gross
distortion of the truth.

Passing beyond the elements, the senses and their objects, taking
hold of the bow whose string is the life of a wandering mendicant
and whose arch is of steadfastness, [armed] with an arrow made of
unpretentiousness he strikes down the ancient doorkeeper at the door
of Brahman (i.e., egoism). [This doorkeeper] whose crown is delusion,
whose earrings are craving and envy, whose staff is sloth, drunkenness,
and wickedness, seizing his bow whose string is anger and whose arch
is greed,—[this doorkeeper,] the lord of self-conceit, [it is who] slays
these creatures with the arrow of desire. Him [the soul] must slay, and,
crossing to the farther side of the ether of the heart, he will enter the
hall of Brahman, even as a miner in search of precious metals enters
into a mine.... Thenceforth pure, cleansed, and void, at rest, bereft
of breath and bereft of "self", infinite, indestructible, steadfast,
eternal, unborn, autarchic, he abides in his own greatness.[21]

Such a soul has passed clean beyond the empirical world of
space and time; all that kept him there has been conquered—
his craving and his greed, his sloth and his envy—above all his
pride, his *amour propre* or self-conceit, which, more than all else,
binds him to a false individuality, which in turn must be cast
aside if his true personality is to be found "in the hall of Brahman." There he realizes his own eternal essence, and contemplating
himself "abiding in his greatness," he beholds the wheel of

[21] *Maitri* Upanishad, 6. 28.

phenomenal existence "like a rolling chariot-wheel." The fragment of the shattered mirror, knowing himself yet to be "in the image of God," has now cleansed himself of all the dirt and dross with which the breaking of the mirror which accompanied man's Fall had bespattered him : the crystal fragment shines again in all its purity with the reflected light of God. Autarchic now, and independent of all things, it looks down upon the wheel of phenomenal existence, and looking down but once, it turns away forever; for it has found its own eternal self. Yet there is something this soul has not understood. It has not understood that the chariot wheel, though revolving senselessly to itself, nevertheless bears on the chariot of human destiny, triumphantly moving forward toward its evolutionary close.

Convinced now that, since it can never die—for it has passed beyond the reach of time—it is almost bound to imagine that it is Brahman itself—not merely one soul among many, splendidly isolated in an eternal isolation from all the purely phenomenal adjuncts it had once mistaken for its "self," but Brahman indeed, the soul of the All, the changeless source of all that comes to be and passes away.

This, then, is the third possibility for the individual soul of fallen man. It is in him to be "like God" in that he can realize his own eternity outside space and time without reference to God, from whom the Fall had in any case cut him off. Thereby he opts out of life, choosing his individual salvation and his own eternity rather than continue the struggle in space and time. And now he can say, "I am Brahman,"[22] and, in saying so, he may think that he is indeed God, not only as he is in his timeless essence, but also as he is in his attributes—the creator and preserver of the phenomenal world. But, as we shall see in our next chapter, in this he is surely wrong.

[22] *Bṛhadāraṇyaka* Upanishad, 1.4.10.

4

Encounter

THE QUEST OF THE UPANISHADS WAS THE QUEST for the eternal both within man and in the universe without. Their whole attitude toward the human being and his response to the divine is totally different from that of Israel and the religions that derive from her. Both Jews and Muslims see God as utterly transcendent—the Lord God of Hosts—a very real and embarrassingly urgent presence whose commands, transmitted to a chosen people through chosen prophets, must be obeyed. God alone is the Eternal, the Ancient of Days; but neither in the Old Testament nor in the Koran is there any conception or understanding of God as being, in his essence, outside space and time and uncommitted to the world of men. His eternity is conceived of rather as extending through and filling out a finite time *sequence,* the beginning and end of which are his creation: he is concerned with what the *Maitrī* Upanishad calls "time with parts" rather than with "timeless time"; his dealings with man are in time and history. For the Hebrews evolution is something that has a beginning in creation and an end in the remaking of all things anew in the last days. The Indians, on the other hand, do not see evolution as a straight-line development from a definite beginning to a definite fulfillment; they see it rather as a rhythmic systole and diastole with neither beginning nor end. The phenomenal world issues forth from the Absolute, evolves to the maximum of its potentialities, and then devolves in steady decline back into the undifferentiated oneness of the Absolute from which it had proceeded and in which all distinctions are lost. This process is infinitely repeated and can have no end.

Yet this is illogical; for the dominant trend of the whole Indian tradition is to identify the microcosm with the macrocosm, and while it is agreed that the salvation of the microcosm, man, consists in his escaping once and for all from this phenomenal world of coming to be and passing away, the macrocosm itself, that is

Brahman or its personification, Vishnu, never achieves total dis-association from the world of matter and time. Even in the so-called non-dualist Vedānta this anomaly remains unresolved : for insist though the Vedāntins may on the absolute unity of Being in Brahman, which is also, in the last analysis, identical with all individual human souls, this absolute unity which they accept as a dogma can never be totally realized so long as one single human soul remains imprisoned in the net of *māyā*, the cosmic illusion which prevents the individual soul from realizing itself as the Absolute. All the Vedāntin is doing in fact is to build a monistic metaphysic on the psychological experience of the absolute oneness of each individual soul in its ontological essence. In this type of mystical experience the soul realizes itself as being an absolutely undifferentiated monad, existing eternally outside space and time; it has dissociated itself completely from both the bodily senses and the mind, and therefore *a fortiori* from their objects, sense data, and discursive thought. If, as many passages in the Upanishads baldly assert, the inmost soul of man is, in its deepest essence, identical with the changeless ground of the universe, then for the soul to realize itself as *a* totally undiffer-entiated monad can mean only that it has realized its identity with the great changeless Being from which all phenomenal being proceeds : it conceives that it must be God in his essence, though not in his attributes, such as creativity, omnipotence, and omniscience, for, according to the Vedāntin dogma, all being is unfractionably one. This wholly irrational idea is liable to take firm grip upon the mind, and nothing on earth will persuade anyone who has had this experience of its absurdity except some further mystical experience that shatters it. Given the metaphysi-cal position of the non-dualist Vedāntin which admits of no being except the One, this is scarcely surprising.

What, however, is yet more surprising, particularly to a Christian whose mystical tradition expresses itself overwhelmingly in terms of passionate love—is the metaphysics of the Sāṁkhya-Yoga as applied to mystical experience. The existence of a personal God, as we have seen, is admitted, but he is not a god of love or one to whom the soul is attracted or with whom he longs for union. He is simply the perfect exemplar of the complete Yogin, isolated in his own eternity for all time. By contemplating God and understanding him in his total aloofness, the human soul takes cognizance of itself as being *like* God and thereby attains its own "isolation in denudation," to use the phrase current among the Muslim mystics, in which it is sufficient unto itself, independent, alone, and free. As an experience this is obviously identical with the Vedāntin undifferentiated oneness, the only difference being the manner in which it is interpreted. For the one the realization of this state of undifferentiable unity means identity with the Absolute, for the other it means no more than the realization by one soul among many of its own essential unity.

Neo-Vedāntism and kindred philosophies have made so deep an impression on large strata of the spiritually dispossessed, particularly in the United States, that it may perhaps be worth our while to show how this perennial and deeply sterile error has been refuted by experience, not by mere argumentation, in every religious tradition in which it has gained a dominant position. I would, then, begin not with the rather complicated Indian phenomenon, but with the experience of a modern Jewish mystic, Martin Buber, whose testimony, added to the evidence we shall produce later, cannot lightly be set aside. I do not apologize for having quoted this passage no less than three times before in published works, since it is one of the clearest refutations from experience of the fatuous claim of would-be mystics that all types of mysticism are reducible to one pattern. This claim, when subjected to analysis, seems to mean that in all mystical experience the mystic in fact realizes himself as the Absolute, and that when he speaks of love, as the Christian mystics habitually do, he is merely accommodating his experience to his dogmatic theology. This extremely naïve view, which is sometimes accompanied by a not very pleasing combination of wishful thinking and spiritual pride, takes no account of the fact that the mysticism of love succeeds to, and supersedes the monistic variety in the Indian tradition itself, or of the fact that a mysticism of love appears in Islam against the strong opposition of the theologians, or of the additional fact that, when monistic ideas were imported into Islam from India, these were in turn refuted, again from further experience, by men of exemplary holiness who realized that the claim of some mystics to *be* God was not only blasphemous but silly. To return to Buber, however, who weighs in against this strange aberration with the immense seriousness we would expect from him :

Sometimes I hear it said that every *I and Thou* is only superficial, deep down word and response cease to exist, there is only the one primal being unconfronted by another. We should plunge into the silent unity, but for the rest leave its relativity to the life to be lived, instead of imposing on it this absolutized *I* and absolutized *Thou* with their dialogue.

Now *from my own unforgettable experience* I know well that there is a state in which the bonds of the personal nature of life seem to have fallen away from us and we experience an undivided unity. But I do not know—what the soul willingly imagines and indeed is bound to imagine (mine too once did it)—that in this I had attained to a union with the primal being or the godhead. That is an exaggeration no longer permitted to the responsible understanding. Responsibly—that is, as a man holding his ground before reality—I can elicit from those experiences only that in them *I reached an undifferentiable unity of myself without form or content.* I may call this an original pre-biographical unity and suppose that it is hidden unchanged beneath all biographical change, all development and complication of the soul. Nevertheless, in the honest and sober account of the responsible understanding, *this unity is nothing but the unity of this soul of mine,* whose "ground" I have reached, so much so that, beneath all formations and contents, *my spirit has no choice but to understand it as the groundless.* But the basic unity of my own soul is certainly beyond the reach of all the multiplicity it has hitherto received from life, though not in the least beyond individuation, or the multiplicity of all the souls in the world of which it is one,—*existing but once, single, unique, irreducible, this creaturely one: one of the human souls and not the "soul of the All";* a defined and particular being and not "Being", the creaturely basic unity of a creature, bound to God as in the instant before release the creature is to the *creator spiritus,* not bound to God as the creature to the *creator spiritus* in the moment of release.[1]

What is particularly interesting in this passage is that Buber regards it as almost inevitable that anyone who has experienced an "undifferentiable unity of oneself without form or content" should interpret it as the "groundless", that is to say, in Indian terminology, as Brahman, the undifferentiable One from which all multiplicity proceeds. This being so, the mystic, thus absorbed in his own unique essence "experiences the cessation of his own multiplicity as the cessation of [all] mutuality, as revealed or fulfilled absence of otherness." In other words, the experience is entirely confined to the individual self and makes impossible all communion with other men or with God; it is the deadest of all possible dead ends.

[1] Martin Buber, *Between Man and Man* (London, 1947), pp. 24–25.

The temptation, however, is overwhelming, for modern psychology is slowly discovering that the human psyche has within it the same immensities that the ancient Hindu sages had long ago attributed to it. We have only to recall the lyrical raptures with which Jung speaks of the "mysteries of the soul" in his later works.

Jung's indebtedness to Indian thought at least for his concept of the "self" is well known. It will be recalled that in the *Maitri* Upanishad liberation was represented as meaning first to pass from self into selflessness, and then, beyond this, to link up with another "self," the very existence of which had not been suspected hitherto—a self that dwells beyond time and space and is thereby immortal. In the terminology of the Vedāntins the first (empirical) self is called *ahaṁkāra* or ego, and the second (transcendental) self is called *ātman* ("self"). So too, in Jung's system, there are two "selves" in every man—the ego, which is the center of the conscious personality, and the "self," "which includes the totality of the psyche in so far as this manifests itself in an individual. [It] is not only the centre, but also the circumference that encloses consciousness and the unconscious; it is the centre of this totality, as the ego is the centre of consciousness."[2] This "self," according to Jung, is the "image of God" in man, and this is precisely what we learn from the Book of Genesis. Jung, however, on purely empirical grounds, finds it difficult to make any clear distinction between God and the "image of God" because it is not his job to busy himself with a purely transcendental God who can scarcely be the object of psychological inquiry. What he is interested in is finding the immortal substrate within man that has its being outside time : this he calls the "God-image" and was at first disposed to identify it with the unconscious *in toto*. Later he modified this view and identified it with what he calls the "archetype of the self" which is itself the archetype of wholeness and immortality. So, at the end of one of his more recent and more controversial works, he says, "Strictly speaking, the God-image does not coincide with the unconscious as such, but with a special content of it, namely the archetype of the self. It is this archetype from which we can no longer distinguish the God-image empirically."[3]

[2] C. G. Jung, *Integration of Personality* (London, 1939), p. 96.
[3] *Id.*, *Answer to Job*, (London 1954), p. 177.

This "archetype of the self" may be regarded as the "image of God" (as in the Sāṁkhya-Yoga) or as the immanent God himself (as in many Upanishadic texts and in the Vedānta) : for Jung it is only a question of terminology, for whatever may or may not be true about God's transcendence—his inaccessibility and remoteness—it can have no interest for the psychologist, for "that which has no effect upon me might just as well not exist." What is important in Jung's eyes is that "the religious need longs for wholeness, and therefore lays hold of the images of wholeness offered by the unconscious, which, independently of the conscious mind, rise up from the depths of our psychic nature."[4] This archetype of wholeness and immortality exists deep down in the human psyche, and it matters little whether we call it "God" or the "image of God," or the "archetype of the self"—unless, of course, we happen to believe, either by faith or experience, that a transcendent God distinct from the human soul exists. Jung himself seems to shrink from the ultimate Vedāntin absurdity, for at the end of his *Answer to Job* he writes, "even the enlightened person remains what he is, and is never more than his own limited ego before the One who dwells in him, whose form has no knowable boundaries, who encompasses him on all sides, fathomless as the abysms of the earth and vast as the sky."[5]

This, I fear, is pure rhetoric, for we are not told whether this infinite One is to be regarded as the One of Plotinus, that is, as the ground of all manifested being, or simply, as Jung maintains elsewhere, as the "image of God" in man. Be that as it may, Jung departs from both the Vendānta and the Sāṁkhya-Yoga in one important respect. His conception of the goal of individual man is what he calls "individuation" or, more comprehensibly, "integration of the personality." And the process of integration seems to be approximately as follows; and here again we must revert to what we have already said about the Fall.

The Fall was the great *Sünde* or *Sonderung*, the catastrophic split between man and God, between man and his fellow men, and between body and soul in man himself. In the light of what India has to teach us about this last dualism we may have to modify our whole concept of the soul. In Indian metaphysics the split is not so much between body and mind, the interdependence

[4] *Ibid.*, p. 178.
[5] *p.* 180.

of which becomes ever more apparent, as between the immortal, undifferentiated essence that lies concealed within all of us and which, once discovered, turns out to have its being outside space and time on the one hand, and the whole psychophysical frame with its mind and emotions, which this essence indwells on the other. The one is necessarily immortal, because it knows nothing of time, the other mortal, because founded on matter, and therefore transient : as is the way with living things, it is born, grows old, reproduces itself, and dies. According to the story of Genesis as interpreted by Christian theology, this dichotomy was due to the soul's inability to impose its will onto the totality of the psychosomatic frame it indwelt.

Since, however, man has no alternative but to face the fact of physical death, the only sensible thing to do, it would appear, is to concentrate on the separation of the immortal from the mortal and to discard the latter at the earliest opportunity as worthless trash. *This* life is in any case under the curse of sin and death; let it go, then, and go in search of the pearl of great price that is within you. This both the Vedāntins and the Sāṁkhya-Yogins did.

Not so Jung : for Jung is a psychologist, and as such concerned with the mental health of his patients here and now; and it is, then, something of a fluke that, in the course of his clinical observations, he should have stumbled onto something that appeared to be immortal, and which religion calls the soul. What depth psychology attempts to do, however, is not to isolate the immortal part of man from his mortal frame, but to integrate the one into the other in one balanced and harmonious whole. His aim and that of every psychoanalyst who knows his job must be first to make the patient whole and then to return him to society, so that he may be integrated again in and with society as such. The integration of the personality is achieved by what Jung calls the transference—the transference, that is, of the center of gravity of the total personality from the ego which had usurped it to the self whose natural birthright it is. The ego is the principle of consciousness : it is what in us says, "I am," that is, an individual with unique characteristics that no other individual possesses. The ego not only asserts its own separate existence, but asserts it at the expense of other egos; it rejoices in individual activity, and is slow to combine with other egos except on its own terms; it is passionately attached to its own individual existence; it is the

seat of *amour propre* and of pride. It is the principal of division
and separation.

The self, on the other hand, apart from being the immortal
substrate of the entire psyche, is totally different from the rest
of the psyche, as it is the Sāṁkhya system. Normally deep down
in the unconscious, its very existence usually remains unsuspected
by the conscious mind, and it is only liable to make its appearance
in normally extroverted people in times of strain. Having its
true being outside time, it takes its immersion in time as it finds
it; it is neither unduly elated in periods of good fortune, nor is
it worried or depressed when misfortune comes its way. It is serene
and calm, and when the storms and stresses of life cause the ego
to disintegrate and to abdicate its usurped sovereignty, it will,
if it is permitted to, and if the unconscious itself is not in
too violent a state of disarray, quietly take over the leadership
and thereby heal and make "whole" the wounded psyche around
itself. It does not isolate itself from its temporal frame, as
the soul of the Sāṁkhya-Yogin does, but consents to remain
within it, bringing peace and quiet acceptance not to
itself only (for such is its perennial state) but to the whole
man. One of Jung's patients who herself had been through
the "valley of the shadow of death" of acute neurosis explains
how she emerged and how all care was lifted off her. She
writes,

Out of evil, much good has come to me. By keeping quiet, repressing
nothing, remaining attentive, and hand in hand with that, by accepting reality—taking things as they are, and not as I wanted them to be
—by doing all this, rare knowledge has come to me, and rare powers
as well, such as I could never have imagined before. I always thought
that, when we accept things, they overpower us in one way or another.
Now this is not true at all, and it is only by accepting them that one
can define an attitude towards them. So now I intend playing the
game of life, being receptive to whatever comes to me, good or bad,
sun and shadow that are forever shifting, and, in this way, also accepting my own nature with its positive and negative sides. Thus everything becomes more alive to me. What a fool I was! How I tried to
force everything to go according to my idea.[6]

To allow the self to take over the control of the whole psyche
is equivalent to "allowing the nature with which one is endowed

[6] *Id., The Secret of the Golden Flower* (London, 1938), p. 126.

to have its free course."[7] It is to allow the immortal substrate of
the soul, which, having its habitat outside time, must therefore
be static, to regulate one's own purely secular affairs in time.
This is Yoga applied to practical life; it is to integrate ego, intellect, will, and emotions around the immortal center of the psyche;
and the latter, if it has already been purged of sin as Yoga
requires that it should be, will itself benefit and increase by the
association. By refusing to opt out of life as the Sāṁkhya and
primitive Buddhism ordain, by refusing to rest quietly in its own
eternal essence which is its own fragmentary image of God, it is
able once again to plunge into the Tao of life and this time to
swim with it in accordance with its own true nature, which is
other than the ego; for its nature is to accept whatever comes to
it of good or evil, and not only to accept, but to welcome and to
bless. It is, I suppose, to realize that one's soul, which, as the
image of God, stands outside time, derives from the same source
and is animated by the same spirit as the world of space and time.
Except for sin and the consequent misuse of intellect as a divisive
rather than a reconciling instrument, both the "within" and the
"without" co-operate in a harmony in which the eternal and the
transient blend, and in which the transient itself gains eternal
value, while eternity is not diminished but enriched by its
association with the transient.

Even in the Sāṁkhya system which makes so clean a distinction between spirit and matter, the two are not regarded as being
in enmity with each other. Sāṁkhya dualism is not at all the
same as Manichaean dualism with its stark condemnation of all
that is material as being irretrievably evil. Soul and matter, in the
Sāṁkhya system, become mixed up together, but not in hatred
and violence; on the contrary, they complement each other, and
their association is one almost of love, except that they know that
the association must come to an end. Matter, the humbler
partner, realizes that, for the time being at least, she can have
part in spirit, and with a touching selflessness she therefore
works for the release of spirit. As the *Sāṁkhya-Kārikā* puts it :

As a dancer, after showing herself to the audience, leaves off
dancing, so does matter reveal herself to the soul, and then disappear.
Though she is possessed of qualities and the soul possesses none, by
manifold means she helps him on though he helps her not at all; she
achieves his goal for him, though achieving nothing for herself.

[7] Chuang Tzŭ, viii. 5.

Nothing is more generous than matter, or so I think. Content that she has been seen by the soul, she never again exposes herself to him.[8]

Together they have co-operated for a while to the mutual delectation of each, and the parting is one of selflessness and peace. One thing only is lacking in the Sāṁkhya concept of matter and soul, and that is that the soul experiences neither loss nor gain from its association with matter. It simply detaches itself from its bodily frame and becomes once again "as it was before it was,"[9] that is to say, an eternal monad locked up within itself. Such a soul is described in the Gospel; it is the man who received one talent and "went and digged in the earth, and hid his Lord's money."[10] This lack of spiritual enterprise which Jesus so roundly condemns, is, however, only natural to anyone who cannot see any connection between life as lived out on earth, and that timeless form of existence which is natural to the soul; content with what Martin Buber calls "the pre-biographical unity ... hidden unchanged beneath all biographical change, all development and complication of soul," such a man will "dig in the earth" and hide it away in apparent safety for fear of exposing it to the perilous vicissitudes of time.

The Sāṁkhya-Yoga in India teaches not only that the soul is individual and immortal but also that it can be realized as such. The Taoist classics in China teach rather that all nature is one and at peace, moving, as it does, in perfect harmony with the Tao, and that the nature of individual men, if left to itself without any interference from man-made ideas, ideals, and ideologies, would automatically adjust itself to the natural order of things. Jungian psychology seeks to combine the two—to integrate man within himself around his eternal center and then to integrate the integrated individual himself into society.

The Sāṁkhya system of philosophy, or rather psychology, lies outside the mainstream of Hindu religious development as represented by the Upanishads. Here it is not a question of isolating the soul, once discovered, but of discovering the nature of the soul and how it is related to the Absolute, the Soul of the All, which is Brahman. The general conclusion that emerges is that the "fine essence" within the heart is, in a manner not yet defined, identical with the Soul of the All, which as pure Being, preserves

[8] *Sāṁkhya-Kārikā*, 59–61.
[9] See below, p. 124.
[10] Matt. 25 : 18.

all else in existence. In the classical formulation of the *Chāndogya* Upanishad, "that which is the finest essence,—this whole [world] has it as its self : that is the real; that is the Self. That art thou."[11] If, however, the whole universe coheres in this "finest essence," what is the relationship of this essence to the personal God who also figures in the Upanishads?

At first no distinction is made : both are the Universal Self or Soul, which is simply another way of speaking of Brahman. And so we read :

This Self is the overlord of all creatures, the King of all creatures. Just as all the spokes are made to converge on the hub and felly of a wheel, so are all creatures, all gods, all worlds, all lives, and all souls ("selves," *ātmānaḥ*)[12] made to converge on this Self.[13]

So too does Jung, when speaking of the individual "self" in the individual psyche, say that it "is not only the centre, but the circumference that encloses consciousness and the unconscious, it is the centre of this totality, as the ego is the centre of consciousness."

Jung's description of man, the microcosm, is then exactly parallel to the *Bṛhadāraṇyaka* Upanishad's description of the "Self" of the universe, the macrocosm. The "self" or immortal soul in man corresponds to the "Self" or God in the universe; for, in this passage, the Universal Self is also personalized as "overlord" and "king"; and as such he is not only immanent as the still center of the soul, but transcendent as extending beyond the universe of space and time. Individual souls are the spokes that individually link the indwelling spirit with the transcendent God : they are the radii through which the divine transcendence elects to commune with the divine immanence : they start and end with the divine in and through the material cosmos. In the beginning is God and at the end is God; in the middle is the macrocosm of living matter, and within the macrocosm of matter is the microcosm, man. Transcendent and "without" is the Father, immanent and "within" is the Holy Spirit, in the middle is the Son of Man and Son of God.

This is perhaps the first passage in the Upanishads in which we meet with the Soul of the World in the form of a personal

---

[11] *Chāndogya* Upanishad 6. 8ff.
[12] My interpolation.
[13] *Bṛhadāraṇyaka* Upanishad, 2.5.15.

God, and we shall now, very briefly, have to trace the development of this idea in the Hindu sacred books and the major commentaries on them. Let us, then, start with the concept of Brahman.

By the end of the Upanishadic period, after successive attempts to pin down the concept of Brahman to "food" (matter), "breath" (spirit), and space (the infinite) had failed to satisfy, it came to be established that Brahman was first and foremost an eternal mode of existence which transcended space and time, mind and matter, cause and effect. In the second place, it was seen to be the unchangeable source of the whole universe of change on the one hand and of human souls which are eternal and do not change on the other. Brahman, then, is (a) an eternal *mode* of existence, and (b) the first cause from which all things, both material and spiritual, both transient and eternal, proceed. As first cause there is nothing particularly mysterious about Brahman; but as to what is meant by an eternal mode of existence, obviously there can be a wide variety of opinions. The non-dualists maintained that what IS absolutely must be absolutely simple : therefore Brahman is One and totally indivisible. Moreover, the human soul at its deepest level is experienced as being undifferentiably one and eternal. Therefore, the human soul, once liberated from all material and mental adjuncts, must be absolutely identical with Brahman. Strictly speaking, the non-dualist Vedāntin has no right to go any further than this. He has a perfect right to say, "I am Brahman," if he has, in trance, experienced the undifferentiable unity of his own soul—though, as Buber has pointed out, he is certainly in error; but he has no right to go on to say, "You are Brahman," for his own experience of undifferentiable unity shuts out not only "you" but the very idea of otherness altogether. The experience is purely subjective, and has no validity for others at all.

Secondly, Brahman may be understood, as the Buddhists understood it, to mean only a *state* of timeless existence which is the soul's condition on achieving liberation. This they usually call *nirvāṇa*, though the Buddha himself is described as *brahma-bhūta*, "become Brahman"; and since the Buddhists do not admit of Brahman as the "Soul of the World," the phrase can only mean in the context "one who has passed into an unconditioned form of existence"—Brahman, then, being a synonym for Nirvāṇa, itself described as the "deathless" and "timeless"; and this is

plainly the sense of the compound *brahma-nirvāṇa* used in the
Bhagavad-Gītā. This state can be identified with the undifferentiable One which is also the ontological first cause of the universe,
as the strict non-dualists do, or it can be likened to an ocean into
which souls are absorbed as rivers are absorbed in the sea, or it
can be regarded as a "category of suprasensuous existence," and
this is, in fact, how Rāmānuja, the founder of the theistic
viśiṣṭādvaita ("differentiated non-dualism") understood it.

From the time of the Upanishads onward Hinduism instinctively understood that the cosmos is a unity and that man not only
shares in that unity but reflects it in his own being; and it understood further that in some profound sense the immortal point
without magnitude deep within the human being was identical
with the eternal ground of the ever-changing cosmos. What was
most "internal" to the whole cosmos—consciousness—was, in
some sense, identical with what was most external—space-time :
both were Brahman. And yet, even this formulation of the unity
of all things could not in the end prove wholly satisfactory, for
though man might intuitively feel that the "greater than the
great" and the "smaller than the small"—the infinite and the
infinitesimal—were ultimately one, the nature of the connecting
link between them was nowhere apparent.

So it came about that the authors of the Upanishads themselves
began to conceive of a personal Being who, standing not only
outside the world of space and time (though at the same time
intimately indwelling it), but outside and beyond the sphere of
eternal substances as well, ordered and controlled them both.
"This whole universe *must* be enveloped by a Lord," the *Īśā*
Upanishad begins—"whatever moving thing there is in this moving world." This Lord, who is also the "Self" and the "Inner
Controller" of the universe, cannot be identified either with extratemporal Being or with transient though never-ending becoming.
This was the pantheistic error of the earlier Upanishads, and
"into blind darkness enter they who worship non-becoming; into
darkness greater than that they who rejoice in becoming. For it
has been said, 'Other is it (the Absolute) than origin and other
than what has no origin.' "[14] The Lord God, then, not only
pervades the world of space and time as well as that of immaterial
essences, but is other than they; he is not only immanent, but
transcendent, not only the hub of the wheel, but the felly, not

[14] *Īśā* Upanishad, 12–13.

only the Inner Controller, but the Lord, not only the Holy Spirit that controls all things, but the Father who creates heaven and earth.

The *Īśā* Upanishad adumbrates obscurely the far clearer theology and cosmology of the *Śvetāśvatara* Upanishad, the only one of the classical Upanishads which is clearly and outspokenly theistic. Standing halfway in the line of development from pantheistic monism to theism is one of the loveliest and most mysterious of the Upanishads, the *Muṇḍaka*. Here again the distinction between the impersonal and the personal God, called here simply *Puruṣa,* the (male) "Person," is maintained. Brahman is described as being—

> Manifest yet hidden: "moving in secret" is his name,
> The great abode. In that is placed
> What moves and breathes and winks.
> What that is know as Being and Not-Being,
> An object of desire, beyond the understanding (*vijñāna*),
> Best of creatures.[15]

Brahman is here the "great abode" which includes both "Being" and "Not-Being," the first meaning eternal essences, the second the phenomenal world as we know it. "Not-Being" is used in the sense of what we would call "contingent being," it is the "matter" of the Sāṁkhya-Yoga, the *māyā* of the *Śvetāśvatara* Upanishad; and it should be noted that the word *māyā* is used there in the sense of "nature" or "matter," not of "illusion." As Being Brahman is both the category of eternal essences and the source of the phenomenal world; as Not-Being it is the phenomenal world itself. It cannot be regarded as the supreme principle, for itself is called the "best of *creatures.*" Above it stands *Puruṣa,* the supreme "Person" :

> Heavenly, formless is the Person;
> He comprises without and within; unborn is he:
> Without breath, without mind, effulgent,
> Higher than the high imperishable.[16]

Here for the first time the absolute transcendence of the personal God is affirmed. He is "without breath," for he has no *physical* life; he is "without mind," for he does not operate through a *physical* brain; and he is higher than Brahman, the

[15] *Muṇḍaka* Upanishad, 2.2.1.
[16] *Ibid.*, 2.1.2.

"high imperishable," whether Brahman be regarded as extra-spatial and extratemporal existence *per se* or as the changeless source of change. God, however, is Maker, Lord, and the Person "whose womb is Brahman" : he not only transcends all spiritual essences, but activates these essences and brings them down into space and time. He is the absolutely transcendent God beyond the Absolute—pure unalloyed Being—and also the maker of heaven and earth : aloof in eternity, he is yet active in time.

This new concept of a personal God who transcends the Absolute is difficult to reconcile with the earlier Upanishadic teaching, particularly in the matter of the fate of the liberated individual soul. Let us see, then, how the *Muṇḍaka* describes this. It declares,

> The ascetics, whose firmly determined aim is knowledge
> of the Vedanta
> Whose being is purified by the Yoga of renunciation,
> They, at the end of time, surpassing death,
> Are all liberated in the Brahman worlds. . . .

> Gone are [all] deeds and the self that consists of knowledge;
> All become unified in the imperishable beyond.

> As rivers flowing into the ocean
> Disappear, leaving behind them name and form,
> So too, the one who knows, released from name and form,
> Draws near to the divine Person beyond the beyond.[17]

The soul, then, liberated from all its bodily adjuncts, enters into Brahman, that is, rejoins eternity, but it is only when it has done so that it can even begin to approach God. Union with Brahman there is, but not union or even communion with God. And this is as true of the much more markedly theistic *Śvetāś-vatara* Upanishad as it is of the *Muṇḍaka*. Here again there are the two kingdoms, the two divisions of the "city of Brahman,"[18] the "perishable" and the "imperishable," the temporal and the eternal, over both of which the Lord holds sway; and here again the individual soul's liberation is never described as "union with God" : indeed, in this openly theistic Upanishad the soul does not even "approach" God as he does in the *Muṇḍaka*. Rather, it is liberated by "knowing God" in exactly the same way as in the

17 *Ibid.*, 3.2.6–8.
18 *Śvetāśvatara* Upanishad, 5.1.

Sāṁkhya-Yoga the soul escapes into its own eternal essence by contemplating God as its perfect exemplar : the soul does not even draw near to him, much less is it united with him. In the *Śvetāśvatara* too liberation is interpreted either simply as "isolation" on Sāṁkhya-Yoga lines, or as a realization of oneness (probably also to be interpreted on Sāṁkhya lines), or as access to Brahman, or as being merged in Brahman. From God, who is the source of Brahman, the soul is still cut off.

It is only when we come to the Bhagavad-Gītā that the possibility of union with God as opposed to union with and in Brahman is even entertained. The God in question is here Vishnu, the supreme Being who becomes incarnate from time to time "for the protection of the good, for the destruction of evil-doers, and for the sake of establishing the law."[19]

The Gītā itself forms one tiny part of India's hugh Epic, the *Mahābhārata*, which tells of the war of extermination fought out between the sons of Dhṛtarāṣṭra and their cousins, the Pāṇḍavas who have right on their side. Vishnu has become incarnate as Krishna, a local prince, who sides with the Pāṇḍavas. During the actual war he acts as the charioteer of Arjuna, the third of the five Pāṇḍava brothers, and the relationship of the God-Man to the hero is so close that not only are they called the two Krishnas, but Krishna speaks of Arjuna as "half his body"[20] and even goes so far as to say that he could not endure the world even for a moment without Arjuna.[21] Arjuna, on his side, fully reciprocates this love "that surpasseth the love of woman"; he is dimly aware that his friend is Vishnu incarnate, but so deep is his attachment to him as a human being that he has not hitherto worried himself overmuch about the implications of his friend's divinity. The gradual revelation by Krishna to Arjuna of his true identity is, then, the main theme of the Gītā in its setting within the whole Epic : it depicts the transition from what had seemed to be a purely human love to a divine one; and into this main theme are integrated the themes of the soul's liberation in Brahman and of how this is to be reconciled with the love of God.

In my interpretation of the Bhagavad-Gītā I follow Rāmānuja, the founder of the so-called *viśiṣṭādvaita* ("differentiated non-dualism") whose traditional dates are A.D. 1017-1137;

[19] Bhagavad-Gītā, 4.8.
[20] *Mahābhārata*, vii. 2808.
[21] *Ibid.*, 2801-2.

and as I have commented on what I believe to be the main message of the Gītā in my *Hindu and Muslim Mysticism,* I will do no more than emphasize once again here the tremendous reversal of Hindu religious values that the Gītā represents.

In the Gītā we once again find reality divided into two—the phenomenal world of space and time and the eternal world beyond space and time. Brahman *is* the latter, and is also the source of the former; and it is the eternal and extratemporal *state* of the liberated soul as well. The first six chapters of the Gītā deal exclusively with the achievement of liberation; they are concerned with the human soul, the *ātman,* and with Brahman, not directly with God. The following four chapters deal with the nature of God, while the eleventh chapter contains the great theophany in which Krishna reveals himself to a terrified Arjuna as the creator and destroyer of the universe. Restored to his human form Krishna then explains how God, terrible though he is, is at the same time a God of love, who not only loves men but, stranger still, yearns for their love in return. Only at the very end of the book does he reveal that union with God himself, rather than realization of oneself as Brahman, is the ultimate fruition of the human soul.

Krishna's instruction of Arjuna starts from the teaching of the later Upanishads. God is both operative in the universe and totally unaffected by what he does. "Know," Krishna says, "that though I am the doer of this, I am eternally a not-doer. Actions do not mark me, for I have no yearning for their results."[22] Thus God is, as in the *Śvetāśvatara* Upanishad and the *Yogasūtras,* the eternal exemplar which man must copy; but, unlike the *Yogasūtras,* he must copy not only his aloofness but also his detached involvement. By contemplating this God whose action keeps the world in being, yet who eternally remains changeless and impassible in his essence, man realizes that he himself, constantly involved in action though he may be, is, at the root of his being, eternally at rest; and this being at rest is "to be Brahman" : but it is not to be God.

In the Gītā the mystical quest for God divides itself into two clearly defined phases. First there is the phase of the integration of the personality around the "self" or *ātman.* This is not quite the "isolation" of the *Yogasūtras,* for the whole of the personality is subsumed and withdrawn into the self, while in the *Yogasūtras*

[22] Bhagavad-Gītā, 4.13-14.

the purely psychosomatic part of man is detached off *from* the self. In the Gītā integration is achieved by withdrawing the senses from their objects, subjecting the mind to the self or soul so that finally all discursive thought is stopped, and the soul shines out alone with its own native light "like an unflickering light standing in a windless place."[23] Such a man is "integrated with the integration of Brahman (*brahma-yoga-yuktātmā*)" : he has passed beyond, being affected by neither pleasure nor pain, and finds his only happiness within his innermost self. "The Yogin, whose happiness is all within—his joy within, his light within— becomes very Brahman and goes to the Nirvāṇa of Brahman. This Nirvāna of Brahman is won by seers who have destroyed all that defiled them, and dispelled all their doubts : they have achieved mastery over their own souls and rejoice in the welfare of all things. Very close is the Nirvāna of Brahman to these seers who know their own souls, for they have become strangers to desire and anger and have learned to discipline their minds." Then such a one "will see himself as abiding in all creatures, and all creatures as abiding in himself."[24] This is the stage of felt omniscience which precedes the achievement of total *"isolation"* in the *Yogasūtras,* and in which all distinction between the perceiving subject and the perceived object seems to vanish away.

Just as the effulgence of the sun is visible before the sun actually rises, so does the preliminary illuminative knowledge which has all things as its object arise before the [supreme] knowledge of the difference [of the eternal from the temporal and the consequent isolation of the former from the latter] supervenes. This being so, he knows everything without recourse to any other form of Yogic concentration.[25]

This is again the identification of the soul with the All, the common experience of the nature mystics and the early Taoists : it is the last stage that precedes the soul's entry into Brahman, that is, an eternal mode of existence.

Having seen all things in himself, the Yogin, by analogy with this very experience of himself, then sees all things in God. This means that to enter into an eternal mode of existence is to realize oneself as partaking in the divine nature; for, says Krishna, "for

[23] *Ibid.*, 6.19.
[24] *Ibid.*, 5.21–6: 6.29.
[25] Bhojarāja on *Yogasūtras* 3.33.

him who sees me everywhere and all in me, I am not lost, nor is he lost to me." And the point would seem to be this, that until the mirror of the soul has been wiped clean of all the nastiness with which the Fall of man had covered it, and until it has polished itself to such a degree of brightness that it can worthily reflect the majesty of God, and until it has realized the time-lessness which, even in its fallen estate, is its own by nature, it cannot hope to have any part in God : only then can the love affair between God and man which was disrupted by the Fall, that is, by man's misuse of his individual consciousness, be renewed and pursued to the end.

The whole sequence in the mystic ascent is outlined toward the end of the last chapter of the Gītā; and the message of Krishna to Arjuna is poignant. Arjuna, who had grown used to Krishna as his bosom friend and companion-in-arms, is told that he must give all this up because an excess of human love is as much a hindrance in the mystic's path as is hatred, envy, and lust : he must lay down his great human love first if he is to find his own soul.

By giving up the ego, force, pride, lust, anger, and acquisitiveness, with no thought of "mine," at peace, so is a man fitted to become Brah-man (that is, to realize his own eternal essence). Become Brah-man, his soul all stilled, he grieves not, nor does he desire. Feeling equanimity towards all creatures, he [then] receives the highest [gift of] loving devotion to me. By his loving devotion he comes to *know* me as I am, how great I am and who. Thence once he has come to know me as I am, forthwith he comes to me.[26]

But it is a very different Krishna to whom Arjuna comes : it is no longer the friend with whom he had gone into battle and with whom he had so lightheartedly caroused, it is none less than the Lord and Creator of heaven and earth to whom obedience cannot be denied. But Arjuna has no cause to despair, for Krishna is the God of grace as well as the God of necessity. But first of all he must realize that God must be obeyed, for he rules with a necessary law which cannot be transgressed. And so it is that Krishna warns him :

Fixing thy thoughts on me thou shalt surmount all difficulties through my grace. But, if, prompted by thine ego, thou wilt not hearken, thou shalt perish. Shouldst thou, relying on thine ego, think, "I will not fight," thy effort is in vain, for Nature will compel thee.

[26] Bhagavad-Gītā, 18.53-5.

Bound by thine own deeds which are born of thine own nature, thou wilt do what, in thy delusion, thou wouldst not, for thou art without mastery. The Lord abides in the hearts of all creatures, and, by his supernatural power, makes them move hither and thither, things caught in a machine. Flee to him as thy refuge with all thy being. Through his grace thou shalt attain peace and an eternal abode.[27]

Thus, Arjuna, forced to give up Krishna as a merely human friend, finds him again after he has first found his own soul, but just as he is himself transformed by realizing his eternal essence as Brahman, so does he find Krishna transformed into the higher than Brahman, the personal God who invites man's love, and, should he fail to get it, takes it by force.

This is, then, the full message of the Gītā. Fallen man can, by his own efforts and by purifying himself from all taint of sin, realize his own eternal being outside time. Prior to this he may have an intellectual knowledge of God, but he will have no direct experience of him. Once he has realized the deep ground of his own soul, however, and subordinated his other faculties to it, God will reward him by bringing him to himself and by enveloping him in his love. First man must kill desire that he may rest in the still depths of his own soul, and it is only then, in the "dark night of the senses," that the "living flame of love" can be kindled. And this to the soul is passing strange, for had not the Lord himself taught him to still desire and led him to believe that, once his soul had found abiding peace, he had attained his final goal? Yet now he sees that this is not the end, for he understands that his God is not only his Lord and perfect exemplar, he is also a God of love and "lawful desire."[28] And since this is so, his own desire must be rekindled and redirected on to the sole object that is worthy of it—God. And this to Arjuna is the miracle of miracles and overflowing joy, for the Lord of heaven and earth turns out to be none other than Krishna, his close companion and dearest friend. And now he understands that only by denying self and, with self, all friendships that retain the slightest trace of selfishness, can the true self be found, and only by subjecting the false self to the true can the total man be made whole, and only by being himself wholly and to the limit of his being can he offer himself wholly in loving sacrifice to God. He understands too that by sacrificing his intimate love for Krishna, the man, he has opened himself to the infinite love for Krishna, the God; and, in

[27] *Ibid.*, 18.58–62.　　　　[28] *Ibid.*, 7.11.

so doing, his love for the man has not been destroyed but fulfilled and made perfect in and through his love for God and God's love for him.

The Bhagavad-Gītā marks a turning point in Indian religious thought; and its real significance, so admirably thrown into relief by Rāmānuja, has consistently been slurred over by modern commentators, both Indian and European. They would have us believe that Krishna is doing no more than introduce a simple religion of loving devotion to a personal God designed for simple people engaged in the ordinary affairs of life; and this is an inferior substitute for the contemplative life that leads to the realization of the soul as Brahman. Krishna, so this school of thought would maintain, is only the *saguṇa* Brahman—the Brahman possessed of qualities, or personal God, who is no more than the phenomenal Brahman acting in the phenomenal world, the phenomenal and therefore ultimately unreal aspect of the *nirguṇa* Brahman—the Brahman devoid of qualities which is alone real. Such a reading of the Gītā is not only wrong but very nearly dishonest; for time and time again Krishna asserts his superiority over Brahman, whether this term be used to mean an eternal category of being or the source and origin of the phenomenal world. And not only this : when he comes to deliver his ultimate message, which is that God loves man, he does so with all possible solemnity, declaring that this doctrine is "more secret than the secret" and "the most secret of all,"[29]—something literally unheard of before in the history of Indian religious thought, something that the incarnate God will reveal only to his bosom friend who is dearer to him than life itself. This new doctrine does not supersede the older doctrine of integrating the human personality around the immortal soul (*ātman*) in the timeless condition of Brahman, but opens up to the liberated soul totally new perspectives of eternal relationships outside time with the personal God who transcends eternity by as much as eternity transcends time. The Gītā is a revelation of God as substantial love, and so new and so startling is this revelation that Arjuna, hitherto bogged down in the multitudinous complexities of contemporary speculation, has the greatest difficulty in grasping the tremendous purport of Krishna's message. The Bhagavad-Gītā is *the* most important document not only in the history of

[29] *Ibid.*, 18.63-4.

Hinduism, but in the history of mysticism as a whole. For Christians too, Krishna, the incarnate God of love, who is yet *rex tremendae majestatis,* prefigures, as no other mythological figure can, the historical person of Jesus Christ, the Word made man who will yet return to pass judgment on mankind.

Hinduism is mystical through and through, and the radical reversal of the dominant trend in the Bhagavad-Gītā is, therefore, of overriding importance; for it smashes the wall of elaborate self-sufficiency that fallen man had built around himself and brings him face to face with God. Both Taoism, Buddhism, and the Sāmkhya-Yoga are religions that opt out of life, reject the world by rejecting individuality and the responsibilities that individuality brings with it. Krishna comes to change all that; for he implies that though, theoretically, there may be nothing wrong in this, it really amounts to a colossal act of spiritual pride; for it means that man, by seeking to be like God in his eternal impassibility and unfathomable peace, spurns to be like God in his capacity of creator and sustainer of the world. This is surely the acme of hybris; for if God is not too proud to keep the world in being, who is man to turn his back on it? And this too Krishna makes very clear to his friend :

Nothing need I do in the three worlds; there is nothing beyond my reach that I should strive to attain it. Yet do I continue to act. For did I not tirelessly busy myself with action, then would men imitate me everywhere. These worlds would run down, were I not to act, and I would be the cause of chaos and the destroyer of these [my] creatures.[30]

The continued existence of the phenomenal world, then, is of importance to God : he cares. Man, then, on his side, has a duty to this transient world as well as to his own immortal soul; and the point that Krishna makes is that the two are not incompatible. Man has his duty to his neighbor (even though it may be to kill him in a just war, as in Arjuna's case) and he has a duty to himself, and through his neighbor and himself to God.

From the purely mystical point of view, however, the Gītā's message is that realization of one's own eternal essence is not the end of the mystic's path: it is little more than a beginning. It corresponds to the *via purgativa* of the Christian mystics, the purpose of which is to wipe God's image clean in preparation for

[30] *Ibid.,* 3.22–4.

its encounter with God himself. To realize the ground of one's
own being is not to realize Being itself, as Buber saw. It is a
mistake that the soul of fallen man is bound to make, and it is
the last refuge of his spiritual pride. This too is the vice that the
Mahāyāna Buddhists detected in the older Buddhist ideal of the
arhant, the liberated sage who, serenely and sublimely, sails into
his own immortality and his own Nirvāṇa, shaking off the dust of
mundane existence from his feet forever and leaving the world to
burn on in agonized despair. Hence the Mahāyānists created a
new ideal, the ideal of the Bodhisattva or Buddha-to-be, the man
who postponed his own Nirvāṇa that he might bring others with
him into the promised land.

Though he has gone beyond all that is worldly, yet has he not moved
out of the world.
In the world he pursues his course for the world's weal, unstained
by worldly taints.[31]

For a Bodhisattva resolves :

I take upon myself the burden of all suffering; I am resolved to do
so; I will endure it. . . . In that I do not follow my own inclinations;
I have made the vow to save all beings. All beings must I set free.[32]

Yet Buddhism, though it developed this sublime ideal of the
Suffering Servant, never made the qualitative leap that the Gītā
makes from the purely static self-sufficiency of the "Nirvāṇa of
Brahman," which, when all is said and done, is no more than rest
in one's own soul, to a dynamic and vital I/Thou relationship
between man and God and the mutual giving and receiving of
divine and human love that is the essence of that relationship.
The Bodhisattva's self-sacrifice is heroic, but it is heroism in a
sterile cause; for unlike Krishna the Bodhisattva does not re-
establish the link with God that had been severed by the misuse
of individual consciousness, the mad desire to set up house alone,
independent of God and Nature, which we call original sin and
the Fall.

Both Hinduism and Buddhism are profoundly mystical religions, but Hinduism went further simply because it asked new
questions and was prepared to accept the new answers as
divinely given when they finally came. Buddhism's refusal to
define Nirvāṇa except as the "deathless" and the "timeless" or,

[31] E. Conze, *Buddhist Texts through the Ages* (Oxford, 1954), p. 130.
[32] *Ibid.,* p. 131.

in the later schools, as "emptiness" or the "Buddha-nature," meant that it never advanced beyond the Hindu concept of Brahman. Unlike Hinduism, Indian Buddhism did not pass on from here to the vision of the living God. This had to await its further development in China and Japan.

The whole concept of Brahman is foreign to the religions of Semitic origin : they do not normally think in terms of an "eternal" mode of existence except in God himself. However, both in Christianity and in Islam we find a similar, though not identical, concept developing. All things and therefore *a fortiori* all human souls are eternally present in the mind of God, and in this sense the human soul must have an extratemporal existence at least in God : this is what Buber calls an "original pre-biographical unity" of the soul—the soul as it is in eternity before it is launched by the hand of God into time. To realize one's soul in this "original pre-biographical unity" is, as perhaps the greatest of all the Muslim mystics, Junayd of Baghdad, puts it, "to be as one was before one was." Elaborating the same theme St. Thomas Aquinas says,

God is the first exemplary cause of all things. In proof whereof we must consider that if for the production of anything an exemplar is necessary, it is in order that the effect may receive a determinate form. For an artificer produces a determinate form in matter by reason of the exemplar before him, whether it be the exemplar beheld externally, or the exemplar interiorly conceived in the mind. Now it is manifest that things made by nature receive determinate forms. This determination of forms must be reduced to the divine wisdom as its first principle, for divine wisdom devised the order of the universe residing in the distinction of things. And therefore we must say that in the divine wisdom are the models of all things, which we have called ideas, i.e., exemplary forms existing in the divine mind. And although these ideas are multiplied by their relations to things, nevertheless, they are not really distinct from the divine essence, inasmuch as the likeness of that essence can be shared diversely by different things. In this manner, therefore, God himself is the first exemplar of all things.[33]

In Christianity, the idea of Brahman is represented by the eternal ideas in the divine mind, and these are one in the one essence of God, but at the same time differentiated in that "the divine wisdom devised the order of the universe residing in the

[33] Aquinas, *Summa Theologica*, Q.44, Art.3.

distinction of things." To realize one's deepest being, then, as an idea of God, "to be as one was before one was," means to realize one's own separate essence in the context of the divine mind—"to become unified in the imperishable beyond," as the *Muṇḍaka* Upanishad puts it.

Thus Hinduism is by no means the only religion in which the conflict between monism and the mysticism of the love of God arises. In Islam this conflict became acute during the ninth and tenth centuries A.D., in Christianity during the thirteenth and fourteenth centuries. In order to impress upon the reader the reality and universality of this conflict we must give a brief account of these internal crises in these two great religious traditions.

Islam is not, one would have thought, a religion to which mysticism would naturally attach itself, so utterly transcendent is the Koranic conception of God. Yet mysticism starts early in Islam, at first as little more than a mildly ascetic protest against the political and sectarian rivalries that bedeviled the first Islamic century, and against a growing worldliness that was inseparable from a career of conquest and loot; then gradually the movement was permeated by the theory of the possibility of experiencing, without intermediary, the love of God, which these Sūfīs, as they were called, learned from the Christian mystics who had preceded them in once Christian lands, now overrun by Islam. In the ninth century, however, all this changed, and very different accents began to be heard in western Khorasan or what is now north-eastern Persia. For there, in the hamlet of Bistām, was born and thrived one, Abū Yazīd, who stunned an outraged Muslim world by declaring that he *was* God. How he came to this very un-Muslim conclusion we must now relate.

His spiritual director was a man of Sind who was a convert to Islam, for Abū Yazīd had to teach him the obligatory ritual duties of that religion in return for which he was instructed in what he held to be the ultimate truths concerning the divine unity. From a comparison of his recorded sayings with some key passages in the Upanishads and elsewhere in Hindu sacred literature, it is clear that the man of Sind who instructed him had been the strictest of strict non-dualist Vedāntins. This particular school of the Vedānta, as we have seen, identified the human soul with Brahman, which, for them, means the undifferentiable One which alone has absolute reality. Translated into Muslim terms Brahman could be identified with God only in his essence : so Abū Yazīd could and did say, "I sloughed off my self as a snake sloughs off its skin; then I looked into myself, and lo! I was he!" thereby roundly identifying himself with God.

The phraseology of this utterance makes it fairly clear that he is reproducing an Upanishadic passage he had learned from his master; and the passage in question runs as follows :

As the sloughed-off skin of a snake lies on an ant-hill, dead, cast off, so does this body lie. But the incorporeal, immortal spirit is Brahman indeed, is light indeed. . . . If a man should know himself and say, "I am He," what could he possibly wish for or desire that would make him cling to his body?[34]

This and a number of other parallels which I have listed and commented on in my *Hindu and Muslim Mysticism* (pp. 94-102) are strong evidence that Abū Yazīd is reproducing purely Vedāntin ideas in Muslim dress. Ignorant, however, of the distinction the Hindus drew between Brahman and "the Lord," that is, the personal creator God, he roundly identifies himself with the Muslim God, whom alone he knew, not only in his essence, but also in his attributes.

Abū Yazīd had the reputation of being not only holy but also slightly mad. He was, then, but little molested by the orthodox, while by his fellow-Sūfīs he was venerated as a saint. Yet the more thoughtful among them, who were yet not prepared to dismiss him as a charlatan, tried to find out just what his experience amounted to and how it fitted into their scheme of things which was centered on union with God through a passion of love. It is clear that if love is to subsist at all, then the distinction between God and the soul cannot wholly disappear; for where there is identity, plainly, there can be no love.

It fell to the lot of Junayd of Baghdad to put Abū Yazīd's experiences where they belonged. He commented on Abū Yazīd's sayings and interpreted them as one who has had similar experiences himself. Time and again Abū Yazīd had laid claim, both explicitly and implicitly, to be identical with God in all respects, and, in the most famous of all his sayings, he had even gone so far as to claim divine honors. "Glory be to me! How great is my glory! So worship me!" he had said—and again this goes back

[34] *Bṛhadāraṇyaka* Upanishad, 4.4.7, 12.

to a Vedāntin original. On this and similar sayings Junayd comments :

He had [indeed] spoken truly of the experience of union except that his words were only beginnings of what might be expected from one who is of the elect.

This he elaborates further, and his analysis of this "monistic" experience agrees entirely with what Martin Buber has said. He writes,

When [Abū Yazīd] says, "I entered into his unity," this represents the first glimpse [only] of unity. He describes what he observed there, —he describes the furthest point he was capable of attaining, [and that is] *the ground of his own finite roots*. All this is only one path among many for those who are called to attain the true experience of union.

Abū Yazīd had made the same mistake as his Vedāntin master (and Junayd knew nothing at all, so far as we are aware, of Indian mysticism) : he mistook the ground of his own single soul for the ground of the All.

According to Junayd, God demands of the soul that it be "as it was before it was," but this is the first, not the last, demand God makes upon the soul. Even this state, however, was attained not by any initiative on the part of man, but by a terrific visitation of God in his overwhelming power. This visitation he calls not only an "overwhelming" but also an "election." God reveals himself to the mystic, and the mystic is stunned by the vision : he is thrown completely off his balance and passes into that form of existence he had enjoyed while yet he was an idea in the divine mind; he passes clean out of time and is isolated within himself, and from this isolation he contemplates the isolation of God. And in this he is doing exactly what the Sāṁkhya-Yogin had done in India—the soul in isolation contemplates its eternal exemplar, God, in *his* eternal isolation. But, unlike the Sāṁkhya-Yoga, Junayd realized that this is not yet the end. The timeless trance passes, and the soul returns from the world of timelessness to the world of time. The vision, however, refuses to be dismissed, and the soul strives ardently to recapture it, and very nearly succeeds; but in reality it succeeds only in doing what Abū Yazīd had done, it reaches only to the "ground of its own finite roots" and thinks (as it is bound to think) that it has become Being itself : it thinks that it is God.

And then, says Junayd,

They become satisfied with what has already appeared to them, lose
all sense of destitution, and abandon all sense of judgment. They
preen themselves on the victory [they think they have obtained] by
their own efforts and power and overweening pride.... And when
God's manifestations appear to them, [God] causes them to take refuge
from him in their own [attributes] so that they exult and glory in their
own isolation. At this stage they go forth without any repining towards him, preferring [to him] that in which their joy is isolated, playing the wanton with him, so sure are they of his forbearance. They do
not see that a return will be demanded of them and that an account will
be exacted from them. When this happens, it is God's guile that encompasses them in a manner they do not understand.

We are now moving in an Islamic, not a Hindu, environment,
and Allah does not take kindly to the spiritual pride of men. At
one stroke he smashes their precarious "unity in isolation"
and reveals himself again as he is in his transcendent majesty
and sovereign attractive power. Then

Their inmost essences are thrown off their balance and their souls
are distraught for life eternal. Their habitual haunts offer them no
refuge nor can their acquired habits hide them [from God]. Desperately
do they yearn for him who causes them to suffer, and bitterly do they
wail at the loss of him who is far away. Their [sense of] loss distresses
them, and their [sense of] finding [God] humbles them as they yearn
and ache for him, longing for him in their ecstasy. Their yearning he
requites with a raging thirst which ever increases and grows in their
bowels, while they strive desperately to know themselves and are lavish
in losing themselves. He gives them a thirst for him and all manner of
mourning and grief. He raises for them all manner of signs(?),
causing them to savour the taste of denudation and renewing for them
the prospect of enduring [yet more] striving; yet even in the aftermath of their troubles they incline [towards him], longing to be
chastised with grief, seeking to be made whole, clinging to any trace
of the Beloved as he reveals himself [to them]. ... So they are completely concealed [from themselves], for they have lost the veil [that
hid God from them], and they are no longer divided from him.
Affliction is removed from them and they are no longer punished.
And how should any veil divide them from him? for they are his cap-
tives, imprisoned before him; and even as they are afflicted, they
find favour with him in that they are destroyed in what is manifested
to them. They no longer aim at looking after themselves, content with
God's love and their dependence on him and their nearness to him.
In the swiftness of their awakening they behold the myriad glances

[that proceed] from him so that the very destruction [of their human individuality] is [itself] drowned in the tide that flows over them in eternal being and violent suffering, until their very suffering is turned to joy and their abiding in it brings them delight in God, for they see that he is near to ward off their suffering and to draw its sting. Then the soul no longer turns away from the burden of suffering out of faint-heartedness, nor is it grieved by it nor chafed. These are the [real] heroes of mystical experience because God has revealed his secrets to them, and they have taken up their abode in his omnipotence, awaiting his command.[35]

I have quoted this passage in full, because it seems to me to illustrate more forcibly than any other I have come across the gulf that separates what another Muslim mystic, Najm al-Dīn Rāzī, calls the "mysticism of the soul" from the mysticism of the love of God. Where there is no contact and no love, but only the still-ness of Nirvāṇa, there the soul rests "in the ground of its own finite roots," "like an unflickering lamp standing in a windless place"[36] : there is no quickening contact with the living God. The impact of God is unmistakable even if, for other mystics, it does not strike with quite the violence with which it struck Junayd, yet, whether it be violent or gentle, the element of suffering is never wholly absent; for, though the pride of the ego may long ago have been subdued, the pride of the eternal "self" which seems to persist even in what the Gītā calls the "Nirvāṇa of Brah-man," has yet to be uprooted and melted in the fire of the Holy Spirit.

Among the Muslim mystics we could quote similar experi-ences from Ibn Ṭufayl and Najm al-Dīn Rāzī, but this must suffice, for these I have dealt with elsewhere,[37] and in any case their spiritual stature falls far short of Junayd's. But before passing on to the similar experience of Jan Ruysbroeck in Christendom, let us quote Junayd for the last time, so admirably does he portray the seriousness, the urgency, and the difficulty of the soul's passage from the immortal "self" to God. He says,

The journey from this world to the next is easy and simple for the believer, but to separate oneself from creatures for God's sake is hard, and the journey from self to God is exceedingly hard, and to bear patiently with God is hardest of all.[38]

[35] Zaehner, *Hindu and Muslim Mysticism* (London, 1960), pp. 223–24.
[36] Bhagavad-Gītā, 6.19.
[37] *Hindu and Muslim Mysticism*, pp. 180–88.
[38] *Ibid.*, p. 153.

The phenomenon of Abū Yazīd with which Junayd had to contend was due to a direct Vedāntin influence upon one individual. Similar phenomena, however, are likely to crop up at any place and time, and the European Middle Ages were no exception. The Blessed Jan Ruysbroeck, whose variety of mysticism for long caused anxiety to the Church, was confronted with exactly the same phenomenon.

There is a mysticism of the soul and a mysticism of love. In the first there is oneness and emptiness, rest and peace : in the second there is yearning and love, union, communion, and—most paradoxical of all—constant activity, constant action and interaction in a world that is yet beyond time; for even the Upanishads teach us that motion in the phenomenal world must correspond to something in the eternal world; for there too the Absolute "moves [and yet] does not move. It is far, and it is near. It is within this universe, and it is outside it too."[39]

To find rest and peace within oneself, to pass beyond space and time into the "ground of one's own finite roots" is still "natural" to fallen man, for God's image, though shattered, had still preserved within it the "breath of life" that the Lord God had breathed into it; and this, being of God, cannot die. And so it comes about that

Whenever man is empty and undistracted in his senses by images, and free and unoccupied in his highest powers, he attains rest by purely natural means. And all men can find and possess this rest in themselves by their mere nature, without the grace of God, if they are able to empty themselves of sensual images and of all action.[40]

And this is, of course the technique of the Yogins of all schools —Sāṁkhya, Vendānta, Buddhist, and Jain. It is, moreover, not only in all men by nature, but is in itself commendable, for, by delving down into the ground of his soul which has its being outside time, man is seeking within himself that which makes him most like God. In the case of the Buddhist or Jain, however, he will be doing this in ignorance of the very existence of God, but he is impelled thereto by his very nature, as the Bhagavad-Gītā itself points out.[41]

Ruysbroeck concedes,

[39] *Isā* Upanishad, 5.
[40] Jan Ruysbroeck, *The Spiritual Espousals* (English translation, London, 1952) pp. 166–67.
[41] Bhagavad-Gītā, 18.59.

In this emptiness rest is sufficient and great, and it is in itself no sin, for it is in all men by nature, if they know how to make themselves empty. But when men wish to exercise and possess their rest without the works of virtue, then they fall into spiritual pride, and into a self-complacency from which they seldom recover. And at such times they believe themselves to have and to be that which they never achieve.[42]

This cultivation of the eternal "self" is no more sinful in Christianity than it is in Hinduism, for by discovering the image of God within him, a man may be spurred on to seek God himself, or, as Junayd would have it, God himself may intervene and smash the vessel of self-contemplation that the eyes may be opened to God. The danger of this method, however, is that the mystic may stop halfway, mistaking his own soul for the living God. Among the Jews Martin Buber has issued solemn warning against this danger, among the Muslims Junayd and many others, among the Hindus Rāmānuja and his successors, while among the Christians it is Ruysbroeck and St. John of the Cross who have both seen the stumbling block and shown how it can be surmounted. And their convergent testimony is surely true.

Mistaking their own souls for God, these men, as Junayd saw, risk being utterly undone by spiritual pride : there will be no goodness in them. Ruysbroeck saw this with equal clarity. He warns,

Observe this with attention, so that you may well understand it. The men who live thus are, as it seems to them, occupied in the contemplation of God, and they believe themselves to be the holiest men alive. Yet they live in opposition and dissimilarity to God and all saints and all good men.... Through the natural rest which they feel *and have* in themselves in emptiness, they maintain that they are free, and united with God without mean, and that they are advanced beyond all the exercises of Holy Church, and beyond the commandments of God, and beyond the law, and beyond all the virtuous works which one can in any way practise. For this emptiness seems to them to be so great that no one ought to hinder them with the performance of any work, however good it be, for their emptiness is of greater excellence than are all virtues.... And thus, according to them, no one is able to give to them or to take from them, *not even God himself*; for it appears to them that they have advanced beyond all exercises and all virtues. ... And therefore they say that they can never increase in virtue, that they can never deserve a greater reward, and also that they can never sin again.[43]

[42] Ruysbroeck, *op. cit.*, pp. 167-68.
[43] *Ibid.*, pp. 170-71.

To mistake this fixing of the soul in a wholly static peace and to suppose thereby that the soul is the unchanging ground of the universe is, for Ruysbroeck, as we have said, the greatest stumbling block to all spiritual advancement; and those who practice it at the expense of good works and the regular performance of their religious duties he compares to the damned in hell!

Monism, then, would seem to be a perversion of the natural hankering after unity and harmony that is present in all men : it is mysticism's dead end and rooted in original sin. It is to mistake that tiny parcel of eternity that is the human soul for the Eternal himself; and it is to separate oneself not only from God, but from one's fellows. It is to reject love and to rule out grace as an ontological impossibility; it is the ultimate refusal to co-operate not only in the fulfillment and enrichment of one's own personality, but in the fulfillment of the destiny of the whole human race. What entropy is in thermodynamics—the reduction of matter to a shapeless uniformity—monism is in the spiritual life : it is, in the most literal sense of the word, a dead end.

Mysticism, like everything else, has evolved; and it has had to adapt itself to the fact of the Fall, the fact of the reality and apparent imperviousness of individual consciousness. Nature mysticism is man's first reaction against individual responsibility which a separated consciousness imposes upon him. Later separated man comes to realize that the ground of his soul has its being outside space and time, and that, by sinking himself in this ground, he can find security and blissful rest. These two ways are always open to him even in his fallen estate. It is, however, only when he discovers God, or rather when God reveals himself to him, that the shell which encases not only his ego, but his immortal "self" as well, bursts and opens like a flower to drink in the sunlight of the love and grace of God : and this opens the way to a fuller development of himself, to a giving of that self to God and a receiving of it back incomparably enriched. And to this process there can be no end, neither in time nor in eternity, neither in the individual nor in the whole mass of the human race. For, as the Zoroastrians saw, humanity must itself be built into God, not only in its individual members but in its total solidarity too, so that at the last the whole may be consecrated as the living temple of the living God.

5

Solidarity in God

In the beginning those two Spirits who are the well-endowed twins were known as the one good, the other evil, in thought, word, and deed. Between the two the wise chose the good, not so the fools. And when these two Spirits met, they established in the beginning life and death that in the end the evil should meet with the worst existence, but the just with the Best Mind. Of these two Spirits he who was of the Lie chose to do the worst things, but the Most Holy Spirit, clad in rugged heaven, [chose] Truth, as did [all] who sought with zeal to do the pleasure of the Wise Lord by [doing] good works. Between the two the ancient godlets did not choose rightly; for, as they deliberated, delusion overcame them, so that they chose the most evil mind. Then did they, with one accord, rush headlong unto Fury, that they might thereby extinguish (?) the existence of mortal man.[1]

So spake Zoroaster, the Prophet of ancient Iran.

Of the Semitic religions it was the Jews alone who succeeded in developing a transcendent monotheism, which, in modified forms, was to make a universal appeal; for from Israel emanated not only Christianity in the direct line, but also Islam indirectly. Of the Indo-European peoples it was only the Indo-Iranians who succeeded in producing religions that had enough of psychological truth to make a universal appeal. The Indian contribution to the religious mosaic that covers the world is far better known than the Iranian; and rightly so, for it has survived for thousands of years both in its own right as Hinduism and in its offshoot, Buddhism, whereas Zoroastrianism, except for the tiny remnant now called the Parsees, has vanished from the face of the earth.

The Indians and the Iranians once formed one people, and their religion was essentially the same and recognizably akin to the religions of the other Indo-European peoples—Greeks, Romans, Teutons, Slavs, and Celts. Their religion was a robust

[1] R. C. Zaehner, *The Dawn and Twilight of Zoroastrianism* (London, 1961) p. 42.

polytheism, this-worldly, outward-looking, and naïve. Their gods were both personified powers of nature and reflections of their own social structure, usually beneficent, sometimes terrible. None of them succeeded in attaining undisputed mastery over the others, and none secured even the precarious, though grudgingly accepted, sovereignty of Homeric Zeus over his immortals. There was nothing particularly remarkable about the religion of the Indo-Iranians before the two peoples divided. It was only after the division that both peoples developed religions that went far beyond a primitive polytheism. The Indians became deeply involved in the "within" of things, the Iranians in the "without." Of the Indian contribution we have already spoken. We have seen how they worked up from the felt experience of the immortality of the soul—the deep center within temporal man that yet transcended time—to the realization of a God who, though himself more immanent that the human soul itself, as being the center from which all individual centers radiated, was yet the transcendent Lord and, more marvelous still, the lover of man's soul.

The development of Iranian religion was quite other than this, for it was dominated by one single personality, the Prophet Zoroaster, just as Islam which arose some twelve hundred years later, was, and continues to be, dominated by the personality of the Prophet Muhammad. But whereas Islam has run a more or less even course during its thirteen hundred years of existence, Zoroastrianism never succeeded in getting properly started. It never developed a continuous tradition; it compromised with the old paganism, was dealt a shattering blow by Alexander the Great from which it never fully recovered, and only after six hundred years of total eclipse did it re-emerge under the royal patronage of the Sassanian kings who ruled the second Persian Empire which lasted from A.D. 226 to 652. Zoroastrianism, then, enjoyed two periods of greatness, first during the first Persian Empire of Cyrus, Darius, and Xerxes (550-330 B.C.), and secondly under the Sassanians. From the purely religious point of view it is only the *Gāthās* or "Hymns" of Zoroaster himself and the developed theology of the Sassanian period that are of enduring interest. Each made its original contribution to religious history, and each contains much that is relevant to the religious situation today.

A religion, in order to satisfy the complete man, must concern itself as much with the "without" as with the "within" of things; and it must also concern itself both with the nature and destiny of the individual soul and with the collectivity of which the individual forms part. In China, Taoism and Confucianism existed side by side, the one concerning itself exclusively with individual "salvation," the other busying itself with the good ordering of human society here on earth. In Zoroastrianism the individual and the collective aspects of religion are emphasized successively in the two periods of its greatness, the individual during the first Persian Empire, the collective during the second. The Prophet Zoroaster addresses himself primarily to the individual, challenging him to make his individual choice between Truth and the Lie—a choice which none can evade. In the Sassanian period the whole emphasis is changed. Certainly, he still has his own fateful individual choice to make, but this choice is made in the context of the whole, for he is primarily a soldier in the army of God, and the army itself is sweeping on to final and inevitable victory over the forces of the Lie. It is no longer individual man that is at stake, but all mankind; and it is the unity of the human race that is destined to bring the powers of darkness tumbling down in fearful ruin.

Truth is one : the Lie is manifold. And it is the unity of the followers of Truth that is bound in the end to triumph over the disunion that is inherent in the Lie; for all things converge with an inexorable logic on the final grinding down of evil beneath the crushing weight of all mankind acting as a single whole. This, however, is to anticipate.

Zoroastrianism, more than any other religion, looks the "mystery of iniquity" squarely in the face. The phrase "beyond good and evil" which Nietzsche had the impudence to put into the mouth of Zoroaster, had no meaning for the Zoroastrian, least of all for the Prophet Zoroaster himself. Evil is something positive which has to be faced and, once faced, conquered. God, unlike the God of Isaiah, does not "make peace and create evil,"[2] he abhors evil, being himself perfectly good. Yet wide awake though Zoroaster was to the fact of evil, he nowhere clearly states whence its origin is. We started this chapter with a well-known quotation which puts before our eyes the fateful encounter at the beginning of time of the Holy Spirit and the Destructive Spirit in which the first chooses Truth, the second the Lie, the first creates life, the

[2] Isa. 45 : 7.

second death—the one being dialectically opposed to the other in
"thought, word, and deed." The contrast is even more vividly
portrayed in an equally famous passage, where the Prophet proclaims,

I will speak out concerning the two Spirits, of whom, at the beginning of existence, the Holier thus spoke to him who is evil: "Neither
our thoughts, nor our teachings, nor our wills, nor our choices, nor
our words, nor our deeds, nor our consciences, nor yet our souls
agree."[3]

The dualism could scarcely be more stark. And yet—in the first
passage we quoted, the spirits are also referred to as "twins"[4]; and
if they are twins, then surely they must derive from a common
origin. Now, Zoroaster's God is called the "Wise Lord," and
the Holy Spirit is not identical with him. He is rather the Spirit
through whom God creates—the *creator spiritus*—and himself
an hypostasis of God, though not identical with God, for he is
elsewhere called his "son." This at once raises the question of
whether the Destructive Spirit, explicitly spoken of as the Holy
Spirit's twin, is not also the son of the Wise Lord. Logically he
must be.

In the *Gāthās* themselves, moreover, the Destructive Spirit is
destructive by choice, not by nature, and God is thereby absolved
from directly originating evil. He permits it because all conscious
creatures are created free to choose between Truth and the Lie,
but he does not condone it. Once the Destructive Spirit has made
his fateful choice, the whole of the divine hierarchy closes its
ranks against him; and individual men on their part are asked
to commit themselves on one side or the other—to fight with
God against the Lie, or to cast in their lot with the powers of
death and falsehood.

Zoroaster's attitude to deity is that of a prophet, not of a sage :
he is not searching for the god within the human heart as the
Indian sages were, he is brought face to face with God—the
"Wise Lord"—a living reality. He *hears* the voice of God who
speaks to him "with the tongue of his mouth," "*sees* him with his
eyes," and *knows* him to be "in Truth the Wise Lord of the Good
Mind and of good deeds and words."

Then did I understand in my mind, [he exclaims,] that thou art
the ancient, thou the [ever] young, the father of the Good Mind,

[3] Zaehner, *Zoroastrianism*, p. 43.   [4] *Ibid.*, p. 42.

when I comprehended thee with my eyes,—[thee,] the very creator
of Truth, Lord of [all] creation in thy works.[5]

For the Prophet this seeing of God and this hearing of his
words is self-authenticating : he has no doubt that he has stood
in the presence of the one true God and has heard his voice. For
Zoroaster, as with other prophets, God is wholly transcendent;
he is "clad in rugged heaven" and is the creator and sustainer
of the world, the author of Righteousness or Truth and of the
Good Mind, of Right-mindedness and the Kingdom, of Wholeness and Immortality—the six entities which are at once
hypostases of himself and his highest gifts to men.

Again, unlike the Hindu cosmos which is cyclic, emanating and
dissolving itself forever and ever, the Zoroastrian cosmos has
a beginning, a middle, and an end. The beginning is marked by
the primordial confrontation of the two Spirits in deadly opposition, the middle by the appearance of the Prophet and his bringing of God's message to man, and the end by the renewal of all
existence in which evil and death, which is the invention of evil,
will be finally annihilated. In the *Gāthās* themselves, however, the
origin of evil is never clearly explained.

In the Sassanian period—the second period of Zoroastrian
greatness—the origin of evil became a matter of much theological
dispute. Mindful of the fact that the Prophet himself had spoken
of the Holy Spirit and the Destructive Spirit as twins, some theologians considered that evil must in some way have originated
in the divine substance itself. This, however, caused some embar-
rassment, for in the course of the centuries God, the Wise Lord,
had become fully identified with the Holy Spirit, and, plainly,
he could not himself be his own son. Hence they hit upon the idea
that the two Spirits, good and evil, or light and darkness, as they
came to be physically symbolized, each derived from infinite
Space-Time, itself neither good nor evil, light nor dark, but the
neutral source of all the opposites and the absolute in which
they all meet, the undifferentiated unity from which all else
arises. Similar to this, though not identical with it, was a second
version of the origin of things, and this was that God himself,
in his infinite solitude, tried to imagine what it would be like
to have an adversary, and from this unworthy thought the Adversary in very deed materialized. Lastly there were the straight

[5] *Ibid.*, p. 44.

dualists who, preferring to sacrifice the unity and infinity of the Godhead to allowing the smallest responsibility for evil to attach to God, whose absolute goodness was the principal article of their faith, opted for a complete and cut-and-dried dualism which divided all being between good and evil, light and darkness, the two pre-existent eternal principles, Ohrmazd, who is the same as Zoroaster's "Wise Lord," and Ahriman, the Destructive Spirit. Evil, then, for the dualists was a separate substance existing from all eternity : for the other two sects it was a hidden flaw eternally secreted in the very heart of God. Yet, different though the premises of the three sects may be, the presence of evil, whether it be eternal or originated, at once limits the Godhead : his omnipotence is infringed. Like his Adversary he is finite, though, unlike him, potentially infinite; and he cannot reach the plenitude of his potentially infinite being except by destroying forever his enemy who is the principle of death.

In the later Zoroastrian texts known as the Pahlavi Books, there is a unique account of the origin of evil, and it is a story of original sin : but the sinner is not man, but God. In our allegory of the first chapters of the Book of Genesis we suggested that the sin of Adam represented the growing of the human race into self-consciousness and the misuse made of that self-consciousness when first it dawned. In the Zoroastrian myth which we are about to consider, the story concerns the growth into self-consciousness of God himself—his passage into time out of eternity and the tragic consequences that this groping from unconsciousness into consciousness entailed. In "infinite time," that is, what the *Maitrī* Upanishad paradoxically calls "timeless time," all is potentiality : the Infinite One (whether it be conceived of as infinite Time, Space, or God himself in his timeless essence) exists in his "power" and "knowledge," but these are as yet purely potential, the first being the potentiality of evolving a material universe, the second the potentiality of developing an intelligible order. Matter and spirit (and by "spirit" the Zoroastrians understand "intellect" and "will," not, as the Indians do, an eternal category of being) are not opposite principles as they are with the Manichees, but rather two facets of one and the same thing. The evolution of matter and the evolution of spirit develop on parallel lines, and the whole trend of the universe is for them to converge ever more closely. In the beginning they were indifferentiably one—the Spirit of God mov-

ing upon the face of the waters. In this One there was neither
movement nor thought; or rather, as in a seed which is the plant
in potency, all movement and all thought was latent within it,
though itself was conscious of nothing at all : God was yet to be
born. We read,

Of knowledge (or, the condition of being a knower), thus is
it taught. By the Creator's marvellous power—in Infinite Time and by
its power knowledge came to know (the immutability of Ohrmazd's
essence depends on Infinite Time). From this [act of knowing] resulted the rising up of the Aggressor, unwilled [by Ohrmazd], to
destroy the essence [of Ohrmazd, i.e., his immutability] and his
attributes, by means of false speech. The immediate result of this was
that [Ohrmazd]'s essence and attributes turned back [in to them-
selves] in order to [come to] know their own ground. So much
knowing was necessary for the Creator [himself] to rise up for the
creative act. The first effect of this rising up was the Endless Light.
From the Endless Light is the Spirit of Truth which derives from knowledge because it has the potentiality of growing into the knowledge of
all things. By knowing all things [Ohrmazd] has power to do all
he wills. Thence creation and the Aggressor's defeat thereby, the
return of creation to its proper sphere of action, and the eternal rule
of Ohrmazd in perfect joy; for it is he who is the origin of all
good things, the source of good, the seed and potentiality of all
that is good. All good creatures are from him as a first effect by creation or emanation, as sheen is from shining, shining from brilliance,
brilliance from light.[6]

Ohrmazd, who is God, is conceived of primarily as being the
divine intellect; in virtue of the fact that his habitat is Infinite
Time, however, he must also be immutable, eternal Being, what
the Indians would call timeless Being. But as "wisdom" and
"knower" he is still potential only, unconscious of himself : he
has yet to be actualized. Something stirs within him : there is a
groping toward consciousness : something wants to "know." And
this groping awareness, moving as it were in a haze, is in search
of an object of knowledge outside itself; but there is nothing
outside itself. So, against the will of the nascent God—so far
as he can be said to have a will at all at this stage—duality arises,
and "in duality is evil."[7] Out of the mists of the divine unconscious emerges the "other," the Aggressor—that which is antagonistic to, and destructive of, the God who longs to reach self-aware-

[6] *Ibid.*, p. 220.
[7] *Ibid.*, p. 212.

ness—the divisive spirit whose impulse is to disrupt and to destroy. The passage of God from the sleep of eternity into full self-awareness is no smooth transition : suddenly it becomes a hideous nightmare, the more hideous for being real. This self-generated object of consciousness, looming up through the thinning mist of semi-consciousness, turns out to be a deadly enemy, the Aggressor now fully actualized. He too has woken out of his timeless sleep, and his awakening is an awakening of mindless misery, and his misery stimulates him to destroy—to destroy everything that all may once again sink back into unconsciousness and death. Above all he must destroy his enemy's essence which now clearly emerges not only as immutable being, but as an ever-increasing awareness of self, an ever surer grasp of the intellect, potentially infinite, of its own infinite being. Ahriman, the Aggressor, cannot operate except in time, for in eternity he is simply not-being.[8] This he knows full well and, because he is the death-wish personified, he seeks to annihilate being itself. This he thinks he can do by imprisoning the infinite in the finite, the eternal in the temporal, God in the world. Having limited God he can then destroy him.

Ahriman, the Devil, then, originates in God's uneasy passage from the unconscious into consciousness; in Jungian terminology —and the whole myth reads like a dream of one of Jung's patients —the birth of the divine, conscious ego is accompanied by the coming-to-be of the "shadow"—the dark, inadmissible side of the divine personality. God's initial failure to reach full self consciousness in one coherent stage puts him in mortal peril; for he risks the loss of his very essence, eternal being, which he now sees to be identical with eternal Knowing or Wisdom. Straightway he makes an effort of total introspection—his "essence and attributes turned back [onto themselves] in order to [come to] know his own ground." Incomplete consciousness revealed to God the dark, aggressive side of his character; and this he immediately recognized as his eternal enemy. To arm himself against this agent of disorder and death he realized that he must plunge back deep into the wells of his own being, and in so doing he realized that this being of his was eternal and therefore indestructible; he realized that his true being lay outside time, and therefore could not die. He realized too that his enemy could not exist at all except in time, and that in time and space he would have to be destroyed.

[8] *Ibid.*, p. 216.

"So much knowing was necessary for the Creator to rise up for the creative act." So God creates the archetypes of the material and spiritual worlds—the Endless Light and the Spirit of Truth —as the first means by which to bring his enemy to bay. Space and time are fashioned forth from the Infinite to form the battle-field on which the struggle is to be fought out, for only in a finite setting can Ahriman, the essentially finite Spirit, be destroyed. Creation, for God, is not only dictated to him by the nature of his enemy who can be destroyed only in a finite setting, it is also dictated by the very nature of God himself, for, in knowing his own ground, God knew that he was good, for "the definition of goodness is that which of itself develops."[9] As Ahriman diminishes God grows into his own infinite stature, he grows into "the knowledge of all things."

In the later Zoroastrian texts God—the Wise Lord—and the Holy Spirit are one and the same Person : but the word used for "holy" literally means "in whom is increase," and this is absolutely basic not only to the Zoroastrians' view of God but to their view of all existence. Though in "infinite Time" God is timeless and eternal, he nevertheless has the possibility, or rather the *necessity*, of growth, development, and fulfilment in him—for he is the Spirit "in whom is increase" : he must develop to the extreme limit of his infinite capacity and "*grow* into the knowledge of all things." Time and eternity, action and effortless rest, are not absolute contradictions any more than they are for Krishna in the Bhagavad-Gītā who, "though in need of nothing" and wholly and blissfully sufficient unto himself, nevertheless "tirelessly busies himself with action." In Zoroastrianism Adam's drama is transposed from the human onto the divine plane. In both cases the first result of the passing from the night of the un-conscious into the dawn of consciousness is to see what is other than yourself as the enemy : Cain slays Abel in the Hebrew account. Ahriman, the Devil—the elder and firstborn of the twin Spirits according to a variant form of the Zoroastrian myth which tells not of the awakening to consciousness of an infinite God, but, in crude mythological terms, of the birth of two Spirits from Infinite Time—is "he whose will is to smite" and "whose will is envy."[10] In each case the first instinct of the newly self-conscious

[9] *Ibid.*, p. 221
[10] See R. C. Zaehner, *Zurvan, a Zoroastrian Dilemma* (Oxford, 1955), pp. 312, 313.

individual, on recognizing what is other than himself, is to strike
it down. And this is only natural; for if it took thousands and
thousands of years for the human species to reach full self-consciousness, this must have taken place by fits and starts, one man
from time to time suddenly dropping out of the collective unconscious of the species and seeing others as separate from himself, menacing in their gregarious concord. Instinctively he fears
them and envies them, and his desire is to smite. And smite he
does, and the human herd turns on him and rends him. And
now is he "cursed from the earth, a fugitive and a vagabond."
He has sinned not only against God whom, perhaps, he does
not know, but also against the Spirit of collective life which still
holds the mass together in the last watches of the night of
innocence and unconsciousness, and the Spirit turns and rends
him. Cain, the premature individual, is the natural victim that
collective man demands of those who separate themselves from
him, and his destruction by the mass might have healed the
breach caused by Adam's fall. But God purposed otherwise.

And the Lord said unto him, Therefore whosoever slayeth Cain,
vengeance shall be taken on him sevenfold.[11]

This verse throws a flood of light on the first chapters of
Genesis. Original Sin, the birth into consciousness and the misuse of self-consciousness, is nevertheless a *felix culpa,* a "happy
fault." It represents an irreversible breakthrough from an un-
defined, though blissful existence, into an existence, aware of itself
and ever more sharply defined, an existence as a person who, as
person, has responsibility, dignity, and freedom—the awful freedom with which the Prophet Zoroaster confronted self-conscious
man, the freedom to choose between good and evil, the freedom
to reject both God and the undeveloped human herd or to work
with God and with one's fellow men in a concerted effort to increase in knowledge and in virtue and to strike down the demon
of "separation in isolation," that original sin which had cut the
individual person irreparably off from his fellows and from God.
The human drama is projected in the Zoroastrian myth onto
the divine nature itself. The first result of cosmic consciousness
emerging out of an infinite and indeterminate unity is not
a coherent and integrated personality but the spirit of naked
aggression—the spirit of envy and fear from which aggression

[11] Gen. 4:15.

grows. It is not the light of intellect but a dull uncomprehending
ache that sees all that is other than itself as menacingly hostile.
The Zoroastrian Devil fulfills all these requirements, for he is
stupid as well as an aggressor: he is "slow to know"[12] and his
reactions are instinctive not reasoned.

God, however, when he reaches full self-consciousness, realizes
his own essence and ground as being pure light, and Truth, and
goodness; and in order to destroy the Spirit of Destruction itself
he must create creatures in his own likeness, so that they, in unison
with himself, may grow, expand, and develop into an infinite
dimension. For, just as he himself emerged from the infinite and
indeterminate into full self-conscious awareness, so must his
creation too be carved out of infinite space-time and given
definiteness and precision. Thus from the infinite and indeterminate One emerge instinctive aggression on the one hand and
consciousness, thought, and a sense of purpose on the other in
the intelligible order, while on the purely material plane are
actualized finite time and finite space which together add up to
the material world. The conditions under which creation is possible are now fulfilled, and God can create heaven and earth as his
first line of defense against the Aggressor.

Creation means diversity and differentiation: but Ohrmazd
conceives of it as a diversity in unity: it is a disciplined and highly
differentiated army designed to act as one unit against the dis-
parate powers ranged against it. It is a growing organism,
developing out of the One, which in this context is conceived
of as primal matter, into the many, and, through increasing
variegation and combination within variegation, growing
into a single close-knit organism which will be known
as the "Final Body" in the last days. In this respect
there is a radical difference between the Zoroastrian cosmogony
and that of the Hindus; for whereas the latter see the evolution
of the cosmos in cyclic terms, the Absolute emanating the
universe in all its variety ever again and the universe as constantly
and as eternally dissolving back into the Absolute, the
Zoroastrians see evolution as an inwardly directed purposive
drive, a constant development from indeterminate beginnings to
a clear-cut and glorious end. As each individual man is destined
to grow into his own plenitude and his own glory, so is the cosmos
itself destined to grow and increase in ever greater complexity

[12] Zaehner, *Zurvan*, p. 313.

and ever more subtle combinations into its own "Final Body."
In this Body it is united with the spiritual world which is
its archetype and with God who is the source of both.

Ahriman, the Devil, counterfeits the work of Ohrmazd, for he
too can create, but he cannot create any material thing, for matter
is the vehicle of life, and Ahriman is substantial death. Like
Goethe's Mephistopheles he is *der Geist der stets verneint,* "the
spirit of pure negation." In "physico-mythology" the substance
of Ohrmazd is said to be hot and moist, and it therefore has the
principle of physical life within it, whereas Ahriman's substance
is cold and dry, and thereby he is debarred from any physical
evolution whatever.[13] Ahriman corresponds exactly to what
thermodynamics calls entropy, the *vis inertiae* that tends to drag
all evolution back into a meaningless and "dead" uniformity.
Over against this devil of entropy stands the universe of Ohrmazd
which, in its purposive drive toward self-fulfilment in ever more
complex forms, corresponds to the law of increased complexity
supporting an ever greater concentration of consciousness. In
this Teilhard de Chardin saw the consummation of the world;
for, without knowing it, Teilhard de Chardin has, among the
moderns, revived the this-worldly optimism of the Zoroastrians
of which the Christian Church, so long astray in a "valley
of tears" of its own imagining, so greatly stands in need.

Ohrmazd creates in space-time, for space and time are the
prerequisites of all matter. "The existence of all [things] has
need of Time. Without Time one can do nothing that is or was
or shall be. Time has need of none of these for anything. That
within which every substance is, yet itself is within nothing, is
Space."[14] Space-time is infinite, but is limited by Ohrmazd for
the purpose of creation. Finite time is destined to last for twelve
thousand years, at the end of which it merges into its source which
is the Infinite, and action, that is, the evolutionary drive within
nature itself, as well as the free actions of men in the fulfilment
of themselves in the context of a universal ferment toward the
perfection of each in all and all in each—this "action" merges
into a final state of rest from which it sprang. But this does not
mean that the universe created by Ohrmazd in all its infinite
variety and all its individual perfections will simply revert back
into the undifferentiated One of primal matter from which it
arose. Far from it. It is true, of course, that all creation, in the

[13] Zaehner, *Zoroastrianism,* p. 204.   [14] *Id., Zurvan,* p. 382.

last resource, depends on infinite time, but this does not mean
that it must be absorbed back into that state of total indetermina-
tion and blind unconsciousness : it means, rather, that every
created thing, simply because it is rooted in the infinite, has thereby an infinite dimension. And so the Zoroastrian can confidently
say, "Those things which Ohrmazd created at the original
creation do not change."[15] For Ohrmazd in creating finite
beings to do battle with Ahriman who can exist only in limited
space and limited time, gives them, through his own participation
in the infinite and his progressive growth back into it, a dimension
in eternity which Ahriman cannot destroy. All the good creation,
then—the material every bit as much as the spiritual—has its
roots in pre-eternity and will realize itself as eternal well-being
and eternal bliss in post-eternity when time will be no more. And
this is what constitutes the "Final Body"—the collective "body"
of all mankind renewed and perfected because purged and de-
livered from the Devil of entropy that would drag it down into a
chaotic conformity that is extinction and death. This "body"
will continue to exist even in eternity, and within it will exist all
the resurrected bodies, now once again reunited with their souls,
of all men reconstituted and transfigured.

In the beginning every material thing was drawn forth from
primal unformed matter, from the shapelessness of infinite space-
time, and every spiritual thinking thing was elicited from an undifferentiated unconsciousness, but their end is very different;
for then all creatures, "possessed of body and conformed to their
own archetypes, will be reunited to their souls, all undefiled, and
together with their souls they will be made immortal, reconstituted as eternal beings in perfect bliss."[16] The end of the cosmic
drama is not, then, simply to return to the *status quo ante* as
in Hinduism : it is not purposeless. For the Zoroastrian, as for
St. Paul, "the whole creation groaneth and travaileth ... waiting for the redemption" not only of our individual physical
bodies, but of the whole mass of human bodies forming the one
"Final Body" which is the "All-man" redeemed and fulfilled.
Each separate creature will have grown and developed to its
highest capacity; in Aristotelian parlance it will have become its
final cause, or, in the words of Junayd, one will come to be "what
one was before one was" : it will have realized what the Iranians

[15] *Ibid.*, p. 315.
[16] Zaehner, *Zoroastrianism*, p. 222.

call its *khwarr*—that perfection of the soul and flowering of the personality designed for man by God which man attains to by fruitful work and simply doing his job. This glorious estate the soul achieves on its own account certainly, but only by dovetailing its own work into the work of all humanity which is also the work of God himself; and that is the total overthrow of evil, the elimination of the Spirit of death and falsehood, aggression and individual pride. This is the grand purpose of Ohrmazd's creation —the reconstruction of all the material cosmos with a consolidated mankind at its head into one living organism united within itself and in constant communion with God, at rest, yet still effortlessly and harmoniously active, for the forces of death and disunity will forever have been destroyed.

Evil, in Zoroastrianism, is personified in Ahriman, who is an aggressor, a destroyer, and a liar. He is entirely spiritual in nature and is, as we have seen, quite incapable of creating any material thing. Matter, then, is in itself good and holy, for it is entirely God's creation, and its goodness lies in the fact that in it is the seed of life and the seed of growth. The Zoroastrians, however, were never crude materialists, for the material world was constructed in the image of a spiritual world which God had created before it—a world not unlike the world of "forms" we find in Plato. This ideal world the Devil cannot touch.

The material world, however, with its capacity for continuous growth and development, is also God's master weapon against his adversary, for it is the bait that lures Ahriman on to attack and the trap in which he is caught once the bait has been swallowed.[17] Once Ahriman is trapped in the material world, the initiative in defeating him passes to man who is the crown and glory of all Ohrmazd's material creation. And what is man?

Man exists at three levels. First he is a pre-existent idea in the spiritual world, both each individual man that ever was or is or is yet to be on the one hand, and the sum total of all mankind on the other. The pre-existent souls of individuals are called *Fravahrs,* while the sum total of such souls is called simply the "Consciousness of the Righteous,"[18] which in turn is identical with the *khwarr* or "function" of the whole Zoroastrian community. This concept, the *khwarr,* both of individuals and of the collectivity represented by the Zoroastrian Church, is of cardinal im-

[17] *Ibid.,* p. 266.
[18] *Ibid.,* p. 265.

portance; and to it we must shortly return. Besides the *Fravahr*, the "idea" of each and every man pre-existing in eternity, there is also the soul proper and the body together with its faculties including mind and consciousness. The soul is not the deep eternal essence of man—the *ātman* of the Hindus—or the "pre-biographical unity" which remains "unchanged beneath all biographical change"—but the directing faculty of the whole bodily and mental organism, itself possessed of right reason—that is, the capacity to distinguish between good and evil—and of free will, the power to choose between good and evil. The *Fravahr* is the immortal and ultimately irresponsible substrate of the whole man,[19] and in this respect it is roughly comparable to the Indian *ātman*, whereas the soul, endowed as it is with intellect and will, is the sole responsible agent within the whole complex that is man, and it alone can merit salvation in heaven or damnation in hell. The body, so far from being evil, is by nature good because it is made up of matter which God alone can draw out from infinite space-time. Moreover, it is the indispensable instrument of the soul, for the soul cannot act except through a material body, and it is through the body's actions that one can know the good or evil quality of the soul. *Fravahr*, then, is the pre-existent idea of a man in the presence of God—exactly parallel to Junayd's theory of souls as pre-existent ideas in the mind of God—while the soul is the responsible "person" which alone can be saved or damned; and it saves or damns itself by the quality of the deeds it performs through the body. The body, then, is the instrument through which salvation or damnation is earned.

Man was created primarily to captain the whole of God's material creation against Ahriman and the Lie and to defeat them on God's behalf. But later Zoroastrianism was never disloyal to the deepest insights of its founder, and one of these is that no rational creature is created by God with an unfree will. The *Fravahr*, as we have seen, alone pre-exists individual man in eternity, and despite the fact that, according to scholastic theology, it is not the responsible part of man, God has no alternative but to turn to the assembled *Fravahrs* to ask them whether they are willing to go down to earth to do battle with the Lie. To enable them to make a valid choice, then, he inspires them with his own wisdom, and thereby obtains their willing consent. Thus—

[19] *Ibid.*, p. 270.

He took counsel with the consciousness and *Fravahrs* of men and infused omniscient wisdom into them, saying: "Which seemeth more profitable to you, whether that I should fashion you forth in material form, and that you should strive incarnate with the Lie and destroy it, and that we should resurrect you in the end, whole and immortal, and recreate you in material form, and that you should eternally be immortal, unageing, and without enemies; or that you should for ever be preserved from the Aggressor?" And the *Fravahrs* of men saw by that omniscient wisdom that they would suffer evil from the Lie and Ahriman in the world; but because, at the end, at the Final Body, they would be resurrected free from the enmity of the Adversary, whole and immortal for ever and ever, they agreed to go down into the material world.[20]

This was man's covenant with God against the powers of evil.

In the *Gāthās* of Zoroaster, as we have seen, the Wise Lord (Ahura Mazdāh or Ohrmazd as he appears in the later tradition) is accompanied by seven abstract entities which together form the divine personality. First there is the Holy Spirit through which he creates and which was very soon to be identified with him completely, next come the Good Mind and Truth or Righteousness, which, with the Holy Spirit, form almost a self-contained Trinity, and finally Right-Mindedness, the Kingdom, Wholeness, and Immortality. Of all these "hypostases" only the Holy Spirit is the inalienable property of God, for it is the Spirit of God made manifest in space-time through the creative act. Truth and the Good Mind can be and are shared by God with men, and it is through the Good Mind, that is, by conforming his own mind to the mind of God, that man can participate in the divine goodness itself. Right-Mindedness is principally man's reasoned response to the divine, and the word is usually—and not at all ineptly—translated as "humility." The Kingdom or sovereignty is the sovereignty that belongs to God by right, but which he delegates to the Persian kings on earth, and below them to the satraps and regional governors, and on the purely individual scale to every soul inhabiting a human body; for the soul too is a king holding sway within its own tiny corporeal domain; so between God and the humblest of souls there is a "communion of kings." Lastly there are Wholeness and Immortality, God's by eternal right, but not his *de facto* since he is limited by Ahriman, the principle of evil. Into these God him-

[20] *Ibid.*, p. 261.

self must grow, and as he grows back into his eternal being, so does his creation grow with him until, like him, it shall be "whole and immortal for ever and ever."

This, however, can be only when Ahriman and all his hordes have been destroyed. In the beginning his first attempt to attack Ohrmazd's spiritual creation totally failed; but when, after three thousand years in which he was reduced to complete unconsciousness, he finally returns to the attack, it is devastatingly successful. Sky, water, earth, plants and fire—all does he defile and ruin; animal life in the form of the "lone-created Bull" he destroys and then comes face to face with Gayōmart, the ancestor of the human race and Ohrmazd's last bastion in the material world. Intoxicated with victory Ahriman cries out :

Perfect is my victory: for I have rent the sky, I have befouled it with murk and darkness and made it my stronghold. I have befouled the waters, pierced open the earth and befouled it with darkness. I have dried up the plants and brought death to the Bull, sickness to Gayō-mart. Against the stars have I set up the planets, frought with darkness. I have seized the kingdom. On the side of Ohrmazd none remains to do battle except only man: and man, isolated and alone, what can he do?[21]

Nothing, it appears, for he too is struck down, and the whole material creation is apparently annihilated. Immediately, however, Ohrmazd counterattacks. The earth is revived and the plants begin to grow again. The seed of the Primal Bull drops into the ground as it dies, and from this seed many plants and all species of animals grow up. Gayōmart, too, in dying, entrusts his seed to his mother, the earth, and from her in due course a rhubarb plant grows up from which emerge Mashyē and Mashyānē, the Iranian Adam and Eve.

The powers of evil have, however, ensconced themselves within the vault of the sky, and the world is now subject to death and decay, concupiscence and sin. Both man's material body and his mind are now at the mercy of "concupiscence," the principle of "disorderly motion," which, by deranging the body, brings on death, and by deranging the mind causes it to think crookedly. The entity in man that concupiscence attacks is his *khwarr*, and this is all-important in the Zoroastrian scheme of things. It is regularly interpreted as *khwēsh-kārīh* which literally means

[21] *Ibid.*, p. 264.

"own-work"; yet the *khwarr* is not created for man, but man for his *khwarr*. What does this mean?

It means that each man is created for the specific job he has to do : each man has his allotted place and his allotted task in God's eternal plan. His dignity as a human person resides in his *khwarr*, for this is what separates him from all other persons and gives him his unique value in the relentless game of chess that God plays against his enemy. In *this* game, however, each piece is unique and irreplaceable, each has his allotted role to play, and each, therefore, has his unique value in the sight of God. But, as in a game of chess, the move of each piece is dictated by the pattern of the whole : each and all are subject to the plan of the player. Man, then was most emphatically not created to retire into his own eternal essence nor to bury his talents in the ground. No, "the Creator created his creation for action, and specified for each [individual] creature his own sphere of action. Any action that contributes to the natural development of a creature is the *khwarr* of that creature."[22] To develop one's talents is the duty of every creature; each must grow into his own full stature, not at the expense of others—for that would be "concupiscence," a disorderly movement incompatible with the Creator's design—but in co-operation and joyous emulation with one's fellows in doing that job which each alone can do. Hence the sterility and stupidity of envy, for none other can do what one has to do oneself; and if oneself cannot perform the task of another, how futile must it be to envy the performance of another in doing a job that oneself cannot possibly do, simply because it does not happen to be one's own "own-work."

To do one's job and to do it with zest is not only to increase in stature, it is also to do one's share in God's work which is to eliminate evil from the cosmos and to bring about the final Rehabilitation in which all will be united in a common joy. For—

The Creator created his creation for action, and creatures are the Creator's agents. Their work can only develop satisfactorily by obtaining a right view concerning their *khwarr*, that is, by doing their own job. By making a success of one's own job one furthers the Creator's work and thereby conforms to his will and pleasure; but by neglecting one's job out of conceit one frustrates that *khwarr* which is the Creator's work, fails to conform to his will, and suffers thereby.[23]

[22] *Ibid.*, p. 151.   [23] *Ibid.*, pp. 151-2.

But it is not only the individual person who has his individual *khwarr,* the individual job he has to do; each household, village, county, province, and country has a *khwarr* in common. The lower unit dovetails harmoniously into that of the higher, and the *khwarrs* of the different countries and nationalities that go to make up the world coincide and coalesce into the *khwarr* of the whole world. The *khwarr* of all "seven climes" strives together to remove the obstacles that stand in the way of a common fulfillment. Since all *khwarr* is from God, the united *khwarr* of all individuals, all households, villages, counties, provinces, and countries—that is, the united personal and communal efforts exercised at every level for the fulfillment of each unit in the context of the larger whole—this united effort which is the driving force immanent in the whole material creation, presses on in one concerted thrust toward its predestined encounter with God.

This buoyant drive toward self-fulfillment grinds down and pulverizes Ahriman and all his hosts who are imprisoned within the wide circle of the sky, and to make his defeat doubly sure the sky itself is girt with the *khwarr* of the Zoroastrian Church triumphant, and this forms an impregnable bastion beyond which the Evil One may not advance.

The ineluctable trend of all Ohrmazd's spiritual and material creation toward the defeat and destruction of the forces of evil, death, and sin, and through this toward the self-fulfillment of each in the collective fulfillment of all, which is the Final Body and the Rehabilitation of all things, is called in Pahlavi the *patvandishn i ō frashkart,* which can best be translated as "the continuous evolution toward the Rehabilitation," or more literally "toward the Making Excellent." Just how this Making Excellent is understood we shall see after we have considered the Zoroastrian view of man as he should ideally be both in the context of his fellows in space and of the intermediate position he occupies between initial defeat and final victory in time.

As for the Jews, man for the Zoroastrian is a compound of soul and body; and once the two are parted, man no longer remains. The soul, indeed, is the center of personality and is therefore the part of man that is rewarded in heaven and punished in hell. But this is a temporary state and is not inherent in the nature of things, for man's destiny is "wholeness" and "immortality" in body and soul, and the separation of the two at death is due to the malice of the Devil, and has no part in God's design. More-

over, even were there no resurrection of the body at the end of
time, as the Zoroastrians believe there is, the Devil's introduction
of physical death has already been frustrated in that the human
race continues to increase and multiply, thereby preserving a collective immortality, whatever may happen to individuals in the
meantime. This however, is only a partial victory over the Fiend,
for God's plan for mankind is that just as it was once one
in Gayōmart, so shall it again be one in the Final Body. But this
Body will have room for all the personal values that have been
built up in every single person and through the person into the
totality of all value from the beginning of time until the consummation of all things. No good, however slight it may be,
whether material or spiritual, is ever permanently lost, for "the
things which Ohrmazd created at the original creation do not
change." And what Ohrmazd created was both spiritual and
material, and even in this corrupted world the link between the
two is immensely close.

Mens sana in corpore sano, "a sane mind in a healthy body" :
this is the ideal expected of the individual Zoroastrian, for the
one conditions the other. There must be harmony between body
and soul, between man and man, harmony too between man and
God. To achieve the first it is essential to understand that
material well-being and this worldly happiness are the most fruitful seedbed in which the moral virtues can thrive. Once this
equilibrium is established self-love is seen as not only permissible
but in the very nature of things, and self-love which is based on
the conviction that an integrated personality is strong enough to
endure without complaint the worst that the Devil can contrive
against you, leads to sympathy with your fellow men; for personal happiness radiates happiness outside itself in ever-widening
ripples, and it is only a happy and united mankind that can
finally vanquish the Lie. All this, however, depends ultimately
on an even balance being preserved between body and soul. And
so we read that

The material body achieves its full worth by the spiritual soul itself
being blessed. The spiritual soul achieves blessedness through the
instrumentality of the body. Material wealth is respected only when
it is accompanied by virtue. Spiritual virtue is won mainly through
material wealth. Worldly honour becomes respectable only if one
strive after spiritual righteousness. Striving after spiritual righteousness derives from zeal for material honour. Earthly kingship is secured

only on the basis of spiritual religion, and spiritual religion is propagated most successfully when it is allied to earthly kingship.
Material generosity receives honour only when it is united to spiritual
wisdom, and spiritual wisdom will show more practical results if allied
to material generosity.[24]

"The man who enjoys bodily health [also] enjoys health of
soul,"[25] we read elsewhere. Or again : "One should make strenuous
efforts to promote prosperity and affluence as well as righteousness and virtue, for this world is linked with the next, and the
next world is linked with this."[26] All this amounts to a complete
rejection of the ascetic ideal, and indeed Zoroastrianism in all
its phases saw in asceticism only a blasphemy against life and
against God, the Wise Lord and Holy Spirit who is the author
of life. "Be yourself to the full extent of your being," is the
Zoroastrian message to man, and leave your *Fravahr,* which,
being an eternal idea of God, can suffer neither increase nor diminution, where it belongs, that is, in the heart of God, and gird
your loins manfully for the serious business of living, for only so
can you return to the living God and lay at his feet the talents
he has entrusted to you not only intact but many times increased.

The man who is really himself is one whose thoughts, words, and
deeds are [in accordance with] his reasoned will. By adhering to
the Zoroastrian religion, he comes to adhere to the highest Lord, the
Creator, Ohrmazd. Following the straight path of his own nature, he
attains to his own plenitude of welfare, his own [appointed] place
of overflowing joy.[27]

To achieve the fullness of one's own personality in humility
and not in pride is to learn to love oneself; and this is all that
God asks of one : for "Ohrmazd asks of man that whatever he
does, he should do it for himself, ... while Ahriman asks him
not to do it for himself." By being oneself and doing one's job,
one conforms oneself to God and partakes of his very nature.
For "among men who pursue their fortune (their *khwarr*) and
protect themselves from misfortune, the most perspicacious is he
who exerts himself most in the performance of his allotted task;
and just as God exerts himself most in the performance of his
task, so among men he who exerts himself most at his task by

[24] *Ibid.,* p. 298.
[25] *Ibid.,* p. 276.
[26] *Ibid.,* p. 277.
[27] *Ibid.,* p. 294.

being what he is shares in the attributes and activities of God and is closest to God in the scale of value."[28]

There is no such thing as a selfless action : the Zoroastrians are cynically firm on this subject. For them Buddhist "selfless-ness" is as selfish as the selfishness of the hedonist; for however much the Buddhist may camouflage the deep core of his spiritual selfishness in the fine-spun tissue of intellectual sophistry, the fact remains that he is after his own Nirvāṇa and nobody else's. It is more honest to face this fact, for it is in no way discreditable. "The man" simply "does not exist who does anything except for himself, whether it be righteous or unrighteous; for whatever a man undertakes, he either increases or restricts his soul [thereby]. In any case [what one does] one does for one's own soul. So we should be very insistent with all men that they desire good for their own souls, not evil."[29] And since body and soul are indissol-ubly linked, any ascetic chastisement of the body can harm only the soul. The body demands material prosperity, a little display and harmless luxury, and pleasure,[30] and these should not be denied it, for a contented body is more likely to minister to the soul's craving for virtue.

"Integrate yourself in soul and body, and love yourself; for once you become indifferent to yourself, you will come to hate yourself and injure yourself both in body and in soul," and that is an affront to the Creator. Love yourself and all who depend on you; so you will learn to love your fellow men by extension, and they to love you. For happiness, which is the state that God designed for man, cannot be enjoyed alone : it is a communal activity in which all men are called to share. Real happiness must be based on mutual love; it is founded on solidarity, not on solitude. This is the message of Zoroastrianism, and it is the direct antithesis of all that primitive Buddhism and the Sāṁkhya-Yoga have to teach.

In Adam all men are one; and this solidarity of the human race is a fact. Facts are things we accept, we do not try to escape them : we try to make good in them what we see to be lacking. And "since the Creator Ohrmazd created creation from one sub-stance, he caused man to be born from one father, so that creation, being of one substance, one man should sustain, provide for,

[28] *Ibid.*, p. 283.
[29] *Ibid.*, p. 280.
[30] *Ibid.*, p. 277.

and help his fellow, and . . . esteem him as his own self. Like affec-
tionate brothers men should do good to each other and ward off
evil from each other."[31]

This is not just a vague exhortation to mutual benevolence;
much less is it merely sentimental. It is part and parcel of what
the Zoroastrian saw to be a "continuous evolution towards the
Making Excellent," the inexorable power of life-bearing matter
and spirit-bearing life to vanquish the *vis inertiae* of entropy and
death—and this through the ever-increasing interlocking of the
individual units that go to make up God's grand army deployed
in faultless order against the hordes of an enemy already doomed,
the author of sin and death.

And so it is inevitable that "when mankind achieves union
firmly based on mutual love, the demons will lose all hope of [ever
again] being able to harm man, nor will they be able to change
their own disunion into union. At the final 'Making Excellent'
the whole of mankind will be firmly and unchangeably linked
in mutual love, and this will mean that the demons will utterly
despair of ever being able to harm man again. They will be
annihilated and prevented from ever again coming together to
take counsel with each other and plotting any new aggression
against the creatures of Ohrmazd. Then there will be a universal
joy for the whole of creation for all eternity; and fear will be
no more."[32]

Mankind, then, is impelled by an irresistible tendency in nature
itself to unite, and thereby to vanquish the powers of disorder
and disruption which are the source of all sin and of death itself.
Against the united front of mankind's solidarity the temporary
union the demons had achieved in their common desire to destroy
man vanishes, and each demon, despairing of ever more being
able to attack individual men, must now play a lone hand; and so
demon falls on demon, each striving to destroy the other in
a paroxysm of destructive and disruptive hatred.

The demons of calumny whose nature it is to incite creatures against
each other by falsehood and lies, since they no longer succeed in incit-
ing the saved against each other, incite the damned against the
damned, and when they can no longer incite the damned against each
other, they incite demon against demon. And Wrath of the bloody
spear, no longer able to stir up strife among the saved, stirs up strife
and warfare among the damned; and when it can no longer stir up

[31] *Ibid.*, p. 280.   [32] *Ibid.*, pp. 280-1.

strife among the damned, it stirs up strife among the demons and lies, and makes them fall on one another. So too the demon of Greed, no longer able to swallow the good, is impelled by her own nature to go and swallow up demons. And so too the Loosener of Bones who deals out death by causing separation, seeing that the saved no longer die and that even the damned among God's creation are no longer subject to death, falls upon the lies and brings them death, which is nothing but the separation of their organs and faculties [which can survive only] in union.[33]

Evil, then, is destroyed by the inner contradictions within itself; and once mankind has achieved a total solidarity based on a mutual sympathy and a mutual respect for the different talents of all, the demons, frenzied with despair, "fight against themselves, strike, rend, tear, and disrupt themselves" until not a particle or a particle of a particle of them remains within the kingdom of the light: they "are vanquished by their own weapons, their own impulse, their own striving, as well by the glorious activity (*khwarr*) of the Creator."[34]

Once the demons are destroyed, the stage is set for the "Making Excellent" or consummation of all things. The bodies of the dead are raised and united with their souls, and "nature is clad in spirit,"[35] and all men become of one mind and one voice. The whole human race is now "solidary" within the one "Final Body," and each individual, purged of sin and error, sees and thinks only what is true, though, no doubt, seeing and thinking it in his own individual way.

We have noted that the Prophet Zoroaster himself associated seven abstract entities with God, who are best regarded as his hypostases. These seven, later called the "Bounteous Immortals," teach mankind, now built into the unfractionable solidarity of the Final Body, how the closest collective unity implies no loss of personality and no diminution of the individual person. They say,

We are seven, but one in thought, word, and deed; and because we are one in thought, word, and deed, we are unageing and deathless, knowing neither corruption nor decay. And when you who are men, become one in thought, word, and deed, then will you become unageing, free from sickness, knowing neither corruption nor decay, even as we, the Bounteous Immortals, are.[36]

[33] *Ibid.*, p. 316.   [34] *Ibid.*, p. 316.
[35] *Ibid.*, p. 319.   [36] *Ibid.*, p. 319.

In the beginning, before the rise of consciousness separated man from man, collective man, "one in Adam" or Gayōmart as the case might be, felt no distinction of persons, for personality had yet to be born. If consciousness there was, it was of the whole, not of the parts, and the loss of worn-out parts by death and their replacement by other parts through birth passed unnoticed in the total Man. The birth of consciousness, however, like all births, was irreversible, and the nostalgia to return to the womb of original innocence, though realizable by individuals for shorter or longer times, proved ineffectual because retrogressive and reactionary. Consciousness, though its first instinctive reaction to the separation of the umbilical cord which had linked it to the group was murder, could not look back. Pushed forward by the directing Spirit inherent in matter, it had no choice but to seek to conquer new fields. Historically, in the West it turned its gaze on the "without" of things; it laid the foundations of philosophy and science, whereas in religion it saw its God "without" as the transcendent Lord of all things "who spake in time past unto the fathers by the prophets"[37] and who spoke too "with the tongue of his mouth" to the Prophet Zoroaster in ancient Iran and revealed himself to his eyes. In the East, and in India especially consciousness turned its eyes "within," and it found within the heart eternal, timeless being. It had found the "image of God within you," which even so great a catastrophe as the Fall could not destroy. The temptation to rest forever in this timeless joy was more than all but a few could resist, for it seemed that there it had reached the ground of Being itself; and so the mystic "began to think that his own essence did not at all differ from the essence of that true Being, but that they were both one and the same thing, and that the thing that he had taken before for is own essence, distinct from the essence of the true One, was in reality nothing at all, and that nothing existed but the essence of this true One."[38] But this, as Junayd saw, was no more than the "ground of the finite roots" of the soul, the "pre-biographical unity hidden unchanged beneath all biographical change," most noble in itself because made "in the image of God," but nevertheless a thing incapable of growth and of combining with the other fragments of the shattered image, being no more than what the Upanishad calls a "half-fragment." This is the dead-end of the

[37] *Heb.* 1 :1.
[38] Zaehner, *Hindu and Muslim Mysticism*, p.186.

mysticism of the "self"; and it takes God himself, incarnate as
Krishna in the Bhagavad-Gītā, to bring the soul back to the
mainstream of life as lived in a material word of space and time
under the guidance of the Spirit. Else, "this misgrounded conceit
of his had like to have firmly rooted itself in his mind unless
God had pursued him with his mercy and directed him by his
gracious guidance; and then he perceived that it arose from the
relics of that obscurity which is natural to body and the dregs of
sensible objects."[39]

The Zoroastrians, unlike their Indian brothers, eschewed individual and partial solutions. On their canvas was written
"solidaire," not *"solitaire."* Man marches forward toward his
triumphant victory over all that is evil, all that separates and
divides, and he marches as an army in which each unit, and within the unit, each individual, has a unique and indispensable
part to play; and all this he does under the obedience he owes to
his Commander-in-Chief, who is God. The final renewal of all
things, the "Making Excellent," as the Zoroastrians call it, means
not only the integration of man with man, but the integration
of matter with spirit and of the total Man with God.

At the transfiguration of our Lord Christ's face is said to have
"shone as the sun, and his raiment was white as the light,"[40] and
this is sometimes taken to be the prototype of the resurrection
body or "glorious body" in which men will be clothed at the end
of time. So too the Zoroastrians saw the final apotheosis of man
as an apotheosis in light as well as in love and joy.

The sun, moon, and stars will [continue to] exist, but there will
be no need for daylight or a succession of glimmering dawns, for the
whole world will be light and devoid of any darkness, and each [in-
dividual] creature will be light. Being light, they will be full of joy.
And all creatures will have but one will and one desire. Individual
men will feel no envy at the joy of the totality of created things, but
will rejoice together with all creatures. The goodness and joy allotted
to each will wax and grow in the glory of the omnipotence of him who
is all-good, [all-]aware, all in all through his overflowing bounty
and perfect skill in means.[41]

The transfiguration of all mankind into the glory of the Final
Body coincides with the defeat of the Devil whose mere existence

[39] *Ibid.*, p. 186.
[40] Matt., 17:2.
[41] Zaehner, *Zoroastrianism*, p. 320.

had made God less than infinite. With the destruction of him and his, God becomes what in Infinite Time he always is—all in all. By limiting space-time and by operating through man, his viceroy in space-time, he not only destroys forever the principle of evil which for all eternity had lain hidden and unknown in the heart of the unconscious God, but elevates his viceroy, man, from the sphere of time to the realm of eternity; but the man he raises up is very different from man as he was first created, for nothing of value that any man has done or earned on earth is lost, for all is fitted into and given its due place in the Treasury of Eternal Benefit, and each, by giving up his own selfish individual will, conforms his will to the universal drive toward fulfillment, thereby both fulfilling himself and pouring his own tiny contribution to the self-fulfillment of all.

6

Solidarity in Matter

ZOROASTRIANISM IS DEAD, AND WITH IT DIED A
this-worldly religion of health and sanity the world could ill
afford to lose. For "this-worldly" it is in contrast to the sublime
withdrawals of the Indian creeds and even to the undercurrent
of other-worldly asceticism that is only now beginning to drain
away from the body of the Christian Church. To call it simply
"this-worldly," however, is to malign it : it is "both-worldly," and
this is what gives it its admirable balance. Christianity, the
religion of the Incarnate Word, was all too soon attacked by
the ascetic virus the most virulent outbreak of which was the
wave of eremetic frenzy that swept the Christian East from the
second to the fifth centuries A.D. This was a very far cry from "the
Son of Man [who] came eating and drinking," of whom they
said, "Behold a man gluttonous, and a wine-bibber,"[1] It was a
radical perversion of the spirit of the New Testament which had
seeped into Christianity from that very Gnosticism against which
the Church herself had waged relentless war. It was an eruption
within the Christian body of that other Iranian dualism, Mani-
chaeanism, which the Church, in her sanity, had condemned as
the *pessima haeresium*, the "worst of heresies," because it saw
in matter, the stuff of which human beings are made, nothing
more nor less than the very substance of a positive and festering
evil. This ascetic ideal makes nonsense of the whole concept of
the "Word made flesh"; for this astonishing phrase means nothing less than that the Word of God who also *is* God and therefore
pure spirit, clothed himself in living matter and thereby united
himself indissolubly not only with the human race but with the
whole universe of matter which from the very beginning had been
in travail with human life and human thought. It is true that
from the moment that "the Spirit of God moved upon the face of
the waters," matter and spirit were locked in close embrace, but

[1] *Matt.* 11:19.

with the Incarnation of the Word of God as man, man's own roots in matter, which Indian and other forms of asceticism had so sedulously and so successfully sought to sever, were triumphantly reaffirmed. Matter henceforth was not to be regarded as a drag upon the human spirit, but rather as the indispensable vehicle through which the spirit must work. This the Zoroastrians had always affirmed, and they had affirmed too that the spirit operates not only on the level of the individual person, but also through the social organisms that together coalesced into the greatest organism known to the Zoroastrian Church—the Persian Empire.

Yet Zoroastrianism, though an Iranian religion and very often most self-consciously so, saw its true fulfillment not in any purely local or national grouping, however large and however imposing, but in the free consensus of all mankind. The reality, however, turned out far different from the dream, for religion and empire came to be so closely identified that the collaspse of the imperial fact brought with it the ruin of the religious ideal. Despite its ascetic aberrations, which were never much more than peripheral, however, the Christian Church, like the Jewish nation and the Zoroastrian empire, saw itself as a single organism in which the individual had his part to play, certainly, and his individual soul to save; but this was at best an episode—and a very minor one—in the Church's mission which is to build the whole human race into the mystical body of Christ. Zoroastrianism fell : but the Zoroastrian ideal of the "continous evolution" toward the "Making Excellent" lives on in the Christian Church, though frequently, and tragically, the main Christian emphasis has fallen elsewhere. Since the Reformation, Christians have been so scandalously divided that the ideal of integrating man within himself through the God-Man, Christ, of integrating him into the "body of Christ" which is the Church, and of increasing and expanding that body so that it will embrace all mankind, has often been allowed to slip into the background. Yet the Church has grown and continues to grow not because of any efficiency of organization, but because, being the body of Christ and breathing the breath of the Holy Spirit, she *must* grow. In the second half of the twentieth century to say this is no longer a paradox. Yet only a hundred years ago Nietzsche and Marx seemed fully justified in predicting the immanent collapse of Christianity, for there seemed to be no life in it. The impact of the breakthrough achieved by the physical sciences and parti-cularly of the Darwinian theory of evolution had taken it com-pletely off its balance, and the Church itself looked very like one of those arrested phylums, like the tapeworms, which evolu-tion had left behind. It might continue to vegetate for a century or two as an interesting survival like the Parsees in India, the sole heirs of the once glorious Zoroastrian faith, but not to be reckoned with as a force in the modern world. A hundred years have passed since then and not only is the Catholic Church not dead—and Christians will no doubt differ as to what the word "Catholic" means—but, wonderfully revitalized, it is the only viable alternative to the new ideology that now controls more than a quarter of the globe.

This, we have been repeatedly told, is the century of the com-mon man; and as usual we have been told a half-truth: it is rather the age of mass movements, and these movements themselves are no more than the expression of one of the deepest instincts in man, the instinct that craves for unity and bids man close his ranks that he may be as he was, one in Adam, the All-man. Hitherto this instinct has never been able to manifest itself or organize itself on any but a local scale because never before has the human race been able to see itself as one. Now it can see itself in no other way; and, as we have learned to our cost, disease in one portion of the body politic immediately affects the whole. It is as if we had woken up, to our astonishment, to find that we are all one body, though composed of many members, and that not only are all the members diseased in themselves, but each is at war with the other. To use an absurd simile, it is as if the liver were at war with the pancreas, each vying with the other in pouring out its own variety of juices, regardless of the fact that this can but result in the total ruin of the digestion, and, through the digestion, of the body as a whole. The age of individualism, both on the personal and the national scale, is drawing to a close, and man, about to enter on a more collective phase of his existence, is as bewildered as he was when first he, as a separate individual, became conscious of himself. Modern man knows in his bones that to live at all fruitfully he must not only live a rich personal life of his own but must be able to live this life in a society to which he can contribute his best and which in turn must be in harmony with himself: he must be able to identify his own interest with the interest of the whole. He must recapture the

Zoroastrian vision of an all-embracing self-love, seeing and understanding his own intrinsic worth as a human being, but seeing too that though, as a partial image of God, he has a dignity almost divine, this image is nonetheless partial and cannot be wholly restored until all the fragments are knit together in a solidarity that will reflect the totality of God. The subjective fragments need to coalesce into a homogeneous whole, and individual "selves" must be brought to see their identity of interest and of purpose within the greater "Self" of the whole. With almost prophetic vision Marx saw this as early as 1844 when he wrote,

> If man draws all his knowledge, sensation, etc. from the world of the senses and the experience gained in it, the empirical world must be arranged so that in it man experiences and gets used to what is really human and that he becomes aware of himself as man. If correctly understood interest is the principle of all morality, man's private interest must be made to coincide with the interest of humanity. ... Each man must be given social scope for the vital manifestation of his being. If man is shaped by his surroundings, his surroundings must be made human. If man is social by nature, he will develop his true nature only in society, and the power of his nature must be measured not by the power of separate individuals but by the power of society.[2]

Marxian Communism, in the eyes of its founders, so far from belittling the role of the individual in society, rather saw capitalist society as it functioned in the middle of the nineteenth century as an outmoded and, in the strictest sense of that much misused word, reactionary society which prevented the individual from developing to the limit of his powers. Thus capitalist society of the nineteenth century could be seen as the modern equivalent of the Zoroastrian Ahriman—a drag on the natural forward drive of evolution. In the interests of the flowering of the human personality itself society had to be changed, and the exploitation of man by man, or of nation by nation, whether open or camouflaged, had to be done away with forever. In the Socialist society which, to their way of thinking, must sooner or later succeed the capitalist, the individual would for the first time in history be in the material position to develop his personality freely in a society in which each would be working for the good of all and all for the good of each. This happy state of affairs, for Marx and

[2] Marx and Engels, *The Holy Family*, p. 176.

Engels, would bring all religion to an end, for, according to them, religion is no more than part of the ideological superstructure which reflects actual economic conditions, and once these were radically changed in a way that would enable each man to fulfill himself simply by contributing to the self-fulfillment of all, his very need for religion would vanish.

Marxism, no less than any other ideology, is an intellectual superstructure reflecting the economic conditions of its time; it is the ideology of the period of transition from private capitalism to state capitalism which some prefer to call socialism; and the rare writings of Marx and Engels on religion reflect their own time and place in history—nineteenth-century Protestant Germany. There, as in all countries that had made one or other of the forms of Protestantism their state religion, the interdependence of the ruling class and the state church was palpable and plain for all to see. Hence it followed that once the ruling class, the bourgeoisie, had been smashed, the religion it supported would go down with it in a common ruin. This had happened in Zoroastrian Persia, and it would surely happen in nineteenth-century Prussia, or for that matter in twentieth-century Russia where the Orthodox Church was as deeply subservient to the Tsarist state as were the Protestant state churches to their own rulers in Europe. Basically Marx's reaction to contemporary Lutheranism was identical with that of Kierkegaard : it was one of contempt for an organization that had ceased even to respect itself, and had long lost all relevance to the actual social conditions of the time. It was not worth destroying : as a living idea it had long since destroyed itself. Thus Engels could write in 1874,

It can even be said of the German Social-Democratic workers that atheism has already outlived itself with them: this purely negative word no longer has any application as far as they are concerned inasmuch as their opposition to faith in God is no longer one of theory but one of practice; they have *purely and simply finished with God.*

Engels made the mistake of identifying religion as such with the state-supported Protestantism of his time, and so he could safely denounce religious persecution as being not so much wicked as stupid. Denouncing the conduct of the Blanquists in 1793, he wrote,

This demand that men should be changed into atheists *par ordre du mufti* is signed by two members of the Commune who have really had opportunity enough to find out that first a vast amount of things can be ordered on paper without necessarily being carried out, and second, that persecution is the best means of promoting undesirable convictions. This much is sure: the only service that can be rendered to God to-day is to declare atheism a compulsory article of faith.[3]

This Engels could confidently write in 1874, and few unbiased persons who had experience only of a state-supported Protestantism would have contradicted him. He would, perhaps, have written with less confidence today. Indeed, the persecution of religion in Communist countries shows not only the enduring vitality of religion as such; it shows too how ideologically unsure of themselves our present-day Marxists are, just as the activities of the Inquisition revealed a latent unsureness of itself inside the Catholic Church. Persecution is the outward and visible sign of an inward and spiritual rottenness.

Marx and Engels' writings on religion are superficial because they more or less identified religion as such with German Protestantism : they knew little about either Catholicism or Non-Conformist Protestantism, less about the religions of Asia. For them religion meant little more than the worship of a highly personal God, the very existence of whom was becoming increasingly doubtful; and they therefore ridiculed Feuerbach's well-meaning attempt to find a religion based on a materialist conception of nature. "If Feuerbach wishes to establish a true religion upon the basis of an essentially materialist conception of nature," Engels wrote, "that is the same as regarding modern chemistry as true alchemy. If religion can exist without its God, alchemy can exist without its philosopher's stone."[4] In fact, most Oriental religions have happily existed without what Engels understands by "God"; they rarely have any idea of God as a Person who acts purposively in history and takes a personal interest in the human race, yet none of them can dispense with an immanent and changeless power that underlies all change. And, despite his jibes at Feuerbach, no more could Engels : for Engels was a religious man.

Engels too was in search of a "true" religion based on the objective structure of the universe itself as science was beginning to discover it. The fact that he always avoids the word "religion" is neither here nor there, for, in his innocence, he did not know

[3] Id., On Religion, pp. 141–42.
[4] Engels, Ludwig Feuerbach (Moscow, 1946), p. 40.

that religions without a personal God were a commonplace in the East, nor could he have known that it was precisely there, and for that reason, that dialectical materialism was to make its most direct appeal.

It was not Christian values that Marx and Engels despised, but the perversion of those values by a soulless and hypocritical bourgeoisie. The Christian heaven might be an illusion, but it was a worthy illusion based on a material reality that had not yet been born—the future classless and propertyless society in which each would lovingly labor for the benefit of all. That the bourgeois revolution was a necessary step on the way to proletarian revolution was part and parcel of Marx's teaching; the bourgeoisie was merely fulfilling its preordained historical role, but, in doing so, it had destroyed genuine human values which religion had formerly kept alive. Thus Marx looks back with a strange nostalgia to the feudal age—the age of faith—when men still lived by what they could produce by their own skills, were still human beings leading a *human* life, and not just things to be treated with neither more nor less consideration than other commodities. It is the destruction of human values and the introduction of a constant element of insecurity into human life that, for Marx, made the period of capitalist expansion so detestable and the manufacturing bourgeoisie so culpable. The old values may have been false values, but they were values nonetheless : the triumphant bourgeoisie had torn down the old values and put nothing in their place. The period of transition, with all its suffering, however, has itself its place in history because, by making a clean sweep of what Marx conceived to be illusory values, the bourgeoisie, which even in being born was pregnant of its own death, was bound, in dying, to make room for real values based on the material realities of human life. With Communism triumphant in a quarter of the globe and with science leaping ahead with a momentum that Marx could not have foreseen, his description of the society of his own time is still applicable today :

Constant revolutionizing of production, uninterrupted disturbance of all social conditions, everlasting uncertainty and agitation distinguish the bourgeois epoch from all earlier ones. All fixed, fast, frozen relations, with their train of ancient and venerable prejudices and opinions, are swept away, all new-formed ones become antiquated before they can ossify. All that is solid melts into air, all that is holy is profaned, and man is at last compelled to face with sober senses his real condition of life and his relations with his kind.[5]

Man's "real condition of life and his relations with his kind"—this is what Marx and Engels set out to investigate and to explain. They were not merely analyzing the economic conditions of their time; they were also explaining how those conditions and any other conditions are ultimately dependent on the inflexible laws by which the whole universe is governed. Religion, as Marx saw it, was the reflection of society in two ways : by condoning the miseries brought on by capitalism as being inherent in the very structure of a world too long dismissed by Christianity as a "vale of tears," the Christian Church reflected the ugly face of the ruling bourgeoisie, and by holding up the image of an ordered happiness in heaven, it prefigured the paradise on earth that man was himself destined to build in the future. Marx did not underestimate the power of religion to console : what he asked was that religious compassion should be transmuted into revolutionary action which alone could do away with the very conditions which necessitated a compensating solace in another unreal world. He writes,

Religious distress is at the same time the *expression* of real distress and the *protest* against real distress. Religion is the sigh of the oppressed creature, the heart of a heartless world, just as it is the spirit of a spiritless situation. It is the *opium* of the people. The abolition of religion as the *illusory* happiness of the people is required for their *real* happiness. The demand to give up the illusions about its condition is the *demand to give up a condition which needs illusions.* The criticism of religion is therefore *in embryo the criticism of the vale of woe,* the *halo* of which is religion.[6]

Perhaps Marx, is merely being rhetorical when he speaks of the "*spirit* of a spiritless world"; but in the whole context of what he says he implies that, just as religious distress is the expression of real distress, so must the "spirit" of religion, though itself illusory, be the expression of a *real* spirit, and by this he can mean only the living Spirit that brings matter itself to life, that same Spirit that "moved upon the face of the waters" and which God breathed into the nostrils of Adam that he might become a living soul. Nor is this merely perverse reading of the

[5] Marx and Engels, *The Communist Manifesto,* ed. Laski, p. 124.
[6] *Id., On Religion,* p. 42.

text; for when we come to study just whom among the ancients Marx and Engels considered to be the true precursors of dialectical materialism, we find not a few who are more usually ranked among the mystics than among the materialists. Of these we need only mention Heraclitus and the Buddhists, and, among the moderns, Jakob Boehme. What is common to these is that they saw reality as a never-ending flux set over against a never-changing ground, and this is the first dogma of dialectical materialism. Engels writes,

When we reflect on nature, or the history of mankind, or our own intellectual activity, the first picture presented to us is of an endless maze of relations and interactions, in which nothing remains what, where, and as it was, but everything moves, changes, comes into being and passes out of existence. This primitive, naïve, yet intrinsically correct conception of the world was that of ancient Greek philosophy, and was first clearly formulated by Heraclitus: everything is and also is not, for everything is in *flux*, is constantly changing, constantly coming into being and passing away.[7]

Here Engels speaks of Heraclitus as one of the precursors of dialectical materialism, and Heraclitus saw himself as a prophet and a seer; and for him the secret of the universe lay in the ultimate reconciliation within the One of all conflicting opposites. Heraclitus, indeed, puts dialectical materialism in a nutshell when he says, "Men do not know how what is at variance agrees with itself. It is an attunement of opposite tensions, like that of the bow and the lyre."[8] But he passes beyond dialectical materialism or, perhaps, formulates the very thought that Engels would have formulated had he not been so very much afraid of being dubbed an idealist, when he says, "Wisdom is one thing. It is to know the thought by which all things are steered through all things."[9] And this "thought" seems to be the power that resolves all contradictions in the mystery of the One. "It is wise to hearken, not to me," he says, "but to my Word, and to confess that all things are one,"[10] for "the One is made up of all things, and all things issue from the One, ... things whole and things not whole, what is drawn together and what is drawn asunder, the harmonious and the discordant."[11] It is simply a question of how

[7] Engels, *Anti-Dühring*, pp. 26–27.   [8] Fragment 45.
[9] Fragment 19.   [10] Fragment 1.
[11] Fragment 59.

you look at them, in detail or as a whole; for "when we look at
things as they differ, we see them to be different; . . . when we
look at them as they agree, we see them all to be a unity."[12] And
once again we are reminded of the *Iśā* Upanishad :

> It moves. It moves not.
> It is far, and it is near.
> It is within all this,
> And it is outside all this. . . .
>
> Into blind darkness enter they
> Who worship non-becoming;
> Into darkness greater still [enter] they
> Who delight in becoming.

Being and becoming are one : they are opposites, but they are
interdependent opposites, and the union of opposites is no less
fundamental to dialectical materialism than it is to Heraclitus,
Taoism, and the Upanishads. The only difference is that dialectical materialism claims to base itself on the findings of
natural science.

The unity of the world does not consist in its being, although its
being is a pre-condition of its unity, as it must certainly first *be*, before
it can be *one*. Being, indeed, is always an open question beyond the
point where our sphere of observation ends. The real unity of the
world consists in its materiality, and this is proved not by a few juggl-
ing phrases, but by a long and protracted development of philosophy
and natural science.[13]

And what, then, is matter? For it is from the Marxist understanding of what matter is that any understanding of Marxism
itself must proceed. Marx, then, is best left to speak for himself :

The first and most important of the inherent qualities of *matter*
is *motion*, not only *mechanical* and *mathematical* movement, but still
more *impulse, vital spirit, tension,* or, to use Jakob Boehme's expression, the *throes* [*Qual*] of matter. The primary forms of matter are
the living, individualizing *forces of being* inherent in it and producing
the distinctions between the species.[14]

Notice the terminology. Matter is not just mechanical movement (and no one is more emphatic in denouncing the purely

---

[12] Chuang Tzŭ, 5.1.
[13] Engels, *Anti-Dühring*, pp. 52–53.
[14] Marx and Engels, *The Holy Family*, p. 172.

mechanistic interpretation of matter than Engels), it is impulse, vital life-*spirit,* and tension—qualities we usually associate only with living things. The total universe too is simply one vast process of transformation—not, however, a mechanistic and meaningless rise and fall on the Indian model—but a transformation that is in comformity with eternal laws : and these eternal laws manifest themselves through changing, vital, living matter in a well-defined and predetermined direction. Within matter there is also immanent will. Engels, as a good disciple of Hegel, does indeed anticipate the new physics in that he sees objective reality not as a collection of things but as an inextricably interconnected series of *processes*; that is to say, nothing can be considered simply in terms of three dimensions in space—to these must be added a fourth dimension in time. Existence is a perpetual flux, and this means not only that the objective world is perpetually unstable, but also that human thought which, according to Engels, is simply a reflection of the objective world, is itself unstable and therefore dependent for its ideas on the material conditions on which it was brought up.

Marxism, despite its claim to have stood the Hegelian system on its feet—for previously it had been standing on its head—nevertheless, and despite its frenzied repudiation of idealism in all its forms, is idealist in this sense that it attributes to matter not only life but also thought. It abolishes the Hegelian concept of an eternally existent Absolute idea, and puts in its place an eternally developing consciousness which will culminate in an infinite "hyper-consciousness," not abstractly conceived, but concretely realized in the sum total of the thinking of all mankind. The break with idealism was only apparent, and though it is emphasized *ad nauseam* in the earlier works including *Anti-Dühring*, it is plain from one memorable passage in the *Dialectics of Nature* that Engels no longer conceives of mind simply as the reflection of matter (a nebulous idea he never bothers to develop logically) but as the final cause and necessary fulfillment of the whole evolutionary process. This is, however, to anticipate.

In theory Engels sees Marxism as a revolution against idealism and he describes his and Marx's philosophical evolution in the following terms :

We comprehended the concepts in our heads once more materialistically—as images of real things instead of regarding the real things as images of this or that stage of development of the absolute concept. Thus dialectics reduced itself to the science of the general laws of motion—both of the external world and of human thought—two sets of laws which are identical in substance, but differ in their expression in so far as the human mind can apply them consciously, while in nature and also up to now for the most part in human history, these laws assert themselves unconsciously in the form of external necessity in the midst of an endless series of seeming accidents.[15]

The "two sets of laws" are identical in substance, but as Engels stresses elsewhere time and time again, the "laws of nature," that is, the laws governing matter, are primary, and the "laws" of thought only reflect them. Transfer this from the process of nature "which is hereby recognized as an historical process of development,"[16] to the history of human societies and it will be found that the material processes, that is, economic processes, will take precedence over the political and ideological, which are but reflections or rationalizations of those processes. Just how, then, the human mind can be in a position consciously to apply laws by which it is itself conditioned is both unclear and contradicted by Engels himself a few pages later. This passage which seeks to establish the interconnections that exist between preconscious and conscious processes of development is of sufficient importance to deserve quotation in full. This is what Engels says :

In one point, however, the history of the development of society proves to be essentially different from that of nature. In nature—in so far as we ignore man's reaction upon nature—there are only blind unconscious agencies acting upon one another out of whose interplay the general law comes into operation. Nothing of all that happens—whether in the innumerable apparent accidents observable upon the surface of things, or in the ultimate results which confirm the regularity inherent in these accidents—is attained as a consciously desired aim. In the history of society, on the other hand, the actors are all endowed with consciousness, are men acting with deliberation or passion, working toward definite goals; nothing happens without a conscious purpose, without an intended aim. But this distinction, important as it is for historical investigation, particularly of single epochs and events, cannot alter the fact that the course of history is governed by *inner general laws*. For here also, on the whole, in spite of the consciously desired aims of all individuals, accident apparently reigns on the surface. That which is willed happens but rarely; in

[15] Engels, *Ludwig Feuerbach*, p. 51.
[16] *Ibid.*, p. 55.

the majority of instances the numerous desired ends cross and conflict with one another, or these ends themselves are from the outset
incapable of realization or the means of attaining them are insufficient.
Thus the conflict of innumerable individual wills and individual
actions in the domain of history produces a state of affairs entirely
analogous to that in the realm of unconscious nature. The ends of
the actions are intended, but the results which actually follow from
these actions are not intended; or when they do seem to correspond
to the end intended, they ultimately have consequences quite other
than those intended. Historical events thus appear on the whole to
be likewise governed by chance. But where on the surface accident
holds sway, there actually it is always governed by *inner, hidden laws*,
and, [concludes Engels—as if it were the simplest thing in the
world,] it is only a matter of discovering these laws.[17]

Science is less self-confident than was the co-founder of Marxian Communism, for the further it advances and the deeper it
penetrates into the mysterious laws of nature, the greater is its
humility in the face of them and the greater its doubt as
to whether man will ever be in a position to comprehend them
in their totality. Engels, on the other hand, when investigating
these laws as they operate in history in spite of and against the
intervention of rational and voluntary human agents, happily
says that "it is *only* a matter of discovering these laws," and is
quite content to leave it at that. All one can in fact discover is
that there is a given trend at work, and that the factors of
"chance," that is, the clashes of individual wills, may obstruct or
accelerate this allegedly inevitable trend.

The inevitability of the trend is, however, what counts and is
what gives Marxism its peculiar dynamism. Although in his later
life Engels got bogged down in the contradictions of his own
thought, the prime purpose of the whole elaborate fabric of
philosophy he erected seems to have been to demonstrate that
the whole of nature and, after the dawn of consciousness, the
whole of history tends ineluctably toward the final abolition of
social classes and the liberation of man from "the struggle for
individual existence."[18] This constitutes the final qualitative leap
and the final "negation of the negation" toward which the whole
evolution of the world had been tending. And the advance in
nature and in history is not merely a progression from point to
point or even a cyclical motion of rise and decline; it is a true

[17] *Ibid.*, pp. 56–57.
[18] *Id.*, *Socialism Utopian and Scientific*, ed. Aveling, London, 1950 (reprint), p. 81.

progress from a lower to a higher form of existence[19] in which thought advances along with it, discovering even higher laws that transcend those hitherto known.[20] The highest stage of evolution that we can conceive of on this planet is the bursting asunder of an outmoded form of society which already stands self-condemned at the bar of evolution, by a new society which will be qualitatively different in that the final contradiction between class and class will have been resolved.

In its economic and social theory Marxism is an evolutionary Messianism with the proletariat cast in the role of the Messiah. In the broader context of the evolution of the universe which fascinated Engels more and more toward the end of his life, the achievement of the golden age on this earth with which nature had for millennia upon millions of millennia been laboring, might appear, within the framework of the space-time continuum, as too insignificant to be noticed, but such was Engels' burning faith (and no other word is applicable) in the supreme dignity of the human person and of human achievement that, against all the scientific evidence of his time, he nonetheless proclaimed the inevitability of human consciousness reappearing ever again in a universe which, according to the second law of thermodynamics, science believed to be running down into a state of chaos and death. There is something touching in the old materialist's declaration of faith in the imperishability of that thought which he had repeatedly affirmed to be nothing more than the reflection or mirror of living matter governed by unchangeable laws. Faced with the newest discoveries of physical science, the old atheist does not shrink from the surprising conclusion that science itself may force us to reckon with the probability of the existence of a personal God. He writes,

Here, either we must have recourse to a creator, or we are forced to the conclusion that the incandescent raw material for the solar systems of our universe was produced in a natural way by transformations of motion which are *by nature inherent* in moving matter, and the conditions for which, therefore, must also be reproduced by matter, even if only after millions and millions of years and more or less by chance, but with the necessity that is also inherent in chance.[21]

It is sad to think that Engels did not live to see his faith in

[19] *Id., Ludwig Feuerbach*, p. 14.
[20] *Ibid.*, p. 31.
[21] *Id., Dialectics of Nature*, p. 52.

the phenomenon that is man confirmed by science itself; for science is now beginning to discover that entropy is not nature's last word, for this ultimate "negation" is itself "negated" by the contrary law of increasing complexity and consciousness. That this affirmation should have come from a Jesuit priest might have given Engels food for thought, for, unlike the Marxists of our day, Engels acknowledged no dogmas, not even those enunciated by Marx and himself.

It would, however, be wrong to suppose that the immensities opened up to the human mind by science diverted Engels from the consideration of the matter-in-hand—and that was the final qualitative leap within human society which nature and history were preparing on this earth here and now. No one had a greater thirst for the Absolute than Engels, and no one exerted himself more strongly to curb it out of loyalty, one feels, to the more practical genius of his dead friend, Marx. There is a certain wistfulness in his regret that the natural science of his day had not penetrated beyond "our" universe to "the infinitely numerous universes outside it," and his rather naïve willingness to make do, for the moment, with this one little universe of ours. Yet the limited advance of the science of his day "does not," he says, "do any essential injury to the practically infinite diversity of phenomena and natural knowledge, any more than history is harmed by the similar, ever greater limitation to a comparatively short period and small portion of the earth."[22]

Marx had on the whole been content to base his theory of the inevitability of the proletarian revolution on the evidence of modern history, and by so doing he never lost sight of purely individual values : he did not conceive of the new classless society as a mass society in which the individual was submerged, but rather as a society in which human beings were treated and valued as human beings and were given free scope to develop to their full stature as parts of a greater whole. Engels, in his purely philosophical work, tends to blur this sense of urgency, for, by overstressing the complete relativity not only of matter but of thought, he, like the Buddhists whom he rightly counted among his precursors, in fact destroyed human personality and reduced it to a tiny and absurdly insignificant process within the wider dialectical process of conscious history which itself is only the apex of the millennial history of the evolution of all nature

[22] *Ibid.*, p. 314.

from the immemorial beginnings of time. The problem and the solution in contemporary terms had been stated by Marx as early as 1845 in classically Heraclitan terms which even the simplest could understand. He writes,

Proletariat and wealth are opposites; as such they form a single whole. They are both forms of the world of private property. The question is what place each occupies in the antithesis. It is not sufficient to declare them two sides of a single whole.

Private property as private property, as wealth, is compelled to maintain *itself,* and thereby its opposite, the proletariat, in *existence.* That is the *positive* side of the contradiction, self-satisfied private property.

The proletariat, on the other hand, is compelled as proletariat to abolish itself and thereby its opposite, the condition for its existence, what makes it the proletariat, i.e. private property. That is the *negative* side of the contradiction, its restlessness within its very self, dissolved and self-dissolving private property. . . .

Within this antithesis the private owner is therefore the *conservative* side, the proletarian, the *destructive* side. From the former arises the action of preserving the antithesis, from the latter that of annihilating it. . . . The proletariat executes the sentence that private property pronounced on itself by begetting the proletariat. . . . When the proletariat is victorious, it by no means becomes the absolute side of society, for it is victorious only by abolishing itself and its opposite. Then the proletariat disappears as well as the opposite which determines it, private property.[23]

The strength of Marxism still lies in the fact that it gives hope, and that this hope is represented as being based on an inevitable trend in history. To aid in the production of the proletarian revolution is to help on history in its ineluctable course, it is to integrate oneself in the stream of the Tao. But the Marxist Tao is very different from the Chinese variety, for it has a well-defined goal, and that is to establish, *of necessity,* "in place of the old bourgeois society, with its classes and class antagonisms . . . an association in which the free development of each is the condition for the free development of all."[24] Or, in Engels' own words, "The possibility of securing for every member of society, by means of socialized production, an existence not only fully sufficient materially, and becoming day by day more full, but an existence guaranteeing to all the free development and exercise of their physical and mental faculties—this possibility is now for the first

[23] Marx and Engels, *The Holy Family,* pp. 51–52.
[24] *Id., The Communist Manifesto,* p. 146.

time here."[25] And this possibility represents "the ascent of man from the kingdom of necessity to the kingdom of freedom."[26]

And what, we may ask, does Engels understand by freedom, and what by necessity? Necessity is the "inner law"[27] that runs through all apparently accidental phenomena, and from this law there can be no escape. "Freedom," then, can mean no more than "the appreciation of necessity," and "necessity is blind only in so far as it is not understood." "Freedom of the will therefore means nothing but the capacity to make decisions with real knowledge of the subject. Therefore the *freer* a man's judgment is in relation to a definite question, with so much the greater *necessity* is the content of this judgment determined; while the uncertainty founded on ignorance, which seems to make an arbitrary choice between many conflicting and different possible decisions, shows by this precisely that it is not free, that it is controlled by the very object it should itself control. Freedom therefore consists in the control over ourselves and over external nature which is founded on knowledge of natural necessity; it is therefore necessarily a product of historical development."[28] Freedom, then, in the sense that Engels uses the term, means no more than to accept and acquiesce in the "inner law" of nature in so far as it can be known, and, on Engels' own admission, the degree to which it can be known in history is very imperfect. The good life, then, consists in living in harmony with the laws of nature; for "we, with flesh, blood, and brain, belong to nature, and exist in its midst ... and all our mastery of it consists in the fact that we have the advantage over all other creatures of being able to know and correctly apply its laws."[29] But this living in harmony with nature will be possible only in the classless society of the future when those forces which had tried to stem the tide of history and are incarnate in the bourgeoisie, have been "negated." For nature's goal is nothing less than "a state of society in which there are no longer class distinctions or anxiety over the means of subsistence for the individual, and in which for the first time there can be talk of real human freedom and an existence in harmony with the established laws of nature."[30]

[25] Engels, *Socialism Utopian and Scientific*, pp. 80–81.
[26] *Ibid.*, p. 82.
[27] *Id., Ludwig Feuerbach*, p. 56; *Socialism Utopian and Scientific*, p. 37.
[28] *Id., Anti-Dühring*, p. 128.　　　　[29] *Id., Dialectics of Nature*, p. 242.
[30] *Id., Anti-Dühring*, p. 129.

To live in harmony with nature is to know its laws, to act in conformity with them, and to make intelligent use of them. But these laws, changeless though they are, seem to be hedged in by "an endless series of seeming accidents,"[31] and, in history, these "accidents" manifest themselves in the actions and volitions of individual men. Individual men have the power to obstruct and impede the inner laws of nature and history, though they cannot do more than postpone their final coming into operation. Until the classless society is established, then, in which man is to live in harmony with nature, he has the power to deflect nature temporarily from her course. In a society which lives in harmony with nature, however, "the free condition of each [will be] the condition of the free development of all," and the individual will of necessity think in harmony with society as a whole, for society will then be in tune with nature as a whole. The consequences of the Fall which separated man from man in thought, word, and deed, will have been transcended, for the final human synthesis in which all contradictions will have been superseded will set in; and this corresponds most exactly to the Zoroastrian conception of the final Rehabilitation when all things will be made new. Personality will not be done away with; on the contrary, it will flower and develop naturally, because in harmony with the inner laws of nature, and through its dedicated association with a society whose interests are its own and through its harmonious integration within it, its death will have no terrors, for, conscious that it has fulfilled itself as a human person, it will be enough for it to know that, in fulfilling itself, it has contributed to the fulfillment of the whole.

It will be a marvelous thing—the true personality of man—when we see it. It will grow naturally and simply, flowerlike, or as a tree grows. It will not be at discord. It will never argue or dispute. It will not prove things. It will know everything. And yet it will not busy itself about knowledge. It will have wisdom. Its value will not be measured by material things. It will have nothing. And yet it will have everything, and whatever one takes from it, it will still have, so rich will it be. It will not be always meddling with others, or asking them to be like itself. It will love them because they will be different. And yet while it will not meddle with others, it will help all, as a beautiful thing helps us, by being what it is. The personality of man will be very wonderful. It will be as wonderful as the personality of a child.[32]

[31] Above, p. 168.
[32] Oscar Wilde, *Collected Works*, London, Collins, 1948, p. 1023.

Such was Oscar Wilde's vision of the personality of man as it would develop under Socialism, and such, in essence, is what Marx and Engels foresaw; it was to put in the place of the illusory heaven of religion a real heaven here on earth. And in this heaven matter herself, once men had learned to live in harmony with her inner laws, would "smile at man with poetical sensuous brightness."[33]

The Marxian paradise is not unlike the Zoroastrian one, but between them there is this difference. For in the Zoroastrian paradise not only is the integration of humanity in thought, word, and deed into a single harmonious organism complete, but this completion receives the added glory of being accepted in infinite time where there is neither death nor decay. The new heaven and the new earth have an infinite dimension which the new era of the Marxist classless state must lack. Further, it needed all the faith of an Engels to suppose that even in a classless society in which that worst of sins, the desire to have, which we owe to the Fall and which breeds all our hatreds and discontents, would be made impossible by law, the apparatus of state would die out,[34] so perfectly would the aspirations of the individual coincide with the good of the whole. To eradicate an instinct which has been native to man ever since he became an "ego" by revolutionary decree is no more possible, as Engels himself saw, than to eradicate the idea of God by religious persecution. Selflessness is something into which man must painfully grow, constrained as no doubt he will be, not all at once but in a period of time that may last many thousands of years, by the power that works in and through matter over which he has no control. Marxism is a very new phenomenon, and, like all young things, it is in a hurry. The Christian Church is less new : it has learned to wait, for it knows that the Spirit takes no account of time.

Yet, even though human cupidity were miraculously to disappear with the advent of a classless society in which the exploitation of man by man would be forever done away with, this society would still lack the dimension of immortality which religion everywhere and always promises in some form or other. And so it was that Engels, instinctively feeling this lack, was led on to ponder over the mysteries of life and death, of the infinite and the finite, of the Absolute and the conditioned.

[33] Marx and Engels, *The Holy Family*, p. 172.
[34] Engels, *Socialism Utopian and Scientific*, pp. 77, 86.

Like the Brahmanism of the Upanishads he realized that Brahman, that is, Being, must be divided into two compartments—first, the world of becoming, the world of matter in which we live and which is conditioned by time and space, and secondly, a world of eternal law, what Engels likes to call the "inner laws of nature" which are beyond change and time. As a good dialectical thinker in the tradition of Heraclitus, however, Engels saw that even this pair of opposites—the eternal and the relative—must itself be relative, for "dialectics has *proved* ... that all polar opposites in general are determined by the mutual action of the two opposite poles on each other, that the separation and opposition of these poles exist only within their mutual connection and union, and, conversely, that their union exists only in their separation and their mutual connection only in their opposition."[35] If this is true, the "inner laws of nature" must be indissolubly interconnected with living matter itself, and the relative must be shot through with the absolute, death with life, and life with death. And such indeed is what Engels begins to tell us in the *Dialectics of Nature* which he did not live to finish; and in these abstract musings on matters he had not perhaps considered overdeeply, he stands ever nearer to Heraclitus and the whole nostalgic tradition of *participation mystique* which permeates so much of the religion of the East.

"Mortals are immortals, and immortals are mortals, the one living the others' death and dying the others' life,"[36] the inspired Heraclitus had said; and Engels, following the same tradition and substituting a scientific for an oracular vocabulary, repeats his thought :

No physiology is held to be scientific if it does not consider death as an essential element of life, the *negation* of life as being essentially contained in life itself, so that life is always thought of in relation to its necessary result, death, which is always contained in it in germ. The dialectical conception of life is nothing more than this. But for anyone who has once understood this, all talk of the immortality of the soul is done away with. Death is either the dissolution of the organic body, leaving nothing behind but the chemical constituents that formed its substance, or *it leaves behind a vital principle, more or less the soul,* that then survives *all* living organisms, and not only human beings. Here, therefore, by means of dialectics, simply

[35] *Id., Dialectics of Nature,* p. 96.
[36] Fragment 67.

becoming clear about the nature of life and death suffices to abolish an ancient superstition. Living means dying.[37]

For matter is uncreated and indestructible : it is not only a moving, but a living and a thinking thing. Hence, despite his wearisome iteration that the mind is no more than a reflection of matter (by which he means no more than the objective world), Engels comes to concede that there must be "a vital principle, more or less the soul" which survives all living organisms, but he does not make it at all clear whether he regards this soul as being individual by nature or as being equivalent to the World-Soul of the pantheists. What he seems to mean is that since life and death are dialectical poles of the one substance, matter, life itself must survive the death of all individual living organisms, for in death too the free development of each is the condition for the free development of all. Whatever else may die, matter itself must live on forever.

Engels had been accused of "mysticism and incomprehensible transcendentalism,"[38] and he did not like it. Yet the old Hegelian in him never died, and his thirst for the Absolute was never quenched. In place of Hegel's absolute Idea he put Marx's "matter"; but matter, for him, was not what Aristotle understood thereby, it was Aristotelian "matter" plus Aristotelian "form," it was (though he would have hotly denied it) matter "informed" and directed by a power that manifests itself as eternal law, and this power is what is normally called "spirit."

And the earth was without form, and void; and darkness was upon the face of the deep. And the Spirit of God moved upon the face of the waters.

And the Spirit of God had kneaded and formed matter in a marvelous way, had brought life to what was dead, and consciousness to what was merely alive; it had brought social organization among conscious beings, and it would bring a still higher consciousness in which human minds would work in harmony in the construction of a literally infinite mind which would be common to the total collectivity of human beings, a mind that will reflect *in toto* the full splendor of those "inner laws" that give motion and life, sense and direction, to the whole cosmic process of which man himself and the society he will build in

[37] *Dialectics of Nature*, pp. 387–88.
[38] *Ibid.*, p. 91.

accordance with natural law will be the crowning glory. Infinite are the capacities of matter and immeasurable the powers of man, the end product of our mother matter. How foolish are we in seeking to circumscribe her who is the infinite flux of all things gravely fulfilling the purposes her own inner laws impose on her. How foolish, then, to say, "We can know only the finite." For this proposition needs to be supplemented by its dialectical opposite, which is, "We can know only the infinite." For—

In fact all real, exhaustive knowledge consists solely in raising the individual thing in thought from individuality into particularity and from this into universality, in seeking and establishing the infinite in the finite, the eternal in the transitory. The form of universality, however, is the form of self-completeness, hence of infinity . . . . The form of universality in nature is *law,* and no one talks more of *the eternal character of the laws of nature* than the natural scientists. Hence when Nägeli says that the finite is made impossible to understand by not desiring to investigate merely this finite, but instead adding something eternal to it, then he denies either the possibility of knowing the laws of nature or their eternal character. All true knowledge of nature is knowledge of the eternal, the infinite, and hence essentially absolute.[39]

But it would be folly to suppose that knowledge of the Absolute is attainable by any purely individual effort; it will have to be the result of the combined and co-ordinated thought of a solidary humanity united in a social system that is in harmony with the laws of nature, and it will be the result (if ever it is achieved) of constant experiment, constant trial and error. For—

This absolute knowledge has an important drawback. Just as the infinity of knowable matter is composed of the purely finite things, so the infinity of thought which knows the absolute is composed of an infinite number of finite human minds, working side by side and successively at this infinite knowledge, committing practical and theoretical blunders, setting out from erroneous, one-sided and false premises, pursuing false, tortuous, and uncertain paths, and often not even finding what is right when they run their noses against it. The cognition of the infinite is therefore beset with double difficulty and from its very nature can only take place in an infinite asymptotic progress. And that suffices us in order to say: the infinite is just as much knowable as unknowable, and that is all that we need.[40]

[39] *Ibid.,* p. 310.
[40] *Ibid.,* p. 311.

Whatever the last sentence may mean—and, as it stands, it means very little—this is the language of religion, of "mysticism and incomprehensible transcendentalism," not of science. It is man's final confession that he can never wholly know the ways of God, whether we choose to call him "matter," "nature," the "Supreme," or simply God. Something can be known, indeed, through science as well as through religion, but this something will have value only if it helps to preserve our hope and our faith in the value and destiny, not of God, but of man. Poor Engels lived at an awkward time, for science was then finding signs that not only our tiny solar system, but the whole of the universe was running down to a dead, inglorious close. At this thought Engels' whole being revolted. "Will the sun's corpse," he asks, "roll on for all eternity through infinite space, and all the once infinitely diversely differentiated natural forces pass for ever into one single form of motion, attraction? 'Or'—as Secchi asks—'are there forces in nature which can reconvert the dead system into its original state of glowing nebula and re-awaken it to new life? We do not know.'"

This "we do not know" Engels will not accept; and here follows his defiant confession of faith not in the supremacy of a material universe which, according to all probability, is running down into the simplest and most banal form of mechanical motion, but in the supremacy of thought, indeed the *consistency* of thought, which has higher claims than the possibly erroneous observations of physical science. No, he says,

We do not know it in the sense that we know that 2 x 2 = 4, or that the attraction of matter increases and decreases according to the square of the distance. In theoretical natural science, however, which as far as possible builds up its outlook on nature into a harmonious whole, and without which nowadays even the most unthinking empiricist cannot get anywhere, we have very often to calculate with incompletely known magnitudes, and consistency of thought must at all times help to get over defective knowledge. Modern natural science has had to take over from philosophy the principle of the indestructibility of motion; it cannot any longer exist without this principle. But the motion of matter is not merely crude mechanical motion, mere change of place, it is heat and light, electric and magnetic tension, chemical combination and dissociation, life and, finally consciousness. To say that matter during the whole unlimited time of its existence has only once, and for what is an infinitesimally short period in comparison to its eternity, found itself able to differentiate its motion . . . and that before and after this it remains restricted for eternity to mere change of place—this is equivalent to maintaining that matter is mortal and motion transient. The indestructibility of motion cannot be conceived of merely quantitatively, it must be conceived of qualitatively; matter whose purely mechanical change of place includes indeed the possibility under favorable conditions of being transformed into heat, electricity, chemical action, life, but which is not capable of producing these conditions from out of itself, such matter has *forfeited motion*; motion which has lost the capacity of being transformed into the various forms appropriate to it may indeed still have *dynamis* but no longer *energeia*, and so has become partially destroyed. Both, however, are unthinkable.[41]

To speak of a scientific probability as "unthinkable" is to speak the language of faith. Moreover, in this passage it is clearer than anywhere else that for Engels matter is not only "impulse, vital spirit, and tension," it is something which has value in itself, and should science ever succeed in proving that it is disloyal to its own law of development from mechanical to vital motion and from vital motion to thought, then it will have *forfeited* motion : the god will have failed; and motion itself, should it succumb to the process of the increase of entropy, would itself have to be written off as an unactualizable potentiality. And this would mean that the whole elaborate structure of dialectical materialism, so ponderously pieced together by Engels in his later years, would collapse in ruins. This, however, is *unthinkable*. In this passage at least, for Engels it appears that "matter" has no value in itself but only in so far as it is the mother of life and thought, and even though the appearance of consciousness may take place only once in millions of years and on only one tiny grain of sky dust in the infinities of space, even so this alone will give point and purpose to what would otherwise be the pointless evolution of a useless machine, made to look the sillier in that it is doomed from the beginning to run down and die. But this is "unthinkable."

[For] it is an eternal cycle in which matter moves, a cycle that certainly only completes its orbit in periods of time for which our terrestrial year is no adequate measure, a cycle in which the time of highest development, the time of organic life and still more that of the life of beings conscious of nature and of themselves, is just as narrowly restricted as the space in which life and self-consciousness

[41] *Ibid.*, pp. 50–51.

come into operation; a cycle in which every finite mode of existence of matter, whether it be sun or nebular vapour, single animal or genus of animals, chemical combination or dissociation, is equally transient, and wherein nothing is eternal but eternally changing, eternally moving matter and the laws according to which it moves and changes. But however often, and however relentlessly, this cycle is completed in time and space; however many millions of suns and earths may arise and pass away, however long it may last before, in one solar system and only on *one* planet, the conditions for organic life develop; however innumerable the organic beings, too, that have to arise and to pass away before animals with a brain capable of thought are developed from their midst, and for a short span of time find conditions suitable for life, only to be exterminated later without mercy—we have the certainty that matter remains eternally the same in all its transformations, that none of its attributes can ever be lost, and therefore, also, that with the same iron necessity that it will exterminate on the earth its highest creation, the thinking mind, it must somewhere else and at another time again produce it.[42]

Marxism, thus, seeks to set itself up as a complete way of life— a philosophy of dying as well as of living, of eternity as well as of time : it is a religion. It has affinities with Taoism, Buddhism, and Hinduism, but whereas these are all, in their different ways, religions of escape—of escape from time into eternity and from action into rest—Marxism, like Zoroastrianism, is a religion of acceptance and fulfillment. Despite the intimations of immortality that, in Engels' later work, refuse to be suppressed, the appeal of Marxism is not so much in its elevation of matter to the rank of an immanent god as in its confident prediction that humanity is marching toward a classless society which will spread across the face of the whole globe and in which all the contradictions which have succeeded each other throughout the millennia in nature's timeless womb, will now, thanks to the inner laws of nature herself and the iron necessity that governs them, be finally resolved; and man at last will be able to develop freely in the conditions in which the free development of each is inherent in the free development of all. The enterprises of men which, since Adam fell, have been individual, unco-ordinated, and rival affairs, will now be dovetailed the one into the other because the interest of all will be the interest of each, and none will need or wish to develop at the expense of his fellows. Marxism evokes the spirit of nature herself, who created life and conscious-

[42] *Ibid.*, p. 54.

ness, to lay the ghost of Cain, who, by the mere fact of becoming self-conscious, started humanity on its fratricidal course. With the conquest of the last pair of contradictions that keep man at war with himself, human brotherhood will at last no longer be synonymous with fratricide. Such is the essence of the Marxist hope.

7
The Convergent Spirit

Let us take a grain of barley. Millions of such grains of barley are milled, boiled, and brewed, and then consumed. But if such a grain of barley meets with conditions which for it are normal, if it falls on suitable soil, then under the influence of heat and moisture a specific change takes place, it germinates; the grain as such ceases to exist, it is negated, and in its place appears the plant which has arisen from it, the negation of the grain. But what is the normal life-process of this plant? It grows, flowers, is fertilized, and finally once more produces grains of barley, and as soon as these have ripened, the stalk dies, is in its turn negated. As a result of this negation of the negation we have once again the original grain of barley, but not as a single unit, but ten, twenty, or thirty-fold.[1]

So does Engels introduce us to his theory of the "negation of the negation" and the "qualitative leap." More simply it was said,

Except a corn of wheat fall into the ground and die, it abideth alone: but if it die, it bringeth forth much fruit.[2]

Man's tragedy since Adam fell is that he is alone: the existentialist's tragedy is that not only is he alone but that he knows that he is alone. Classical Buddhism tells us how to be alone, but it does not tell us how to "bring forth much fruit." Marxism tells us how to bring forth much fruit, but it does not tell us how to put back a heart into a heartless world.

The civilization of a technological age will not leave us alone. We are still free to opt out of life into our own little Nirvāṇas, but even this freedom will shortly be taken from us. The religious conscience of modern man stands at the crossroads, for his religious roots seem to have been cut from under him. Primitive religion had its roots in nature, and through nature man appre-

[1] Engels, *Anti-Dühring*, p. 152.
[2] John, 12:24.

hended the divine; and though the religions of India and China differ greatly in emphasis, they agree in this, that though nature may be infinitely varied, in its essence and ground it is one; and to realize its oneness in one's own consciousness is salvation and bliss.

Modern science cuts away the roots of "natural" religion. In direct contradiction to the Taoist's loving acceptance of, and submission to, Nature's Tao, modern science dissects the Tao itself, demanding that it yield up its secrets and reveal its eternal rationality. The universe is ceasing to be mysterious, but reveals itself, with every step that science takes forward, as being governed by the same mathematical laws that govern human thinking. Physics (the science of nature) comes increasingly to depend on mathematics (the science of mind); and the priority of mind over matter, or, in Marxian terminology, of the "inner laws of nature" over nature itself becomes ever more clear. Modern man has outgrown the childhood of the human race; he does not seek to commune with Nature or to be at one with her, he demands that she be understood. This is a trend that no amount of wishful thinking can reverse; and it is a trend that all religions must take into account. How they will emerge from this encounter we have yet to see, but, with the possible exception of Christianity, they seem ill-equipped for the brutal trial ahead; and Teilhard de Chardin is perhaps not wide of the mark when he says,

For almost all the ancient religions, the renewal of cosmic outlook characterizing the "modern mind" has occasioned a crisis of such severity that, if they have not yet been killed by it, it is plain they will never recover. Narrowly bound to untenable myths, or steeped in a pessimistic and passive mysticism, they can adjust themsleves neither to the precise immensities, nor to the constructive requirements, of space-time. They are out of step both with our science and with our activity.[3]

And broadly speaking this is true : the Eastern religions can scarcely stand up to the assault of Western science. Despite the sublimity of the concepts, no purely mythological deity, no Krishna or Bodhisattva, can for long hold the allegiance of modern man, nor can the mysticism of escape any longer satisfy, for it concerns the individual alone, and mankind is tiring of individuality and demands a religion that provides for the sal-

[3] Teilhard de Chardin, *The Phenomenon of Man*, p. 296.

vation and sanctification of the whole human race. Thus, while
it is possible that the Neo-Vedānta and Zen Buddhism may
satisfy some individuals for a short time, they plainly can never
be integrated into modern society. Neither Confucianism nor
Taoism was able to stand up to the impact of a militant Marxism,
for Marxism brings with it not only a hope of salvation of each
in the activity of all, but also an ideal of the collective fulfillment
of all mankind in an Absolute conceived of as the totality of all
conscious thought. Islam, too, has become muscle-bound in its
medieval traditions, and all attempts to bring it into harmony
with the modern age have so far failed. It was within a Western
Christian setting that our technological civilization came to birth,
and this was no accident, for Christianity is both "this-worldly"
and "other-worldly"; it has always taught that the universe of
matter is a rational construction, rationally ordered by a rational
as well as suprarational Being. And Catholic doctrine has in
addition taught that the order of grace does not contradict but
complement the order of nature, and that in the Incarnation
the two orders combine to build up the mystical body of the risen
Christ. From the very beginning the Holy Spirit had been working
in the order of nature, preparing the material world, through the
rise of consciousness and its misuse, which constitutes Adam's
Fall, for the entry of God himself into history to retrieve what
was lost and to attract all his creation back to himself. With the
Incarnation of God in Christ the material world was called upon
to share in the supernatural order of grace. And on the first Whitsunday the same Holy Spirit which, in the order of nature, had
"moved upon the face of the waters" before time began, is
poured forth upon the infant Church to bring it grace and a more
than natural destiny.

The history of the Church has to be seen in the light of evolution, and in evolutionary terms its two thousand years of existence
can measure no more than its early childhood; but the miracle
of Pentecost reversed the tide of evolution itself, for from this
moment, and at first very slowly, it could be seen that the
Church's destiny was to rebuild mankind in the image and unity
of Christ. The scattering of the nations represented by the Tower
of Babel, when men's tongues became confused, was annulled at
Pentecost when each understood his fellow, though speaking unknown tongues. The convergence of humanity upon itself had
already begun.

The service Teilhard de Chardin has rendered to Christianity is that he has shown how the Christian Church can be regarded as the logical fruit of evolution itself. He has explained Christianity in Marxist, because evolutionary, terms : he fulfills and perfects and baptizes the insights of Marx and Engels, and brings the heart of Christ into a heartless world.

Teilhard de Chardin was a scientist and a mystic. As a scientist he brought a wholly new approach to the mystery of Christianity, and as a mystic he found in the very matter he studied as a scientist that same Spirit that sanctifies the soul in the Church. As a mystic, too, he was able to distinguish between the different types of mysticism that writers on this subject so repeatedly confuse. He was well aware that there was the mysticism of *participation mystique,* the mysticism of the isolation of the soul in its eternal essence, and the mysticism of the love of God. Beyond all these, however, he conceived of a new type of mysticism, that of the mass of mankind converging upon itself and upon God in what he calls the "noosphere," and by this he seems to have meant a slow integration of the mind of all mankind around its center, Christ, in rational adoration; and this is what Christians mean by the Communion of Saints.

Teilhard de Chardin has been criticized for "explaining" the Christian "mystery" in purely evolutionary terms : he has been accused of ignoring such fundamental doctrines as Original Sin and the Fall : and this is true, for *The Phenomenon of Man* reads rather like a "spiritualization" of the *Dialectics of Nature;* it is the reformulation of Christian doctrine in Marxist terms. We must now return again to the Fall and to the interpretation of it by one who strangely prefigured Teilhard in that she saw salvation in terms of the whole human race rather than in terms of the individual, I mean, Blessed Julian of Norwich, who was vouchsafed a vision of the Fall in the year of our Lord 1373. She writes,

For the first [sight], thus, I saw two persons in bodily likeness: that is to say, a Lord and a Servant; and therewith God gave me a ghostly understanding. The Lord sitteth solemnly in rest and in peace; the Servant standeth by, afore his Lord reverently, ready to do his Lord's will. The Lord looketh upon his servant full lovingly and sweetly, and meekly he sendeth him to a certain place to do his will. The Servant not only he goeth, but suddenly he starteth, and runneth in great haste, for love to do his Lord's will. And anon he falleth into a slade, and taketh full great hurt. And then he groaneth and moaneth and waileth and writheth, but he neither may rise nor help himself by no manner of way.

And of all this the most mischief that I saw him in, was failing of comfort: for he could not turn his face to look upon his loving Lord, which was to him full near,—in whom is full comfort;—but as a man that was feeble and unwise for the time, he gave intent to his feeling and endured in woe.[4]

Such was Julian's vision of the Fall, and this is how she interpreted it :

The Lord that sat solemnly in rest and in peace, I understood that he is God. The Servant that stood afore the Lord, I understood that it was shewed for Adam; that is to say, one man was shewed, that time, and his falling, to make it thereby understood how God beholdeth *All-Man* and his falling. *For in the sight of God all man is one man, and one man is all man.* This man was hurt in his might and made full feeble; and he was stunned in his understanding, for he turned from the beholding of his Lord. But his will was kept whole in God's sight;—for his will I saw our Lord commend and approve. But himself was letted and blinded from the knowing of this will; and this is to him great sorrow and grievous dis-ease : for neither doth he see clearly his loving Lord, which is to him full meek and mild, nor doth he see truly what himself is in the sight of his loving Lord. And well I wot when these two are wisely and truly seen, we shall get rest and peace here in part, and the fulness of the bliss of Heaven, by his plenteous grace.[5]

For Julian of Norwich Adam is not just one man, the common ancestor of the human race : he is humanity in the mass as it emerges into the light of consciousness. And humanity falls through an excess of zeal : "suddenly he starteth, and runneth in great haste, for love to do his Lord's will." He longs to know, and he knows that God wishes him to know, but he thinks he can do it all himself so eager is he to show his real value to his Lord; and so he tries to run before he can walk. His will is all right, but he becomes "stunned in his understanding." He is dazzled by the light of consciousness, falls, and in falling he is not only stunned but ricks his neck so that he cannot turn his head to see God in the new light of consciousness. He is permanently injured and retains only a dim image of God in his head which from now until

[4] Julian of Norwich, *Revelations of Divine Love* (London, 1952, 2nd ed.), pp. 91–92.   [5] *Ibid.*, pp. 94–95.

God's own assumption of human flesh, he will try to reflect ever more truthfully. "O happy fault," indeed, that was man's first step from individual consciousness toward the ultimate reunion with his Lord. The Fall of Man is, then, not so much his inability to adjust himself to the full light of consciousness as his confidence in his own unaided ability to do so—and that all for the love of God! It is not his heart that is at fault but his childish self-confidence which some call pride.

But let us go right back to the beginning again when "the earth was without form, and void; and darkness was upon the face of the deep. And the Spirit of God moved upon the face of the waters." Here, surely, we find "in the beginning" those contrary forces which modern physics discerns will bring about the end. There is the shapelessness and emptiness to which, we are told, the process of the increase of entropy will ultimately reduce the whole universe, and there is the Spirit of God which broods upon this shadowy material, kneading it and molding it until, moved by an obscure instinct to unite with what is other than itself, it forms a living cell—and life is born. Thence, through millions upon millions of years, it gropes obscurely toward consciousness, until consciousness itself breaks forth, and there are men to say "I am." Yet evolution does not move in a straight line, it gropes forward tentatively, and can break through only to a new and more complex form of development when it finds the ideally adapted formation of matter. Either, then, it will seem as if life and, after life, consciousness, are the result of an unbelievable series of accidents, or it will appear that the Spirit of God is itself uncertain of where it is going. Yet the fact remains that there is something in matter which, against all probability, has produced not only life and thought, but also an awareness of beauty and a conscience which can distinguish right from wrong; and these are things which no so-called "materialist" philosophy can explain. Hence we must assume the presence of Spirit, of an "inward" type of energy that works *pari passu* with the "outward"—one Spirit that manifests itself both in natural law and in moral law. As natural law it operates from the beginning, as moral law it makes itself felt only with the dawning of consciousness in man.

Both Christians and Hindus are familiar with the doctrine of divine incarnation; and this unique marriage of heaven and earth, of spirit and matter, is surely no more than the crystallization in time of a process eternally present in the space-time continuum. For just as Christians believe that God the Son became incarnate in the man Jesus, thereby embracing and making his own the transient and ever-changing envelope that goes to make up the flesh of man, so did God the Holy Spirit from the beginning quicken and guide the whole material universe toward forms, ever more complex and ever more conscious, until the stage of *homo sapiens* was reached. And just as it remains a mystery how it is possible for the Maker of heaven and earth, the all-seeing and all-knowing God, at the same time to be an unconscious embryo in Mary's womb, so must it remain a mystery how the Holy Spirit, the "Lord and Giver of life," should for so long remain apparently lifeless in the immensities of swirling matter. Yet, if it is possible for God the Son to grow and mature in the Virgin's womb, to be born, to rise to full self-consciousness as a child, to die, and to rise from the dead, then it can scarcely be accounted surprising that God the Holy Spirit should conceal himself in the womb of matter and be born into life, consciousness, responsibility, and full maturity. This is not surprising at all, indeed, but almost a self-evident truth. For even the Marxists, shy of the Spirit as they are, cannot but admit that the universe and this world of ours which distinguishes itself from every other part of the universe by its having given birth to self-consciousness, is propelled by a force they attribute to the "inner laws of nature," but which is nothing less, according to their own account, than an immanent will pursuing the ends of a mind innate in nature herself. And this Christians are wont to call the Holy Spirit.

We are finite creatures, and we are dazed by the infinite; but we cannot get away from it, nor can we ever understand it; for "the gods love the obscure and hate the obvious." We cannot understand how the Holy Spirit can *both* operate in matter, thrusting it forward to consciousness and perhaps beyond to what Teilhard de Chardin calls the "hyper-consciousness" of the whole human phylum, *and* remain outside it all as the bond of unity that welds together the Godhead itself. We cannot understand this at all unless we can imagine that it should please an absolutely perfect being not only to raise up to himself children who should in the end become "like him" in that they should share with him his eternal mode of existence, but also to assume to himself their very nothingness and weakness that he might himself bring them back to his own perfection. Hence God is a Trinity, "Alpha and Omega, the first and the last," but also the middle point between the infinitely great and the infinitely small, for he became man, the mid-point between spiral nebula and electron. He is Alpha the Holy Spirit that "moved upon the face of the waters," he is the mid-point incarnate in the man Jesus Christ, and he is Omega, the end-point and eternal Father to which Adam, the All-Man, is destined to return.

But Adam sinned, not understanding what he did, and the result of sin was a dislocation within the All-Man. In his over-anxiousness to grasp the fruits of knowledge, man became so intent on improving *himself* that he lost sight of God; and in losing sight of God he lost his own internal unity. One man became many, each trying to master his fellow. In so doing he not only cut himself off from God and his fellow men, he introduced a dislocation within himself—a disastrous disharmony between the body, the mortality of which could no longer be concealed, and the soul, immortal still, yet unable to establish contact either with God or with his fellows. "Neither did he see clearly his loving Lord . . . nor did he see clearly what himself was." For he had sinned, and sin is *Sünde* and *Sonderung*—separation, disunion, and dis-ease.

Humanity was no longer one. The All-Man, the Image of God, was shattered into mutually hostile fragments, each fragment, indeed, preserving its own parcel of eternal life, but quite unable to share in the eternal life of God or of his fellow men. Man had now but two alternatives : to seek his own immortality in isolation, or so to integrate himself in the life of his nation and the nation's collective response to God as to rise superior to his particular mortality. The first was the way of India, the second the way of Israel : and both were only half-solutions. No complete solution could come until man was reconciled to God, and through God with his fellow men.

To regard the Fall as an unmitigated disaster is to disregard the facts of religious history : it was a *felix culpa*, a happy fault, not only because it made redemption possible, but be·ause personal self-consciousness is itself a good. To be oneself, and to be oneself more fully "increased and fulfilled through the Holy Ghost,"[6] is man's highest fruition as man; and it is a far nobler state than to lapse back into the collective unconscious of all

[6] *Ibid.*, p. 112.

living things, better far than passively to submit to the rhythm of the Tao. But to be oneself fully does not mean to develop at the expense of others, for the personality of man "will not be always meddling with others, or asking them to be like itself. It will love them because they will be different. And yet while it will not meddle with others, it will help all, as a beautiful thing helps us, by being what it is." This is profoundly true, and any attempt to develop one's personality at the expense of others or by seeking to use others as things, is not only an outrage and a violation of what is most sacred in the other, his personality; it is a boomerang that with the inevitability of Engels' own "inner laws of nature" recoils upon oneself, lacerating and warping the very personality one had sought to fill out. This lust for power, on however small a scale, is the direct result of Original Sin, for it is to seek to be like God in his omnipotence, and that is an attribute of God in which man can never share. The Muslim theologian, al-Ghazālī, though he did not subscribe to the doctrine of Original Sin, was more right than he knew when he wrote, "Because of the exceedingly intimate relationship that exists between the soul and [God's] Dominion, to seek dominion is man's very nature, and everyone has a secret desire to say with Pharaoh, 'I am your Lord the most high.' "[7] And this is the sure result of Original Sin.

How, then, is Original Sin a happy fault? The stock Christian answer is that without the Fall there would have been no redemption; man would have remained no more than a rational animal and, like all animals, unfree. In the Zoroastrian legend, it will be remembered the pre-existent souls of men were given the free choice between remaining forever unharmed in eternity or of going down to earth "to do battle with the Lie." They chose to go down because they saw that, so far from being diminished and demeaned by their entry into space and time, they would prove their worth and return enriched and fulfilled by their achievement in time. Like the "released" soul of the Buddhist or Yogin they could have enjoyed their timeless being forever without growth or diminution, and perfectly at rest; but guided by the infused wisdom of God, they saw that to do this was to acquiesce in being forever a spiritual and immortal vegetable : better far, they thought, to be a mortal man, rooted in matter and endowed with reason and a free will, with all the risks that that entailed.

[7] See Zaehner, *Hindu and Muslim Mysticism*, p. 169.

So the souls of men chose to go down to earth "to do battle with the Lie."

In Genesis too man chooses the knowledge of good and evil, though little knowing the consequences : yet the achievement of personality is a qualitative leap and a vast advance prepared from time immemorial by the Holy Spirit's action within matter. Only in the abuse of personality was sin present. So God drove man from the Garden of innocence and childhood into the hard world of responsibility and adult life. Man had to learn to grow up : and God watched his growing with joy : for "mightily he joyeth in his falling for the high raising and fullness of bliss that Mankind is come to, overpassing that we should have had if he had not fallen."[8]

Et incarnatus est: "and became flesh." God the Son became man. Just as God the Holy Spirit had "become" matter "in the beginning," so did Christ, the "Mid-Person,"[9] become man, the mid-point in the material world between spiral nebula and electron. In the beginning God the Holy Spirit entered the macrocosm : with Christ God enters the microcosm—Christ who is God and man, God the Son and the second Adam, Son of God and Son of Man; and because he is both God and Man be brings a whole new dimension not only into the life of fallen man, but also what would have been the life of man if he had not fallen, for Adam did no more than walk with God as with a companion. Through Christ he has the chance and destiny of being built back into the very substance of God. The Spirit had always been within him; but now he is given the Son. Thus does he not only begin to restore and rebuild the image of God that was shattered when Adam fell, not only does he start to re-form the body of Adam around Christ, the second Adam, he is given the unique and incredible privilege of building up the life of the Holy Trinity itself in time. Molded by the Holy Spirit into the Son, incorporated into the Son, and guided as before by the Spirit, he advances, with many a fall and many a backsliding, but advances still, gathering around him all those who were lost, toward that point at the end of time where the Father, his End as well as his beginning, waits to receive him.

The Fall of man, as we have seen, resulted in three separations :

[8] Julian of Norwich, *op. cit.*, p. 105.
[9] *Ibid.*, p. 108.

the separation of Adam, the All-Man, from God, the separation of each man from his fellow, and the separation of body from soul. Only in man is the last separation possible, for man alone possesses an immortal soul that has its being outside time. In the rest of the material universe matter and spirit are so inextricably mixed that science has the greatest difficulty in defining matter at all; and if matter is reducible to energy, then it already stands very near to spirit. In man, however, the spirit is both static and dynamic : it operates not only in the same way as it does throughout the whole realm of matter, it also dwells in each man as a timeless entity which even the Fall could not destroy; it both "works" in time and "rests" in eternity. Hence the Indian religions diagnosed the nature of man as being an unnatural amalgam of an immortal spirit and a perishable psychophysical apparatus; and they concentrated all their religious energy on realizing this immortal essence in its naked "prebiographical unity," beyond all the vicissitudes of time. There was nothing else to do, for there was no contact either with God or with the souls of other men; and seeing no purpose in the world, there could be no sense in trying to improve it. So they sought their individual "liberations" and their individual "Nirvāṇas" in contemptuous isolation from the world.

Christ, however, came not only to save individual souls, but to found a Church of which he was to be the head, she the body. He brought not only the soul's salvation outside time, but the promise of a solidarity of bodies and minds concurring in him who claimed to be the Way, the Truth, and the Life. By becoming man he not only sanctified the human body and mind, he drew all human beings to himself, making them co-heirs with him in the kingdom, members of the same body, stones in the same temple of which he is the corner, "to whom coming, as unto a living stone, disallowed indeed of men, but chosen of God, and precious, ye also, as living stones, are built up a spiritual house."[10] The coming of Christ marks not only the beginning of the divinization of individual man, but the building of the House of God of living stones in which alone "the free development of each [will be] the condition for the free development of all"; free because "no more a servant, but a son; and if a son, then an heir of God through Christ."[11]

Christ is the cornerstone which the builders rejected, and as

[10] I Peter, 2:4-5.   [11] Gal., 4:7.

such he is the nucleus and foundation around and on which the new Adam, the new All-Man, must be built. Original Sin led to the disintegration of the human race; and salvation could no longer be thought of in terms of one single human mass, united by a common purpose and a common mode of thought: now the best that could be hoped for was a *sauve qui peut*—"be saved who can": and salvation could come about only by man himself piercing down to the deep wellsprings of his being which guard his own fragmentary image of God, for he could no longer "turn his face to look upon his loving Lord." Christ came, as the second Adam, to integrate what had been dispersed. But he came not as Adam did, the All-Man or total human phylum emerging into consciousness under the wings of the Holy Spirit: he came as one among millions in no way different from the rest except in that he was without sin, and that he was also God. Being without sin, he was without separation, a unity in himself—God and man—and man in the fullest sense, with body, mind, and immortal spirit: and not only was he one and whole, integrated within himself, he was also the bond of union that was to draw all men together into his own body which is the Church. His mission was not only to reunite man with God, but to heal the lesion between soul and body in individual men, and to build them into the integrated whole which is the Church. We have seen how Zoroastrianism conceived of this ideal, and how the seven divine hypostases who together form the Godhead announced the ultimate solidarity of all things human and divine, saying,

We are seven, but one in thought, word, and deed; and because we are one in thought, word, and deed, we are unageing and death-less, knowing neither corruption nor decay; and when you who are men become one in thought, word, and deed, then will you become unageing, free from sickness, knowing neither corruption nor decay, even as we, the Bounteous Immortals, are.

One thing only was lacking in the Zoroastrian vision of the solidarity of mankind as it is lacking in the Marxist vision of the future classless state: both lack any center from which the various members can draw their strength and in accordance with which they can co-ordinate their activities. Both edifices lack a corner-stone made of living rock, and so the one collapsed as the other must in its turn collapse unless and until it grafts itself on to the temple that has for two thousand years been growing up upon the rock of Peter, and beyond Peter, Christ. Zoroastrianism's center was the Persian King of kings, the successor of Cyrus, the Lord's anointed, but the Empire fell and with it the King, and once the King had gone, the religion he had sustained collapsed with him. And this was bound to be, for no religion that depends on the succession of temporal kings can grow into its full stature even if the line were to last forever, for all religion, however "this-worldly" it may be, has no eternal life unless it is anchored to a foundation that is itself eternal and independent of the passage of time. How much less, then, can Marxism last, moored as it is in no visible or invisible center, yet knowing in its bones that without such a center it must be dissipated and disintegrate as Adam did of old. Stalin was no fool when he established himself alone as such a center upon which he grounded the monolithic structure of the Soviet State and the ancillary Communist parties, for he saw that unless and until men of themselves and of their own free will become "one in thought, word, and deed," then they would have to be made such, and the living stones of *his* temple would have to be riveted to-gether with bands of steel lest, by reverting to an outmoded in-dividualism, they should ruinously fall apart. Stalin, more than anyone else in the whole history of the world, realized "the ex-ceedingly intimate relationship that exists between the soul and [God's] Dominion," and therefore had no difficulty in proclaiming himself the "Lord most high." But Stalin, like the vast organi-zation of which he was the apex, was a man, and only a man, and, unlike the Zoroastrian kings, he had no successors, so that world Communism now lacks any real center to which it can turn; for already the fissiparous tendencies that were at work in the Tower of Babel, are nibbling at the roots of the Communist structure; for apart from the established center in Moscow a separate center asserts itself in Peking, not to mention the still, small center in Belgrade which so obstinately refuses to conform. And these fissiparous tendencies, the sure sign of what is not of God, will in the long run destroy the Communist edifice, even though the destruction be delayed for hundreds of years.

Christ was one man among millions, and as such of little account—a stone of so little account, indeed, as to be rejected by the builders, yet destined nonetheless to become the "headstone of the corner." And this was possible because, being himself God and man, he could alone reconcile man with God; and so "if any

man be in Christ, he is a new creature : old things are passed away;
. . . all things are become new. And all things are of God, who
hath reconciled us to himself by Jesus Christ, and hath given to
us the ministry of reconciliation; to wit, that God was in Christ,
reconciling the world unto himself."[12]

Through Original Sin, the "happy fault" that had given rise
to individual consciousness, man became separated not only from
God but from his fellow men : and until the bond between God
and man had been restored, there could be no real communion
between man and man. But how was the bond to be restored?
How could man be persuaded that God is not just a lawgiver
who sets him impossible and incomprehensible tasks against
which his very reason rebels, not just an arbitrary employer who
pays the workmen whom he employs at the eleventh hour just as
much as those who have toiled through the grilling heat of the
midday sun? How could man be made to believe the unbelievable,
namely, that, despite the hatred, cruelty, and unmerited suffering he sees on every side, God nevertheless *is* love?

There seems to be no other way but for God himself to become
man, and for him to display on earth as God the Son and Son
of Man, the divine life itself as lived in eternity by the
Holy Trinity : for the life and death of Christ not only shows man
what love really means, it also shows what kind of life God lives
in eternity and how that life must be three in one, because love
is impossible except between a lover and a beloved. To love is to
give, and to give in abundance, to give, if need be, what is most
precious to all men, life itself; for "greater love hath no man than
this, that a man lay down his life for his friends."[13] But even this
is not the ultimate sacrifice, for the sacrifice is not Christ's alone
but God the Father's too : for whereas there always have been and
will be men who will lay down their lives for their friends, it needs
a God to sacrifice his own Son in order to become reconciled not
only with that Son's friends but with his mortal enemies. So God,
who never acts on the human scene either in the lives of
individuals or in the life of the human race as a whole in a way
that anyone chould expect or foresee, does not only what he does
not demand of any man, but what he has expressly forbidden
anyone to do : he sacrifices his only Son as a peace-offering to be
an everlasting covenant between man and himself—a covenant

[12] II Cor., 5:17–19.
[13] John, 15:13.

sealed in the blood of his Son. If God were not love, this would
be an act of monstrous cruelty and immeasurable injustice, but
love knows nothing of justice as men understand it, it knows only
how to give what it cannot afford to lose. So God gives his only-
begotten Son, that man in him may once again find the lost principle of unity—union within himself first, and union of one man
with another through participation in the universal victim
second. And that the giving and the self-sacrifice of God might
be complete, it was necessary that man, for whom God was giving himself wholly on the Cross, should surpass himself in sin and
declare himself openly the enemy of God. Had he not done so,
how could he understand, let alone obey, Christ's impossible command to love your enemies? For if it was possible for God to
love man even in the paroxysm of his sinning, then man, if he
accepts redemption in the blood of Christ, has no choice but to
love his enemy—and not only his own enemy, but the enemies
of his God, both the Father who gave his Son wholly and the God
who died. For in the tragedy of Calvary all mankind takes part—
each and every one of us crucifying our Redeemer because our
pride will not admit that we have ever been in the wrong.
Throughout the whole scene sin follows sin in mechanical proces-
sion: the loutish sloth of the chosen three in the garden of
Gethsemane beside which the betrayal of Judas has at least the
cleanness of singleness of purpose; Peter's pitiful panic in the hall
of Caiaphas; Pilate's self-righteous refusal to accept responsibility; the blood lust of the mob; and most terrible of all,
the urbane callousness of the scribes—the dons, lawyers, and
intellectuals of their day—wagging their heads and whispering
to each other with a marvelous self-righteousness, "He saved
others, himself he cannot save."

But from this total defeat of the Cross in which human sin,
human stupidity, and human self-righteousness conspired to
crucify the God of love, arose the body of the Resurrected Lord.
Yet from the day of the Resurrection it must have been clear that
the body of the Risen Lord, though the body of the man Jesus
still, was at the same time something infinitely more. For though
he ate and drank with his friends, he vanished from their sight
at will, proving thereby that he transcended the laws of space and
time. By conquering death Christ raised up matter from its very
condition of transience and "clothed it in spirit." The Resurrection of Christ was not just the guarantee of the survival of our

souls, for the experience of the soul's eternity had long been a
commonplace in India; it was the guarantee that the total personality of each human individual would survive not simply as
an idea within the mind of God or as an undifferentiated eternal
monad, but also as it had grown and flowered and borne fruit
in time : and all that it had added to itself in wisdom and love,
in creativity and compassion, would not be taken away from it,
but would be sanctified forever through Christ in God.

The Crucifixion of Christ means the total giving of self : translated into Indian terms this does not mean just giving up the
"ego" and all love of possessions—of "I" and "mine" as the
Buddhists say—it means also the crucifixion of the eternal essence
which is the very ground of the soul and a final refusal to accept a
timeless beatitude apart from God. This means not only to die to
the world and to self, but to die the second death—to die to that
immortal essence which Original Sin could not slay, and which so
often claims identity with God—for in this essence rest "is sufficient and great" and no need or desire for anything or anyone is
any more felt. Man knows himself to be "like God" in his eternity,
and as such he would forever remain. Comfortably ensconced
outside space and time he no longer cares how the world is pushing forward to a common destiny in which all mankind is being
knit together in an ever-increasing coherence around its common
center, Christ : he prefers his own rest which is "sufficient and
great," he prefers to live as the "horn of a rhinoceros, alone."[14]
It is this, the ultimate selfishness of a solitary Nirvāṇa, the more
selfish because it believes itself to be selfless, that is crucified with
Christ on the Cross. It is the symbolical abrogation of the *Hina-
yāna* or "defective vehicle" of the Buddhists and the inauguration
of the *Mahāyāna* or "great vehicle" in a real historical setting.
For the Mahāyānists saw that the old ideal of the *arhant* who
abandons the world to sink himself into a featureless Nirvāṇa
was radically selfish and a betrayal of the Buddha's own compassion, for the Buddha himself had refused to abandon the world
until he had fully expounded his message of salvation. Yet the
Mahāyāna too had its weaknesses, for its Bodhisattvas are all
purely mythological beings, and its Nirvāṇa is as void of positive
content as is the older one. Christ, on the other hand, is
the historical Bodhisattva, no less than the historical Messiah,
and the "Nirvāṇa" he offers includes both union with God

[14] *Suttanipaṇa*, iii.

through him and union and communion with all men in and through his mystical body which is the Church.

Hinduism, too, in the Bhagavad-Gītā, had turned away from the ideal of an impersonal Absolute and in the person of Krishna had embraced a personal god of love with whom communion and union were possible. And in the Passion of Christ God shows just what this love means : it means to give up everything of yourself without residue or remainder not only for your friends but for the very enemy who nails both Christ and you to the Cross. By the example of the Cross each individual is summoned to deny himself that he may find himself again in God. Here at last the shell of his individual consciousness breaks open to let in the flood of God's love and, through God, the love of man, his image.

Yet this total self-abnegation of Christ on the Cross is only the necessary prelude to the rebuilding of the "All-Man" into the new Adam, who, as a living organism, is nothing less than the body of the risen Christ. No man need any longer stand alone, for each is called to play the part that he alone can in the rebuilding of the All-Man not this time simply "in the image of God," but soldered together in the body of God made man.

From the Fall of Adam until the coming of Christ human history in its own way followed the pattern of the animal species. True, the human phylum did not split up into separate subspecies as has been the case of the other animal species, but it did split up into different religions and cultures, each having its own particular flavor, and each separated from the rest. With the outpouring of the Holy Spirit in the order of grace on that first Whitsunday the scattering of man which is symbolized by the Tower of Babel comes to an end : the Church of Christ is born and the symbol of unity and union is found.

From the beginning matter was animated by the Holy Spirit, and through the secret power of that Spirit moving matter burst into life, and from life into consciousness : and man was born. Through the misuse of his consciousness the universal trend initiated by the Spirit which is toward ever closer cohesion, was reversed and inhibited, so that a second irruption of the divine into matter became necessary. So the second Person of the Holy Trinity, the Son and the Word, the rational principle of the universe, took on the form of matter in its most complex and highly organized state, the form of thinking and self-conscious

man; and he thereby inaugurated the second phase of purely
human evolution, the irreversible trend toward unity, the molding
of a humanity which was to become "one in thought, word, and
deed," because it would be, though many, yet one in the body of
the Church whose head is Christ. From the very beginning this
doctrine was clearly understood and enunciated by St. Paul. Because the Church is one body under one head, Christ, the "free
development of each" is guaranteed by the "free development of
all." The Church is a living organism operating here and now in
this world, and not, as poor Marx thought, a purveyor of
"illusory happiness" in an illusory world : it is the *only* religion
into which the ideal Marxist world-state could *naturally* fit;
for its ideal is a collective ideal which would "secure for every
member of society ... an existence not only fully sufficient
materially, and becoming day by day more full, but an existence
guaranteeing to all the free development and exercise of their
physical and mental faculties"[15] within the framework of a
universal state and a universal Church, which is the body of
Christ. And in this body each organ has its part to play, and none
can play the part of another. Each must develop with and not
against the development of all.

For the body is one, and hath many members, and all the members
of that one body, being many, are one body: so also is Christ. For by
one Spirit are we all baptized into one body, whether we be Jews or
Gentiles, whether we be bond or free; and have been all made to drink
into one Spirit. For the body is not one member, but many.

If the foot shall say, Because I am not the hand, I am not of the body;
is it therefore not of the body? And if the ear shall say, Because I am
not the eye, I am not of the body : is it therefore not of the body?

If the whole body were an eye, where were the hearing? If the whole
body were hearing, where were the smelling?

But now hath God set the members every one of them in the body,
as it hath pleased him. And if they were all one member, where were
the body? But now are they many members, yet but one body.

And the eye cannot say unto the hand, I have no need of thee: nor
again the head to the feet, I have no need of you.

Nay, much more those members of the body, which seem to be more
feeble, are necessary: and those members of the body, which we think
to be less honourable, upon these we bestow more abundant honour;
and our uncomely parts have more abundant comeliness. For our
comely parts have no need: but God hath tempered the body together,

[15] Engels, *Socialism Utopian and Scientific*, pp. 80–81.

having given more abundant honour to that part which lacked: that there should be no schism in the body; but that the members should have the same care one for another. And whether one member suffer, all the members suffer with it; or one member be honoured, all the members rejoice with it.

Now ye are the body of Christ, and members in particular.[16]

This building up of the body of Christ in which each community and each individual has its individual part to play, is paralleled in Zoroastrianism in the building up of the "Final Body," through which evil is finally eliminated from the world. And as in Christianity, Zoroastrianism too has its own sacrament of unity and immortality, the so-called Haoma sacrifice in which the god-plant Haoma is pounded in a mortar as a pure oblation to his father, Ahura Mazdāh, the Wise Lord, and the juice that flows from its bruised limbs is consumed by the faithful "unto life eternal." And at the end of time when evil is finally destroyed, there will be a final "sacrifice of the raising of the dead, and in that sacrifice the bull Hadhayans will be slain, and from the fat of the bull the white Hoama will be prepared, [the drink of] immortality, and it will be distributed to all men."[17]

So too, in Christianity, Christ institutes the sacrament of bread and wine on the night before he himself offers himself up as a human sacrifice for human sin with the words, "This is my body," "This is my blood," and distributes the consecrated elements to the twelve, the nucleus of his Church. In so doing he consecrates and converts into himself the whole of the material universe that converges upon man, the rational apex of the evolutionary tree, who alone has the power to unravel the laws that govern matter and convert them to his use and the greater glory of God.

"To think, we must eat," as Teilhard de Chardin has reminded us. Lest we should think that, after the coming of Christ who "came eating and drinking," we may ever again maim and warp our bodies and minds; lest we should think that we may the better rest in the timelessness and emptiness of our immortal souls without thereby rejecting the God of total love once and for all revealed in the tortured body on the Cross, Christ identifies our daily food and drink, the bread and the wine of the sacrament, with his own body and his own blood without which there can

[16] I Cor., 12:12–27.
[17] See Zaehner, *Zoroastrianism*, p. 318.

be no eternal life. For if we are all members of the body of Christ, each one a living cell within the one body, then Christ is not only the total body, but the blood that courses through the body bringing life and sustenance to every living cell, and the blood itself is ever renewed by the breath of life, the Holy Spirit, who from the beginning indwelt this whole universe of matter : for the same Spirit who "moved upon the face of the waters," is the same Spirit by whom the man Jesus was conceived in the Virgin's womb, the same Spirit who launched the Church on her stormy mission on that first Pentecost when he appeared as a "rushing mighty wind" and as "cloven tongues of fire."

From the beginning the Spirit moved within matter, and each stage in man's development is marked by a new influx of the Spirit. Man attains to the knowledge of good and evil, and he is led thereto by the temptation of the serpent, the Spirit of the Earth, from which man's life and consciousness had burst forth. Man sins through pride and foolish self-conceit, and the human race degenerates into separate and divided cultures and separate and divided individuals, each despising his neighbor, until the Spirit overshadows the Virgin Mary, the "matter" from which the new Adam, Christ, is to be born. Finally, when God the Son has achieved his task and demonstrated the totality of God's love for man upon the Cross, has risen from the dead, and ascended into heaven in a visible body, it is the same Spirit that speeds the infant Church on its way—the Church that is itself the material as well as the mystical body of the risen Lord.

The same Spirit too, working through the same evolutionary process that brought matter to life, and life to consciousness, kneads this human matter together into ever closer harmony and cohesion, directing the total body of Christ toward its final point, its Omega, which is God the Father who, transcending time and space and all change, awaits the redeemed All-Man at the end of time.

Thousands upon thousands of years, we are told, it took for consciousness to dawn in man; and for only two thousand years now has man converged upon himself in the body of Christ, and this is an inconceivably short time. The coming of Christ reversed the fissiparous trend in man symbolized by the Tower of Babel, and it also reversed the same trend in the spirit of individual men; for by the Incarnation of Christ the breach between man and God was healed, and men were no more simply "half-fragments" of the shattered image of God. No longer did man need to submerge himself in the preconscious stream of life, the Tao that has no definite form, and no longer did he need to seek his rest in the primordial unity of his own soul, for this splendid isolation, blissful though it may be, was shattered by the Living Flame of Love that blazed upon the Cross; and mysticism itself has, since the time of Christ, taken on a new form in which there can no longer be any talk of isolation or "identity," but rather of union and communion in which all is giving and receiving and giving again and again. Christian mysticism, and the Hindu mysticism initiated by the Bhagavad-Gītā, as well as what is most authentic in Islamic mysticism, is essentially and always an outpouring of the spirit between two poles and their total harmonization in the act of Love, which itself is the Holy Spirit.

Teilhard de Chardin, who in that wonderful book *Le Milieu Divin* shows how the mysticism of the love of God and the active, creative life are but the two poles of one single phenomenon, is right when he says, "In [God] and in him alone does the mad vow of every love come true,—to lose oneself in what one loves and plunge into it more and more."[18] This is true, but it is true of man's approach to God alone, for though God demands that every trace of selfishness be put away, he nevertheless raises the soul up to a higher power and yet more distinct form of personality, for it is God's nature to give and to increase as the Zoroastrians alone among the pre-Christian religions clearly saw.

The soul as it issues forth from the hand of God is indeed a very wonderful thing, and to have discovered the beauty, the worth, the timelessness, and the seeming boundlessness of this "fragment" of God, as the Bhagavad-Gītā calls it, is the marvelous achievement of Indian religion, yet the increase and enrichment of this virgin soul through its habitation in a transient body is yet more wonderful; for through Christ who is the "body" of redeemed mankind, the body itself is given an eternal dimension, as even modern physics is beginning to discover, for now "each individual finds himself henceforth (actively and passively) simultaneously present, over land and sea, in every corner of this earth."[19] Julian of Norwich too understood how both

[18] Teilhard de Chardin, *Le Milieu Divin*, p. 165.
[19] *Id., The Phenomenon of Man*, p. 240.

matter and spirit work together toward eternal life, and that the body itself is the vehicle through which eternal life is obtained. She writes,

> What time that our soul is inspired into our body, in which we are made sensual, all so soon mercy and grace begin to work, having of us care and keeping with pity and love: in which working the Holy Ghost formeth, in our Faith, Hope that we shall come again up above to our Substance [i.e., God], into the Virtue of Christ, *increased and fulfilled* through the Holy Ghost. Thus I understood that the sensuality [i.e., the life of the senses] is grounded in kind [i.e., nature], in Mercy, and in Grace: which Ground [en]ableth us to receive gifts that lead us to endless life.[20]

Through the Incarnation, then, not only is man reunited to God in the body of Christ through the Holy Spirit: the rift in himself too is healed, body is subsumed into spirit and the two conspire in union toward the greater union of the Whole Man in his evolutionary ascent to the living God. And this ascent has already begun in the Catholic Church in which men, even today, are "one in thought," if not in word and deed. This convergence, too, which shows itself *in parvo* within the Church is now becoming increasingly plain in the world at large; and because the natural urge to unite is so strong the kicking against the pricks of union appear all the sharper—and the more futile, for everyone now knows that the human race can progress together only as members of one body or destroy itself as one body. And what more natural? For perhaps the evolution of mankind has reached a stage which the whole universe must itself reach in time. As Sir James Jeans says,

> Entropy must forever increase: it cannot stand still until it has increased so far that it can increase no further. When this stage is reached, further progress will be impossible, and the universe will be dead. Thus, unless this whole branch of science is wrong, nature permits herself, quite literally, only two alternatives, progress and death: the only standing still she permits is in the stillness of the grave.[21]

But science is coming more and more to admit "the persistent march of things towards greater consciousness, and the paradoxical solidity of what is most fragile," and these two tendencies

[20] Julian of Norwich, *op. cit.*, pp. 111-12.
[21] James Jeans, *The Mysterious Universe*, (London, 1930 reprint), p. 144.

"gravitate against the tide of probability towards a divine focus of mind which draws it onward. Thus something in the cosmos escapes from entropy, and does so more and more."[22] And this is only natural if the whole of evolution is indwelt by the spirit of God, for in adopting ever more complex and more fragile forms matter approximates ever more closely to spirit.

Whether or not mankind is indeed progressing to an ever more intimate convergence upon itself in what Teilhard calls "the wholesale internal introversion upon itself of the noosphere," that is, in the dovetailing of individual minds into a universal mind, which, for Christians, is the Word or Christ, it is too early to say; but, as Engels pointed out, the insights of philosophy and of religion not infrequently adumbrate what science subsequently confirms; and it would seem that the Zoroastrian vision of a "Final Body" and Engels' own vision of the sum total of human minds, working together in space and time and converging in an infinite mind, must have in them something of truth, and something of all this is perhaps already with us in the Catholic Church, the unity of whose faith and thought is habitually called the "mind" of the Church.

And this is what the Church, for all its palpable defects and frequent stupidities, stands for and offers : the ultimate solidarity of each in all and all in each—the ideal of Marx which the Marxists themselves can never achieve—an organism of persons in all their variety united around the Person who is the center and the circumference of them all, Christ, and impelled by the Holy Spirit toward the consummation of all things, which is the encounter with the Father.

If, then, it is true, as Teilhard de Chardin and many other scientists maintain, that evolution itself is driving mankind into convergence in unanimity and thereby to an immortal life that joins not only individual souls to God, but also welds together all the millions of human souls that form the one body of Christ in union and communion with each other, then we are justified in viewing present disharmonies and present hatreds as the last, and therefore the most virulent, manifestations of that spirit of separation which Christians call sin and Zoroastrians the Devil : and we will not be dismayed. For we know that these are the death throes of a dying age of individual selfishness, though we dare not say the death agony of sin and death itself. United round

[22] Teilhard de Chardin, *The Phenomenon of Man*, p. 271.

one center we can now look forward in hope to the Communion of Saints, the co-ordination of all our thinking and hoping and all our adoration. The present existentialist pessimism with its morbid preoccupation with individual destinies and individual commitments can thus be seen for what it is, what Lenin called in another context an "infantile disease."

The prospects opened up by a technological civilization are not only tremendously exciting but tremendously worthwhile, for technology is creating conditions which make individual effort futile and closest co-operation inevitable : it forces unity upon us on the material plane, and it is the function thrust on her by history and evolution itself and not only a duty of the Christian Church to expand into that universality she has always claimed is hers. Then, in very deed, she will have grown into the full stature of the body of Christ, the concrete and material manifestation of the same Spirit with which matter has been in travail from the beginning. Thus the Marxist jibe that religion represents an "illusory happiness" artifically superimposed upon a real "vale of woe" will cease to have any meaning; for the material mass of Christ's mystical body must inexorably move forward to rejoin what Teilhard de Chardin calls "point Omega" and what Christians have long been accustomed to call God the Father, who is Alpha and Omega, the first and the last.

Because we live under the constant threat of atomic annihilation, we will in the long run—and it may be a very long run indeed since the spirit has all eternity to work in—be forced to unite; the two economic blocs—the Capitalist and the Communist —will be forced, in their struggle to gain the confidence of the uncommitted world, to abandon their sillier and more sinful shibboleths—the sordid pursuit of gain on the one side and the frightened suppression of creative thought on the other. This done, they will be astonished to see that they, like the linguistic philosophers they both despise, are quarreling about words not realities. Then, perhaps, co-existence will grow into peace, peace into understanding, and understanding into the formation of a solidary mankind reconciled to God in Christ and Christ's body, the Church. If and when this happens, the words of the Zoroastrian apocalypse will no longer seem absurd :

Individual men will feel no envy at the joy of the totality of created things, but will rejoice together with it. Their goodness and joy will

wax and grow in the glory of the omnipotence of Him who is all-good,
[all-] aware, all in all, through his overflowing bounty and perfect
skill in means.

It would perhaps be foolish to look for any such consummation
for many hundreds of years to come. The fact, however, remains
that we are entering on an era totally different in kind from any
that has gone before—the era not only of scientific revolution but
of unwilling co-operation enforced on us by the shadow of total
death, and neither of the protagonists in the present ideological
struggle—the Communists on the one side and the Christian
Church on the other—is permitted by their dogmas even to contemplate mass suicide. Against this ideological tension the
Church will continue to grow quietly and perhaps all but un-
perceived; but she will grow nonetheless, slowly attracting to herself all the craving toward unity that lies deep down in the heart
of every individual man. The Church herself, casting off the
last vestiges of a Manichaean aberration and proclaiming ever
more insistently the indissoluble marriage of Spirit and matter in
Christ, and rejecting as emphatically all private attempts at personal spiritualization, will appear ever more *solidaire*—so
"solidary" indeed and so centered on her divine Founder that all
other organizations, because they lack such a center and because
they are strangers to a sacramental system that nurtures each
individual with the lifeblood of the whole and the blood itself
with the Spirit, must inevitably feel the strange attraction she
cannot help exercising. That she will be resisted to the last no sane
person would doubt, but that this resistance will weaken as
humanity converges ever more insistently on itself, we have every
reason to hope. The "existentialist" movement which has
mirrored the economic disruption of our times, can no longer have
any *raison d'etre* (if ever it had one) once the world's economy
settles down to the inevitability of co-existence and, beyond co-
existence, peace.

And what of Marxism? Perhaps Marxism still has its part to
play in providing a more rational and indeed a more just road
to the full industrialization of underdeveloped countries, but it
lacks now, what it lacked much less in the beginning, a rational
vision capable of cementing together not only men's bodies in
an ordered society, but also men's minds and souls in a common
sense of purpose, a common drive toward human fulfillment in

which the "free development of each will be the condition for the free development of all." This alone the Church can provide, for the matter of which the Church is built is not only charged with spirit as is the whole material universe : it is built upon the Son of God, who, as the second Adam, the second "All-Man," is the magnet of human unity, upon which all strivings toward unification must ultimately converge. Such a magnet Marxism can never supply—and to supply this need Teilhard de Chardin stepped on the scene; for he places matter in the very center of his vision, showing us how God works through matter itself for our common sanctification. He shows us how defective and somehow out-of-date are the ancient Oriental techniques designed to procure the soul's release from matter, and in their place he puts a truer Christian mysticism which sees in the total gift of self to God no depersonalization, but on the contrary the transcendence of self into something greater and even more personal than self.

Divine and human love are not, of course, identical, but they are analogous, as the mystics' figure of the soul as the bride of Christ clearly shows. What is most characteristic of love is giving, and it stands to reason that if a total surrender of self—a total self-giving—is the perfection of love, then the more of you there is to give, the greater will your love be. Christ demands not only that we should lose our lives in order to save them, but that we should develop our talents to their highest power and not bury them in the ground. This means that each individual must contribute the utmost of what is uniquely his in the interest not of himself but of all men who constitute the body of the All-Man, Christ; for in so doing he will forget himself, "diminish" himself, as Teilhard puts it, as a single center, while increasing as an indispensable part of a whole that itself is moving on to self-perfection. To diminish as an ego, to grow as an organically interconnected cell—this is the essence of the mysticism of Teilhard de Chardin. True, each immortal soul has its own "prebiographical unity" which cannot be taken away from it, but this does not mean that this unity cannot develop and grow, cannot be combined and fused with other prebiographical unities through the supreme attraction of the central focus of all creation which is God. And this combining and fusion takes place in and through the body of Christ, which is the Church. Yet in the order of grace as in the order of nature there can be no perfection until the "end," when what Teilhard calls point Omega is reached; and this for the simple reason that just as nature is plagued by disease, so in the order of grace is the Church plagued with sin. It follows, then, that the Church must to the end of time be sick in some of its members, and the sickness and sin of the one of the parts cannot but affect the health of the whole. Neither individual salvation nor the reconstitution of the total Man in Christ are automatic processes. The first can be achieved only by a constant vigilance and striving on the part of the individual in his desire to co-operate with grace, the second only by the joint striving of all in their convergence upon the divine center of all things. So much did Teilhard de Chardin see.

At the beginning of this book I expressed my debt to Fr. Teilhard de Chardin and the whole new perspective he had opened up for Christianity. And now, at the end, I find I have directly cited him but little; and that for two reasons. First, his thought is so rich that it needs to be quoted *in extenso*. Secondly, his terminology is so original and obscure that one hesitates either to reproduce it for fear of being misunderstood or to rephrase for fear of distorting his meaning. To compare great things with small I feel about this man of visionary genius what St. Peter, the first Pope (no genius himself), felt about St. Paul and what St. Peter's successors tend to feel about men of startling originality. St. Peter writes,

Account that the longsuffering of our Lord is salvation; even as our beloved brother Paul also according to the wisdom given unto him hath written unto you; as also in all his epistles, speaking in them of these things; in which are some things hard to be understood, which they that are unlearned and unstable wrest, as they do also the other scriptures, unto their own destruction.[23]

Yet we cannot refrain from quoting his vision of the end in which he sees a final spiritualization of all human matter as the Zoroastrians did before him :

Now when sufficient elements have sufficiently agglomerated, this essentially convergent movement will attain such intensity and such quality that mankind, *taken as a whole,* will be obliged—as happened to the individual forces of instinct—to reflect upon itself at a single point; that is to say, in this case, to abandon its organo-planetary foothold so as to pivot itself on the transcendent centre of its increasing

[23] II Pet., 3:15–16.

concentration. This will be the end and the fulfillment of the spirit of the earth.

The end of the world: the wholesale internal introversion upon itself of the noosphere [the shared soul- and mind-stuff of mankind], which has simultaneously reached the uttermost limit of its complexity and its centrality.

The end of the world: the overthrow of equilibrium, detaching the mind, fulfilled at last, from its material matrix, so that it will henceforth rest with all its weight on God-Omega.[24]

"Conquered" too "by the sense of the earth and human sense, hatred and internecine struggles will have disappeared in the ever-warmer radiance of Omega." And how could it be otherwise, if Teilhard's vision is true? Man, despite all his betrayals and his denials, cannot forever resist the attractive force of God. Impelled by the Holy Spirit from the beginning, saved from the egoism and selfishness into which the misuse of individual consciousness had drawn him by the divine Consciousness itself incarnate in Jesus Christ, he has no alternative but to share in the building up of the "body" of the Holy Trinity itself in space and time, in the making manifest on earth of that indissoluble Unity that subsists forever in eternity, in which the Father is forever welded to the Son in the incandescent flame of the Holy Spirit, who is that substantial love without which Deity itself would fall apart. Man, assumed like his mother Mary into the heart of the divine life, will not thereby cease to be man, nor will "each" be swallowed up in "all," nor "all" in God; for each will see himself only in the context of all, his individual will transformed at last into the will of God. Then, when the "All-Man" is once again made "one in thought, word, and deed," we shall understand what is meant by the "Communion of Saints."

[24] Teilhard de Chardin, *The Phenomenon of Man*, pp. 287–88.